Afghanistan

George Arney works as a j
BBC's Pakistan and Afgha
for two years, 1986 to 1988. He has spent a
considerable amount of time with the mujahedin
guerillas and was reporting from Kabul during
the Russian occupation.

At Trinity College, Cambridge, he specialised in
Modern Indian History and went on to do an
MA in South Asia Area Studies at SOAS. He has
lived in India, Pakistan, England and Israel and
travels frequently.

GEORGE ARNEY

Afghanistan

Mandarin

A Mandarin Paperback

AFGHANISTAN

First published in 1990
by Mandarin Paperbacks
Michelin House, 81 Fulham Road, London SW3 6RB

Mandarin is an imprint of the Octopus Publishing Group

Copyright © George Arney 1989

A CIP catalogue record for this book
is available from the British Library
ISBN 0 7493 0196 1

Phototypeset by Input Typesetting Ltd, London
Printed in Great Britain
by Cox & Wyman Ltd, Reading

Contents

Acknowledgements

Special thanks are owed to Gordon Adam, Professor M. Ishaq Negargar and Dr Abdul Ali Argandawi for their time and invaluable suggestions, and to members of the BBC Pashto Service generally for their friendly encouragement. I am grateful to friends and colleagues too numerous to mention in Islamabad, Peshawar and Quetta for the generous help and information they provided during my stay in Pakistan. I would also like to acknowledge the unwitting contribution of experts whose published works I have shamelessly pillaged for the early chapters of this book, particularly Louis Dupree, the American scholar and lover of Afghanistan who died in March 1988. Above all, my thanks to Cal Stockbridge for her endless patience, support and cups of tea, and for ensuring that Mungo still has a vague recollection that he does, after all, have a father.

List of illustrations

Picture 1 reproduced courtesy of the British Library's India Office Library; pictures 2, 3, 4, 6, 9 and 11 by David Stewart-Smith, reproduced courtesy of Insight Photographers; pictures 5, 13 and 14 by Julian Gearing; pictures 8, 10, 12 and 15 reproduced courtesy of Rex Features Ltd.

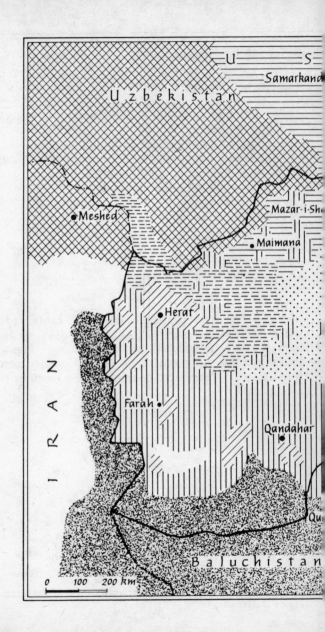

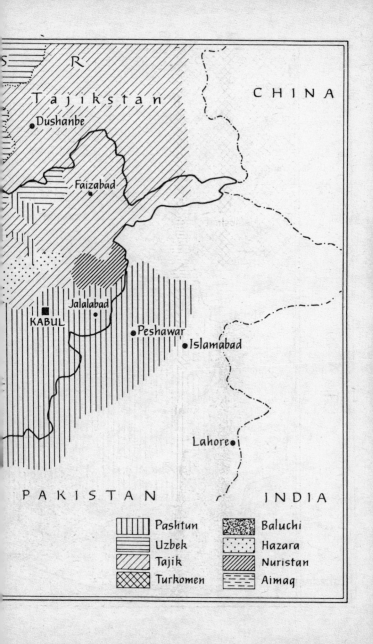

CHINA

Tajikstan

Dushanbe

Faizabad

KABUL
Jalalabad
Peshawar
Islamabad

Lahore

PAKISTAN

INDIA

▕▎▏▕	Pashtun	░░░	Baluchi
▤	Uzbek	⋰⋰	Hazara
▨	Tajik	▧	Nuristan
▨	Turkomen	▤	Aimaq

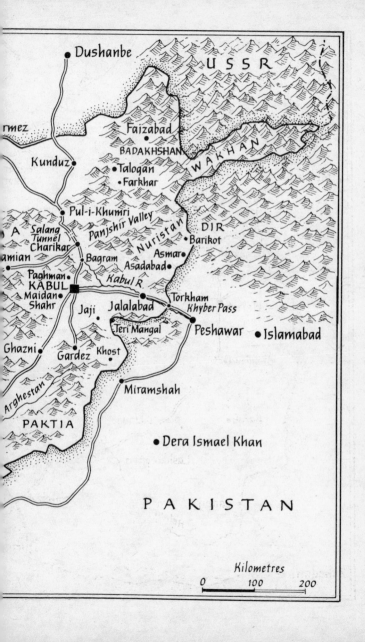

ONE

Birth of a Nation

Under a bright winter sun in mid-February 1989, a jeep pulled up in the middle of a river bridge in Central Asia. A lone figure got out, and walked, with head held high, to the far side. For weeks, thousands of trucks, tanks and troop carriers had been rumbling across the same bridge, spanning the Amu Darya river. Headlights full on and klaxons blaring, the Soviet army was travelling northwards for the last time, out of Afghanistan.

General Boris Gromov, overall Soviet commander, was the last to leave. Not surprisingly, he didn't look back. After more than nine years of Soviet occupation, Afghanistan was in smouldering ruins. Once-thriving villages lay devastated and abandoned. Orchards, vineyards and terraced hillside fields had reverted to wildernesses. Farms and mountain trails were littered with millions of mines. Half the population had been uprooted from their homes, and a third had been driven into exile, in one of the greatest human exoduses of the century. Green flags fluttered in the breeze over hundreds of thousands of Afghan graves.

'With one stroke, a world which billowed with fertility was laid desolate, and the regions thereof became a desert and the greater part of the living dead and their skins and bones crumbling dust.'[1] That lament, written in the aftermath of the cataclysmic arrival in Afghanistan of Genghis Khan and his 'roaring ocean' of Mongolian horsemen, serves equally well as an epitaph to the Soviet invasion seven hundred years later.

Apart from the indescribable devastation, the invasion

achieved little. When Leonid Brezhnev took the decision to invade in late 1979, he was determined to preserve the faltering dominion of communism across the Soviet Union's southern borders. Communism is now more loathed in Afghanistan than ever before. Islamic fundamentalism, which Brezhnev wanted to prevent spreading from Afghanistan into Soviet central Asia, is now more deeply entrenched and more aggressive. The Afghan civil war, which Soviet troops were dispatched to extinguish, continues unabated. Only General Gromov knows what thoughts passed through his mind as he crossed the Amu Darya into Soviet territory on 15th February 1989. But the diary of a British officer, written in 1842 when a British invasion force was forced to retreat from Kabul, may give a clue. 'Everything,' he recorded bitterly as he packed his bags, 'is reverting to the old state of things, as it was before we entered the country.'[2]

Compared to the destruction it inflicted on Afghanistan, the Soviet Union's own losses pale into insignificance: less than 14,000 Soviet lives, and an expenditure of $70 billion.[3] The intangible costs, though, may be considerably more. Mikhail Gorbachev's decision to abandon the communist regime in Kabul to an uncertain fate sent a potent signal to his country's other socialist allies, with dramatic consequences throughout Eastern Europe and within the USSR itself. The fifty million Muslims of Soviet central Asia have been reminded that their own subjugation to Moscow is less than a century old. 'For Soviet Muslims,' an Azerbaijani scholar commented shortly after the withdrawal, 'the impact of defeat in Afghanistan – a small, Muslim, Third World country – will be enormous, incalculable.'[4] It's possible that future historians will identify Moscow's Afghan war as one of the chief catalysts in the disintegration of the Soviet empire.

Since before recorded history began, wave after wave of invaders have swept down through the high mountain passes of the Hindukush, or east across the Iranian plateau, before heading on southwards to the rich, river-fed plains of northern India. In the 2,500 years before the Soviet invasion, scholars have identified at least twenty-five different ruling dynasties. Genghis Khan and his Mongols were preceded by Persians, Greeks, Scythians, Parthians, Indians, White Huns and Turks, all of whom incorporated parts or all of present-day Afghanistan into vast but often short-lived empires stretching from the Mediterranean to the Indian subcontinent, or from India to the steppelands of central Asia. The British and the Russians are only the latest of the country's would-be rulers, and amongst the least successful.

Isolated and backward though it seems today, Afghanistan was for thousands of years one of the great crossroads of Asia. Trade and ideas followed in the footsteps of the imperial armies and nomadic tribes. Camel caravans and missionaries criss-crossed its deserts and mountains, exchanging the riches and philosophies of India with those of Persia, Rome, central Asia and China. The hymns of the Rigveda, Hinduism's ancient scriptures, may have originated in the Afghan hills. Zoroaster is thought to have been born and to have died in the far north. In the south, Greek, Roman and Indian influences fused in the Peshawar valley to produce the rich Buddhist culture of Gandhara. It was through Afghanistan that Buddhism surged northwards into China, Mongolia and Korea, and a huge monastic centre thrived in the Bamiyan valley, west of Kabul, for 500 years.

The huge, faceless Buddhist statues carved into Bamiyan's sandstone cliffs by pious monks some time between the third and fifth century AD still dominate the valley today. But it was the culture of Persia which left the most enduring imprint on the land now known as Afghanistan. Although the last Persian conqueror, Nadir Shah, died in 1747, Dari – the local name for Persian – is still the language of educated Afghans and the country's main lingua franca. Islam was firmly established as the region's predominant

3

religion by Turkish and Persian adventurers who overthrew the last Hindu kings of the Kabul valley four hundred years after the death of the Prophet Mohammad. As late as the fifteenth century, one of the most brilliant Muslim civilisations the world has ever seen flourished in the western Afghan city of Herat.

Ethnically, Afghanistan is an anthropologist's nightmare. Each new invasion or migration left behind its own ethnic deposit in the form of settlers, who either inter-bred with the original inhabitants or forced them to retreat deeper into the mountains, creating over the centuries an ethnic mosaic of bewildering complexity. The name itself – Afghanistan, or land of the Afghans – conjures up a totally false impression of homogeneity. Strictly speaking, there's no such thing as an Afghan. It's a name used by other communities to describe the country's dominant ethnic group – but that group calls itself Pashtun and is known to the outside world as Pathan. Besides the Pashtuns, there are at least twenty-one other distinct ethnic groups, speaking upwards of thirty different languages, and to make matters more complicated still, their linguistic and cultural loyalties frequently transcend Afghanistan's modern frontiers. Far more Uzbeks, for instance, live in the USSR and China than in Afghanistan. Like the Tajiks and Turkomen, they have their own Soviet republic. The Baluch of the southwestern deserts also inhabit Pakistan and Iran, while the Pashtuns are divided almost equally between Afghanistan and Pakistan.

Each group preserves the awareness of its separate origins in its folklore. Some Pashtun tribes cherish a mythical pedigree stretching back to King Saul and Nebuchadnezzar. The blue-eyed Nuristanis who live in the high mountains along the eastern frontier believe they sprang from the loins of Alexander the Great's Macedonian soldiers, while the Hazaras of the central highlands claim descent from the Mongol armies of Genghis Khan. Sayyeds, found throughout Afghanistan, claim pure Arabian blood as direct descendants of the Prophet, while in the north the Uzbeks look back to an ancient Turkish past. In this melting pot of cultures, Islam is the only common denominator and tensions are never far from the surface. Hazaras – who are mainly Shi'ite Muslims – are held in especial contempt by the Sunni majority. The highest form of praise a recent Western traveller through Hazara country could wring out of his Pashtun guide was that 'there are some good-looking ones that seem almost human'![5] Tajiks, the second largest ethnic group, have an old proverb which warns them to 'trust a snake before a harlot, and a harlot before a Pashtun'.

The political history of the modern state of Afghanistan is primarily the story of the Pashtuns. Pashtun tribes have been inhabiting the south of Afghanistan since at least the sixth century AD, and probably long before. Clear references to them are extremely scarce, though in 1333 an Arab travelling through the area was harassed 'by a tribe of Persians called Afghans' who 'hold mountains and defiles, possess considerable strength and are mostly highwaymen.'[6] Other Pashtuns hired themselves out to passing armies as soldiers of fortune, and several of them went on to carve out kingdoms of their own in northern India. In their mountain homelands, though, they remained divided into numerous warring clans, too rebellious for outsiders to subjugate for long, but equally incapable of uniting. Bemoaning the repeated incursions of the Indian Moghul kings, the great seventeenth century Pashtun poet Khushal Khan Khattak wrote with customary boastfulness:

The Afghans are far superior to the Moghuls at the sword
Were but the Afghans, in intellect, a little discreet,
If the different tribes would but support each other,
Kings would have to bow down in prostration before them.[7]

By the early eighteenth century, amidst the welter of Pashtun tribes and sub-tribes which had spread throughout the south, two clans had risen to prominence, the Abdalis and the Ghilzais. For 200 years, they had been kept more or less in check by their own bitter feuds, and by three powerful foreign empires which met and fought in Afghanistan: the Moghuls, the Persian Safavids, and the Uzbek rulers of central Asia. But in 1747, when the blood-crazed Persian conqueror Nadir Shah was assassinated, all three empires had run out of steam. Seizing their chance to fill the political vacuum created by Nadir Shah's death, the Abdali clans chose as their paramount chief a dynamic young warrior who had served in Nadir Shah's army, Ahmed Khan. Crowned king with an ear of wheat placed in his turban, he took the name Ahmed Shah Durrani.

Ahmed Shah was the archetypal Pashtun. A contemporary described him as 'tall and robust, and inclined to be fat. His face is remarkably broad, his beard very black and his complexion moderately fair. His appearance on the whole is majestic and expressive of an uncommon dignity and strength of mind.'[8] Conscious of the fierce jealousies of the tribes, he kept his interference in local affairs to a minimum, and ruled through a tribal council, which he consulted on all important matters. Within the space of three years, Ahmed Shah had spread his authority from his capital at Qandahar throughout present-day Afghanistan, as well as to most of modern Pakistan and parts of eastern Iran.

Ahmed Shah is considered by most historians to be the founder of the modern Afghan state, and his conquests – including ten invasions of India – confirmed the Pashtuns as the region's foremost power. Yet although during his lifetime he managed to unite the heterogeneous people of Afghanistan under a loose Durrani overlordship, his empire disintegrated after his death amidst a series of fratricidal tribal wars. Impatient as always of central control, his numerous offspring and rival tribal chieftains asserted their independence, once more carving the country into several

6

warring principalities. Surveying the Afghan scene a century after Ahmed Shah's death, a British general, Sir Henry Rawlinson, wrote that 'the nation consists of a mere collection of tribes, of unequal power and with divergent habits, which are held together, more or less closely, according to the personal character of the chief who rules them. The feeling of patriotism, as known in Europe, cannot exist among Afghans, for there is no common country.'[9]

It was European imperialism, more than anything else, which eventually gave Afghanistan a semblance of national cohesion. Not long after Ahmed Shah embarked on his career of conquest, Clive's victory at Plassey started Britain on its relentless march to dominion over India. By 1849, after two wars with the Sikhs, British rule had advanced right up to the turbulent Pashtun territories nominally under the control of the Amir of Kabul. Czarist Russia was embarking around the same time on its equally inexorable southward expansion through central Asia. By 1885, Moscow had extended its control, either by conquest or by treaty, over most of the Muslim territories north of the Amu Darya river.

The rivalry between these two great imperial powers shaped the course of Afghanistan's history in the nineteenth century. To Kipling, it was 'the Great Game', in which Afghanistan was a troublesome pawn. Paranoid about Russian designs against India, British armies invaded Kabul twice in the space of forty years, only to discover that the costs of occupation far exceeded the gains. On both occasions, the British were forced to withdraw within a few years, leaving the country in a more dangerous state of anarchy than before.

The first Anglo-Afghan war was both unnecessary and disastrous. Shortly after Lord Auckland arrived in 1836 to become India's new Governor-General, he received secret instructions from his masters in London to 'watch more closely, than has hitherto been attempted, the progress of events in Afghanistan, and to counteract the progress of

Russian influence'. What perturbed the British most was Moscow's alliance with Persia, which was once again casting covetous eyes on the city of Herat, long an outpost of the Persian empire. Leaning heavily on the discretion of their man on the spot, the directors of the East India Company authorised Auckland, if he deemed it necessary, to 'interfere decidedly in the affairs of Afghanistan'.[10]

Two years later, Auckland did just that. In 1837, a Persian army, accompanied by Russian advisers, laid siege to Herat. Ignoring Kabul's initial pleas for help, Auckland gathered together a large army and dispatched it in November 1838 across the river Indus, which then formed the boundary of British India. The siege of Herat was lifted even before Afghan territory was reached, but the Army of the Indus rolled on. Nine months later, having occupied Qandahar and Ghazni en route, it entered Kabul in triumph and placed on the throne a puppet ruler, Shah Shuja, who had been deposed thirty years before after a brief and unhappy reign, and who had lived quietly every since as a pensioner of the British.

Like the Soviet army 140 years later, the British denied any aggressive intention, claiming that they were merely supporting Shah Shuja's troops (which formed less than a third of the whole) 'against foreign interference and factious opposition'. The original intention had been to send the bulk of British and Indian troops home once Kabul had been won, but Shah Shuja, never a popular ruler, was now utterly detested for having returned to power with the help of foreigners and infidels. It was evident that he would never be able to survive without British support; but the British presence provoked a state of permanent unrest and sporadic revolt which eventually spread to Kabul.

In January 1842, the once-mighty Army of the Indus, led by the inept and senile General Elphinstone, began its retreat. Of the 16,500 troops and camp-followers who began the march, only a handful of Indian sepoys and one exhausted British army surgeon got through to the safety of the

8

British garrison at Jalalabad. The rest were either captured or massacred in a series of ambushes as they struggled through the snowbound passes south of Kabul. The honour of British arms was restored later that year by a swift-moving expeditionary force which seized Kabul and blew up its famous bazaar before retreating. But the overall costs of the adventure to British India were enormous. According to a contemporary enquiry, they included 'the exhaustion of her treasury; complete stop to internal improvement; loss of the lives of fifteen thousand men; destruction of fifty thousand camels . . . loss of England's character for fair dealing; loss of her character of success; the Mussulman population rendered hostile.'[11] The Kremlin should have taken note.

The lessons of history, though, are notoriously hard to learn. Even the British quickly forgot the outcome of their first disastrous intervention in Afghan affairs. For the next fifty years, British policy vacillated between two extremes. One school of thought favoured leaving the turbulent peoples on India's north-west frontier more or less to their own devices. The other argued that India would never be secure unless its frontiers were advanced northwards to the natural barrier of the Hindukush. The resumption of Russia's southward drive in the 1860's strengthened the hand of the advocates of what became known as the 'forward policy', and in 1878, provoked beyond endurance by the arrival of a Russian diplomatic mission in Kabul, a British army invaded Afghanistan for the second time.

The second Anglo-Afghan war was a bizarre and rather inconclusive affair. Although British troops successfully occupied Kabul and Qandahar, and forced the Kabul amir to abdicate, they found, like the Soviet army after them, that it was far easier to seize the towns than control the surrounding countryside. With tribal resistance growing, with chieftains of the royal clan gathering strength in the north and west, and faced with the prospect of the ruinous costs of an indefinite occupation, Gladstone's newly elected

9

Liberal government ordered a withdrawal from Kabul after only eight months. In the words of the new Secretary of State for India, 'as the result of two successful campaigns, of the employment of an enormous force, and of the expenditure of large sums of money, all that has yet been accomplished is the disintegration of the State which it was desired to see strong, friendly and independent.'[12]

Even more ironically, the man who became Kabul's new ruler, Abdur Rahman Khan, arrived straight from Russia, wearing a Russian uniform, and with offers from Moscow of military aid. A nephew of the former amir, he had spent eleven years in exile as a guest of the Russian government. Britain, though, finally seemed to have learned that Afghans could be trusted to put their passion for independence before their obligations to their foreign patrons. Looking around desperately for chieftains strong enough to restore some order amidst the chaos it had created, Britain reluctantly recognised Abdur Rahman as amir of Kabul, mounted a new expedition against Qandahar, and then withdrew its troops.

Amir Abdur Rahman began his reign in a position of weakness. His authority did not extend beyond Kabul and the surrounding area, and he was forced at the outset to accept a treaty which ceded to Britain a large swathe of border territory, as well as control over his country's foreign relations. Britain used its new power to draw up a series of international agreements demarcating Afghanistan's northern and southern borders, largely irrespective of Abdur Rahman's wishes. For the next forty years, until the third Anglo-Afghan war of 1919, Afghanistan remained a *de facto* British protectorate.

Yet it was only now that Afghanistan began to emerge as a coherent political entity. As a British observer, Sir Thomas Holditch, noted in the year of the Amir's death, 'We have contributed much to give a national unity to that nebulous community which we call Afghanistan [but which Afghans never call by that name] by drawing a boundary all round it and elevating it into the position of a buffer state between ourselves and Russia.'[13] Hemmed in by two mighty empires, Abdur Rahman was forced to turn his considerable talents and energies inwards, to the creation of a rudimentary nation state.

A cruel, sardonic man with a massive black beard, Abdur Rahman recalled in his autobiography, with untypical Afghan understatement, that 'when I first succeeded to the throne of Kabul my life was not a bed of roses. Here began my first severe fight against my own relations, my own subjects, my own people.'[14] Military campaigns began immediately, and lasted throughout most of his twenty-year reign. In turn, the Pashtun tribes of the south were subdued, then the Uzbeks and Turkomen of the north, the Hazaras of the central highlands, and finally the heathen Nuristanis of the east, who were forced to embrace Islam at swordpoint.

The unification of the country was only achieved through extreme ruthlessness. Each new rebellion was followed by mass executions; the Hazaras were sold into slavery; political enemies were blown up by cannon; and bandits were thrown into iron cages and left to die slowly as a warning to others. But Abdur Rahman mixed his cruelty with innate shrewdness and a talent for administration. Exploiting the age-old rivalries of different tribes, he forcibly deported thousands of Ghilzai Pashtun enemies to new lands north of the Hindukush, where their rebelliousness was neutralised by their even greater hostility to the native Uzbeks and Tajiks. Unlike earlier rulers, he kept his sons safely by his side, appointing loyal followers as provincial governors in their stead. He began building a modern army and bureaucracy, made the roads safer for trade, and tentatively began to exploit the country's resources. Abdur Rahman's success in cowing his rebellious subjects and forging a strong central government can be measured by the fact that on his death in 1901, his eldest son Habibullah succeeded to the throne without any of the usual opposition.

Abdur Rahman harboured no illusions about the delicacy of his country's position. 'How can a small power like Afghanistan, which is like a goat between two lions, or a grain of wheat between two strong millstones of the grinding mill, stand in the midway of the stones without being ground to dust?' he asked in his autobiography. The only answer he could offer his successors was to follow a careful policy of neutrality, to avoid antagonising either of Afghanistan's giant neighbours, and prevent them from intervening in the country's internal affairs. The eleven years he spent in exile in Russia seem to have convinced him that the greatest threat to Afghan independence came from the north. 'The Russian policy of aggression,' he wrote, 'is slow and steady, but firm and unchangeable . . . Their habit of forward movement resembles the habit of an elephant, who examines a spot thoroughly before he places his foot upon it, and when once he puts his weight there is no going back, and no taking another step in a hurry until he has put his full weight on the first foot, and has smashed everything that lies under it.'[15]

Ten years ago, Cold-War warriors seized gleefully on Abdur Rahman's warning to support their contention that the Soviet invasion of December 1979 was part of a calculated long-term strategy in pursuit of 'Russia's historic destiny . . . the domination of Europe and the civilised world.'[16] But brutal though the Soviet occupation has been, Afghanistan's problems did not begin with an act of unprovoked military aggression by an expansionist evil empire. The roots of its woes go deeper. Afghanistan is the victim of its belated collision with the twentieth century.

Abdur Rahman's instinctive response to the pressure of external forces was to keep his country in a state of enforced purdah. He turned down repeated British proposals for advisers, telegraphs, railways, commercial treaties and diplomatic missions. Afghans were required to seek official permission to travel inside and outside the country. But the modern world could not be kept at bay indefinitely. As in all backward countries, Afghans could not help but be influenced by the overwhelming technological superiority of the West. The European armies pressing up against their borders were deeply impressive, even if they had problems subduing the wild tribesmen of the hills. Modern military techniques and hardware were the first things to be borrowed. Afghans saw their first aeroplane only in 1919, when British pilots carried out a desultory air raid during the final Anglo-Afghan war. Yet within ten years, Afghanistan had its own air force.

It was impossible, though, to embrace Western technology without being influenced by Western ideas. The first modern (i.e. Western-style) school was opened in Kabul by Abdur Rahman's son Habibullah in the early years of this century. Culturally and economically, Afghanistan had been stagnating for centuries, and a tiny educated élite soon grew up in the towns which was deeply influenced by Western secularism and concepts of progress. In the 1960's, inevitably, some of them turned to communism. Others, reacting against Western values, turned to radical Islam in a bid to achieve modernisation without spiritual pollution.

The bitter struggle between these two tiny élites for control of the state apparatus eventually engulfed the entire country and precipitated the Soviet invasion. Outside interference magnified, but did not create, the conflict; and although Soviet troops have now withdrawn, Afghanistan's painful birthpangs will not cease until its disparate peoples manage to reconcile the contradictions between their ancient traditions and allegiances, and the ever greater encroachments of the modern world.

TWO

A Clutch of Kings:
from Amanullah to Daoud

Habibullah, who ruled from 1901 until his assassination in 1919, had a modern, even a futuristic turn of mind. He loved motor cars, cameras and the science-fiction novels of Jules Verne, which he had translated into Persian. He also commissioned American engineers to build Afghanistan's first hydro-electric generating station. I imagine him, after a hard day of palace intrigue or hunting, reading *Twenty Thousand Leagues Under the Sea* by the flickering electric lights which he had installed in the royal palace.

Habibullah's son, Amanullah, was an even more modern man, who was besotted with the outward trappings of the West. Although there are photographs of his father in European dress, Amanullah was the first Afghan ruler who habitually wore Western clothes, and he once caused a scandal by performing his prayers in Cairo's Azhar mosque wearing a fashionable grey top hat. But unlike his father, Amanullah was also fired by a passion to drag the rest of Afghanistan with him, kicking and screaming if need be, into the twentieth century.

Young, ambitious, idealistic and impetuous, Amanullah took less than ten years to reduce Afghanistan to chaos and anarchy. Seventy years on, the reforms which he tried to introduce seem admirable. But he was a man ahead of his time, and like the Afghan communists of the seventies, thought he could work a magical transformation on a semi-tribal and deeply conservative society. Concentrating at first on streamlining the administration, he soon turned his attention to grand but ill-conceived development projects, such as the construction of a modern capital along the lines of Ankara or New Delhi on the outskirts of Kabul. It was never completed. Nor were the roads which he started to build across the treacherous passes of the Hindukush in an attempt to fulfil the old ambition of connecting Kabul to the remote north of Afghanistan.

Far more risky were the next projects on his list, educational reform and the emancipation of women. Foreign-language high schools were opened in the capital, and schemes were hatched for making universal education compulsory. With the zeal of the true reformer, Amanullah also dispatched teachers to travel with Afghanistan's nomad population who, no doubt, viewed their city-bred cousins with bemused disdain. Women were another target of his progressive ambitions. Unlike his father, who had four wives and a bevy of concubines, Amanullah contented himself with a single queen, Surraiya, and was, according to one chronicler, 'exemplary in his domestic life'.[1] If he had stuck to reforming the royal family's personal habits, his reign might have been longer. But instead, he set about trying to better the lot of women generally, upgrading their legal status and introducing compulsory female education.

The fiercely conservative Pashtun tribes of the south, already angered by the abrupt termination of their traditional subsidies from the royal coffers and by changes in the system of conscription to the army, were enraged. The first serious tribal revolt against Amanullah was ignited in the spring of 1924 by the lawless tribes around Khost. It continued for nearly a year and was only put down after spreading from the Pakistani border to within thirty-five miles of the capital. In the end, two World War One aircraft, sold to the amir by the British and piloted by Germans, helped bring the rebellious tribes to their senses. But it was Amanullah who lost the peace. The royal treasury, already seriously stretched by his grandiose building projects, was virtually bankrupted. Helplessly, Amanullah convened a Loya Jirga, or Grand Assembly of the Tribes, a

Pashtun institution traditionally summoned to decide matters of exceptional national importance. The delegates agreed that the legal rights Amanullah had tried to extend to women should be cancelled, while only pre-pubescent girls should be given the opportunity of a basic education.

Whether through simple determination, revolutionary fervour, or arrogance, Amanullah was undeterred. Even after colliding head-on with the bed-rock conservatism of his people, he persisted with his drive towards modernisation. It gained fresh impetus from a six-month tour of Europe which he undertook in 1928, the first time the king (a title Amanullah had adopted five years earlier) had crossed the borders of his own country.

The tour was a huge personal success. The crowned heads of Europe laid on lavish receptions for this oriental potentate with a military moustache and weak chin from the wild mountains half a world away. After progressing through Cairo, Rome, Paris, Brussels, Bern and Berlin, the royal couple finally arrived in Britain, where the red carpet was rolled out. The Prince of Wales was on hand to receive them when their ship docked at Dover, and King George V himself escorted his guests from Victoria station to Buckingham Palace. There ensued a three-week whirl of banquets, factory visits and trips to the Boat Race and the Grand National. The might and majesty of the British empire was on full display. They watched army manoeuvres on Salisbury Plain, naval manoeuvres at Bournemouth, and Royal Air Force displays at Hendon, until Queen Surraiya, who preferred her shopping sprees in Maples department store, asked her hosts, 'Why do you want to show us so many ways of killing people?'[2]

Whatever his queen thought, though, the king, reflecting on his own primitive nation, must have been deeply impressed. In 1928, despite the imminence of the Great Depression, London and other European capitals were bright with bustle, gaiety and pomp. Motor cars thronged the boulevards, and electric street lighting transformed night into day. There were railways, trams, trolleybuses, telephones and telegraphs; modern factories turned out a dazzling array of goods, and modern hospitals treated the sick. By contrast, Afghanistan in 1928 was virtually untouched by industrial development. Workshops turned out little more than guns and artillery, boots, leather, soap, saddles and candles. Trade was conducted by camel caravans threading their way along thousands of miles of dirt tracks, impassable in winter or after the rains. Even the streets of Kabul were unpaved. One of Afghanistan's main provincial towns, Jalalabad, had changed little since the late nineteenth century when a British visitor described it as 'a dirty little place, surrounded by dead donkeys and camels, whose essences made the live air sick'. If the Afghans were a sturdy race, it was simply because only the strongest survived childhood. Tuberculosis, malaria and other diseases were rife, and in the huddled, hostile villages of the countryside, opium-smoking was the only available means of pain relief.

The creation of a European-style civilisation in Afghanistan must have seemed virtually unattainable, even to Amanullah. But two other Muslim nations were already demonstrating that it was possible to bridge the gulf between East and West. The early 1920's saw the emergence of the most successful of progressive Muslim leaders, Turkey's Mustafa Kemal Ataturk. From the crumbled ruins of the old Ottoman empire in 1918, Ataturk was forging a new, secular Turkish nation which was at the same time Westward-looking and anti-imperialist. In 1924, the same year that Amanullah was battling with his rebellious southern tribes, the Caliphate was formally abolished, and, with the help of a well-disciplined army and a well-organised political party, Ataturk was sweeping away the centuries-old bureaucratic and religious resistance to change. On Turkey's eastern borders, Ataturk's example had inspired a Persian military careerist, Reza Khan, to set about the forcible modernisation of another tradition-encrusted society, creating a centralised bureaucracy, banning the chador and veil for women, and forcing men to wear a wide-brimmed hat specifically designed to interfere with the rituals of prayer.

Amanullah already had strong ties with Turkish radicals, and, after diplomatic relations were established in 1921, he granted spacious grounds in central Kabul for the building of a Turkish embassy, which is still there today. Before his accession, Amanullah had been a member of a group of young Afghans who met secretly to discuss ways and means of modernising Afghanistan, modelling themselves on the Young Turks, who shortly afterwards overthrew the Ottoman Sultanate and shaped modern Turkey. In 1921, British officials, still smarting from the humiliation of losing control over Afghanistan's foreign relations after the third Anglo-Afghan War, were appalled to discover a Turkish military mission in Kabul, helping to train the Afghan army. Meanwhile Amanullah – always fond of intrigue – was secretly corresponding with the former Young Turk, Enver Pasha, who was trying to forge a new Turkic-speaking state out of the chaotic vacuum left in central Asia by the simultaneous collapse of the Ottoman and Czarist empires.

The Turkish connection was reinforced by Amanullah's father-in-law, Mahmud Beg Tarzi. Tarzi belonged to an Afghan family exiled by Abdur Rahman, and he spent his formative years in Damascus, the intellectual centre of opposition to the floundering Ottoman Empire, where his progressive views were shaped by his encounters with the Young Turks. He first set out his ideas about the necessity of social and political reform when he was only twenty-five. Later in life, expounding his views on the need for Islam to harness Western science in order to survive, he wrote, 'If Islam is worthwhile, it is worthy of challenge'. Not surprisingly, Tarzi was not popular with the religious bigots of his day, who considered, like their modern equivalents, that the Prophet's seventh-century injunctions should be applied literally to contemporary life.

Returning to Kabul at the turn of the century, Tarzi

18

became a trusted adviser to King Habibullah. He had even more influence over Amanullah, who married one of Tarzi's daughters, and when Amanullah seized power in 1919, he quickly implemented some of his father-in-law's pet reforms, such as the creation of a cabinet of ministers based on the Turkish model. But unlike Tarzi, Amanullah's idealism was not tempered by pragmatism. The king was dazzled by his visits to Turkey and Iran in 1928, and against all advice, decided on his return to emulate them. A British official, W. K. Fraser Tytler, who spent thirty years serving on the North West Frontier and in Afghanistan, was in Kabul when Amanullah finally returned from his foreign tour. He wrote later that the king's visits to Turkey and Iran had sealed his fate:

> In Tehran the Afghan party did not impress the Shah and the Court, who considered that their treatment in the European capitals had gone to their heads. They talked altogether too big and imagined that a few weeks in Europe could turn an Afghan into a civilised being. The King, however, seems to have won the hearts of the Persian people by his affability and graciousness, which contrasted so strongly with the sullen bearing and arrogance of their own rulers. Their applause and acclamations were still ringing in his ears as he set forth on the last stage of his journey across the Afghan border to Herat, and may well have fortified him in his determination to win similar acclaim from his dour and suspicious subjects who awaited his return.[3]

It was not to be. While he was away, conservative conspirators stepped up their campaign to portray the king as a Western decadent, and his reforms as un-Islamic. Rumours were spread about the king's new plans to undermine Afghan traditions, and photographs of Queen Surraiya unveiled and wearing an evening gown were secretly distributed. The same tactic was still being used by Islamic zealots

19

sixty years later, when photos of a decolletée Begum Bhutto dancing with Gerald Ford were used to discredit her daughter Benazir during the 1988 Pakistan election campaign.

Undeterred, and disregarding the advice of Ataturk, Tarzi, and the British Minister in Kabul, all of whom warned that large-scale reforms should be postponed until the administration had been reorganised and the army strengthened, Amanullah unleashed a new programme of reforms. It included the creation of a constitutional monarchy and an elected assembly, a secular judiciary, the complete emancipation of women, the introduction of monogamy and compulsory education for both sexes. An increase in taxation was proposed, and plans for co-educational schools were unveiled. So were women, who were forbidden to walk the streets of Kabul unless they went bareheaded. Men were barred from wearing Afghan caps and the baggy, comfortable pyjamas called *shalwar*; second-hand clothes dealers in the capital made their fortunes out of visiting tribesmen who were compelled to put on Western dress for the duration of their stay.

The crowning absurdity occurred at the end of August 1928, when a Loya Jirga was assembled in Kabul to endorse the king's reforms. Sensitivity was clearly not one of Amanullah's strongest qualities. Among the entertainments laid on for the tribal delegates, according to Fraser-Tytler, were cinema shows, theatre plays and 'a variety entertainment which included a scantily clad lady contortionist [which was] particularly well patronised.' But the king's final undoing was the reform programme itself, which he presented before a collection of dumbfounded tribal elders, whose irritation had been greatly exacerbated by having to dress in morning suits and black ties.

The proceedings lasted for five days. Amanullah delivered a long tirade against his country's superstitions and backwardness, which was interspersed with film shows of his foreign tour. Lady Humphrys, the wife of the British minister in Kabul, Sir Francis Humphrys, who was in the audience, wrote later in her diary: 'The most dramatic moment of all was when Amanullah wound up an impassioned appeal to his people to free their women with a wave of his hand towards his Queen, saying, "Anyway, you may see *my* wife," and she pulled down her veil before the assembled multitude.'[4]

Thoroughly outraged, the religious establishment could stand no more. The head of the city's most prominent Sufi order, the Hazrat Sahib of Shor Bazar, was arrested for whipping up opposition to the king's reforms. Further arrests followed. And as the Loya Jirga delegates returned to their towns and villages to inform their clansmen of the king's ludicrous reforms, the general unease turned to revolt, fired by the preaching of the mullahs. In mid-November, Shinwari tribesmen burned down the royal palace and the British consulate in Jalalabad before setting off for Kabul, 100 miles to the northwest, picking up recruits as they went. Amanullah dispatched the army south to deal with the tribal *lashkar*, or war-party, but the disaffection was so widespread that even his regular troops deserted en masse to join the rebellion.

Kabul, exposed and largely undefended, now lay vulnerable to attack. The man who took advantage of the situation was a small-time Tajik bandit from one of the valleys north of the capital, nicknamed Bacha Saqao, 'Son of a Water-Carrier'. Despite his lowly origins, his uncouth appearance and his lack of education, Saqao was – at least for Tajiks – something of a Robin Hood figure, with a reputation for robbing wealthy travellers and royal officials and distributing a share of the loot to the poor. As the unrest started, he spotted the chance to extend the range of his philanthropic activities, and began to raid government treasuries with his ragged band of followers.

In the second week of December 1929, Saqao and his by now well-armed retinue captured a strategic fort at the mouth of the Salang valley, and then moved south towards the capital itself. Fierce fighting raged for more than a month before the depleted royalist forces were overwhelmed. Starting just before Christmas, aircraft of the Royal Air Force based in Iraq carried out the first mass airlift in history, evacuating first the wives and children of the foreign legations and finally the diplomats themselves. The British legation had been badly damaged in the crossfire, and it was only the pipe-smoking sangfroid of the British minister Sir Francis Humphrys, which kept the rebels at bay.

Dick Gould, then aged six, still remembers the two-month-long siege, during which he, his brother Bob and the rest of the embassy staff and their families survived on a diet of bully-beef and Christmas pudding. 'Bob and I spent most of our days under the table in the billiard room. I remember long hours playing there with a Christmas present, which I had been allowed to open early. This was a large First World War tank, a parallelogram with rubber tracks driven by clockwork and capable of scaling formidable objects. We boys were excited rather than frightened; my father remembers that I called to him one day to cross the room to where I was: "You can hear the bangs much better this side!" '[5]

A fortnight after the evacuation was completed, Saqao's forces captured the aerodrome, and Amanullah, hoping to rally the Durrani tribesmen of the southwest to his cause, hurriedly abdicated in favour of his oldest brother Inayatullah, and fled by Rolls-Royce to Qandahar.

Inayatullah lasted just three days before he too fled. Winter snows delayed the final royalist attempt to regain Kabul until the spring, when Amanullah's tribal levies, marching from the southwest, were easily defeated at Ghazni. Amanullah fled for a second time and settled in Italy, a precedent followed forty years later by another ousted king, Zahir Shah. Saqao (who had been re-titled by the Kabul religious establishment as 'Ghazi Habibullah,

Deen-e-Rasoolullah', or 'Holy Warrior Habibullah, Servant of the Faith') was left in control of the Afghan capital.

Amanullah's ten-year reign was in many ways an early rehearsal for the upheavals of the late 1970's and 80's. Activists of the People's Democratic Party of Afghanistan frequently depict themselves as liberal reformers in the tradition of Amanullah, and critics of today's mujahedin draw comparisons between them and the band of adventurers, religious figures and reactionary tribesmen who brought Amanullah down. Certainly, many of Kabul's present-day citizens, while indifferent or hostile to the PDPA regime, seem fearful that its overthrow could be followed by another interregnum of reaction and terror, like the one instigated by Bacha Saqao. For despite a varied career, which included short spells in the Afghan army, as a tea-vendor in Peshawar, and in a British jail for petty theft, Saqao was ill-qualified for kingship. Even the ecstatic clerics who had welcomed him to Kabul quickly turned against him, despite the decision to put religious scholars, or *ulema*, on the government payroll. Normal life in the capital came to a standstill. Schools were closed down, and Saqao's lieutenants indulged in unrestrained looting and murder. Kabul and its environs suffered a nine-month-long reign of terror, while the rest of the country, refusing to acknowledge the son of a Tajik menial as their ruler, lapsed into its preferred state of anarchy.

In spite of the persistent belief among Afghan nationalists that the British engineered Amanullah's downfall in retribution for his victory in the third Anglo-Afghan War of 1919, the chaos across its north-western border was dangerous for British India. Having learned the bitter lesson of the preceding century that direct interference in Afghan affairs did not pay, the Government of India was reluctant to take sides openly. Yet it was also afraid that the resurgent Soviet empire would not remain so aloof.

The Bolshevik Revolution of 1917 had aroused hopes among the Muslims of central Asia, cynically encouraged by Lenin, that they could regain the independence lost when their kingdoms were annexed by the Czar in 1868. But within months of the Revolution, Red armies were on the move to re-assert and expand Soviet authority. In 1918, Soviet troops entered the 'protected' Muslim emirate of Khiva, whose ruler fled southwards to Kabul. Eighteen months later Soviet troops invaded Bokhara. Despite pledges to respect the independence of both emirates, both were formally annexed by the Soviet state in 1924; and after seizing Kabul five years later, Bacha Saqao threatened to help his fellow Tajiks in Bokhara restore their independence (a theme still echoed by mujahedin zealots today).

At the time of Amanullah's downfall, Soviet troops were already prowling along the northern bank of the Amu Darya ready to strike against the last bands of the Basmachi, central Asian Muslim rebels, some of whom were using the sanctuary of Afghan territory to resist the annexation of their homelands.

Equally worrying to the British were the activities of Amanullah's ambassador to Moscow, Ghulam Nabi Charkhi. The father of the three Charkhi brothers had been one of Abdur Rahman's most powerful generals, and his sons formed a powerful conservative clique at Amanullah's court. After the king's overthrow, Ghulam Nabi Charkhi, with Soviet advice and backing, travelled south from Moscow and collected a mercenary force from both sides of Afghanistan's northern border. He may even have been accompanied by a contingent of disguised Russian soldiers. Although he got no further south than Mazhar-i-Sharif during his first attempt, Ghulam Nabi remained encamped near the border, waiting to seize his chance to recapture Kabul and restore the monarchy.

While Ghulam Nabi dithered on the northern border, another contender for power was rallying support in the south. The strongest opponents of the Charkhi faction at Amanullah's court in the 1920's were the five Musahiban-brothers. The oldest brother, General Mohammed Nadir

Khan, became one of the heroes of the third Anglo-Afghan War, when, as Commander-in-Chief of the Afghan army, he struck deep across the frontier into British-administered tribal territory. Eventually, though, the Musahibans lost their influence at court. Innately conservative, they were strongly opposed to Amanullah's reform programme, and in 1924 Nadir Khan met the fate of many influential Afghan dissidents, and was posted off as ambassador to Paris. Two years later, on the excuse of ill-health, he relinquished the post and retired to the south of France to brood and bide his time.

Early in 1929, Nadir Khan and two of his brothers arrived in India and sought British backing for an attempt to re-take Kabul. For the British it was a God-sent opportunity. Despite instructions from London which forbade them to intervene directly, British officials turned a blind eye to the recruitment of supporters from among the tribes on the British side of the frontier. By mid-October, Nadir Khan had collected a sufficiently large *lashkar* or tribal army to defeat Bacha Saqao's army and occupy and sack the capital. Saqao himself fled back to his stronghold in Kohistan; despite assurances of a reprieve, he was soon recaptured and, a fortnight later, was publicly executed alongside his chief lieutenants. Pashtun honour was finally vindicated the following summer, when Nadir Khan sent his undisciplined frontier tribesmen to put down a simmering revolt among the Tajiks of Kohistan, which they did with extreme brutality.

With hindsight, it seems unlikely that Nadir Khan ever intended to restore Amanullah to his throne, despite earlier professions of loyalty. He certainly had no intention of proceeding with his royal cousin's reforms. Shortly after entering Kabul, he was acclaimed Mohammad Nadir Shah, King of Afghanistan. As a soldier born and bred, his first priority was to make his new title a reality by stamping his authority on the rest of the country. This he had virtually achieved by the end of 1931, through a careful programme of pacification in the south and military campaigns in the west and extreme north, where the last great Basmachi leader, Ibrahim Beg, was driven over the Amu Darya into the hands of his Soviet enemies.

As the pacification of the country proceeded, Nadir Shah was able to turn his attention to consolidating his authority in the capital and laying the foundations of a stable dynasty. His first step was to co-opt the support of the religious leaders who had played such an important part in fuelling the anti-Amanullah agitation. Following the example of his predecessor, Bacha Saqao, the new king put the imams of the capital's mosques on the government payroll. He also handed out lucrative posts to prominent religious leaders, and created a special board of *ulema* to ensure that all schooling was carried out according to 'Islamic' principles. The first article of the new 1931 constitution decisively turned its back on Amanullah's tentative moves towards a secular state, and declared the religious law of the Hanafi sect of Sunni Islam to be the law of Afghanistan.

The constitution introduced a quasi-parliamentary form of government, in which the king presided over a cabinet which was theoretically accountable to an elected assembly. In an effort to appease the still-vocal pro-Amanullah faction, the new king was also careful to include concessions to liberal sentiment, including the abolition of slavery and imprisonment without trial, and the establishment of compulsory primary education. But he had little intention of respecting the constitution's human-rights provisions, and none of allowing real power to pass into anyone else's hands. Well before the constitution was promulgated, the king had set up a cabinet, led by his loyal brothers, and manned by other friends and relatives. The Loya Jirga which confirmed him as king in September 1930 also selected a National Council, which in effect was little more than a rubber-stamp for the decisions of the Musahiban family.

Nadir Shah's main contribution to nation-building was as a man of action rather than of ideas. Although still partly dependent on his tribal levies, he built a regular army of 40,000 men and replenished the royal treasury by collecting taxes with military efficiency. During his reign, the malarial swamps of northern Afghanistan were drained and turned into fertile agricultural land, and the economy was strengthened by his decision to give free rein to the country's first major agro-industrial entrepreneurs. He also accomplished what Amanullah had failed to do, and built an all-weather road across the mountains of the Hindukush, creating a relatively direct route to the remote provinces of the north for the first time in Afghanistan's history.

Nadir Shah lived to see the Great North Road completed, but only just. In November 1933 he was shot dead in the grounds of his own palace by a young student, probably as a result of his blood-feud with the Charkhi family. It was a measure of the stability he had restored and the loyalty he inspired in his brothers that no power-struggle ensued. Nadir Shah's nineteen-year-old son, Prince Zahir, was unanimously acclaimed king on 8th November 1933. But Zahir Shah was no more than a figurehead who for the next twenty years reigned in the shadow of his uncles. Mohammad Hashim, first appointed Prime Minister in 1929, continued in the same post until 1946, when he was succeeded by his youngest brother Shah Mahmud. It was an unremarkable period in which the king's uncles devoted themselves to the preservation of the status quo: maintaining law and order, strengthening the army and starting to develop the national economy were their main priorities. The family maintained an iron grip on power: royal cousins not in the government were appointed as generals in the army, and all dissent was stifled.

Prince Zahir and his cousin Daoud, who was later to overthrow the monarchy and establish a republic, were barely out of their teens when Nadir Shah was assassinated in 1933. The two cousins were brought up together. Both got their schooling in France, and they continued their education as classmates in Kabul's Afghan Military College.

As members of the stern Musahiban family, the two young princes were not brought up to be pampered. Fraser-Tytler recalls seeing them taking part in the annual Independence Day parade as common infantrymen shortly before Nadir Shah's death. But it was Daoud, rather than Zahir, who had the temperament to be an Afghan ruler. He was a military man and an autocrat, with a violent temper and an unshakable belief in his own destiny. Zahir, on the other hand, was of a gentler disposition. He was ostentatiously pious, and had quiet, courteous manners. An Indian diplomat who was posted in Kabul in the latter part of his reign still remembers King Zahir's favourite way of relaxing from the weighty matters of state. A fine horseman, he would ride out early in the morning to the summer palace at Paghman, twelve miles west of Kabul, where he would spend the day, stripped to the waist, working in the royal gardens.[6]

Overthrown by his cousin Daoud in 1973, Zahir Shah went into exile in Italy, and is now in his late seventies. In recent years, visitors to his villa outside Rome have found that the old king's memory of the royal gardens is the only thing about Afghanistan which still animates his conversation. Nevertheless, Zahir Shah is still seen by many Afghans as the only man capable of re-unifying their country. Both Moscow and the Najibullah regime in Kabul have sent emissaries to talk to him in Rome, and moderate guerilla politicians in Peshawar have often told me that if he were to fly to Islamabad, the roads leading to the Pakistani capital would be jam-packed with Afghan refugees hurrying to acclaim him as their leader. Privately, some of them have even fantasised about crossing the border with Zahir Shah at their head and re-capturing Kabul without opposition, in a repeat performance of Nadir Shah's 1929 expedition against Bacha Saqao.

Zahir Shah himself, though, has never shown any great desire to abandon his comfortable Roman retirement for the maelstrom of Afghan politics. Apart from occasional appeals for unity among the resistance and meetings with moderate mujahedin leaders, he's so far resisted taking an active role in the struggle for power. He's well aware that his reappearance on the scene would be bitterly opposed by fundamentalist guerilla leaders who are determined to prevent the old Durrani Pashtun aristocracy from re-establishing the 200-year-old dominance it enjoyed until 1978. And the same temperamental detachment from the hurly-burly of politics which Zahir Shah displayed in 1973 by abdicating without protest after Daoud's coup, has grown with his advancing years. The chances of the old king ever returning to Kabul, except as a private citizen, remain remote.

THREE

Embracing the Bear:
Foreign Policy 1919–1973

Afghanistan declared its formal independence from Britain in 1919. But either because of their fierce love of liberty, or because of the encroachments of the outside world, twentieth-century Afghans have viewed most of their rulers as foreign puppets. Even King Amanullah is now seen by ideologues of the Afghan resistance as a prototype communist; he was the man who employed Soviet technicians to fly and service the thirteen aircraft donated by Moscow to form the nucleus of the Afghan air force; he also allowed Russian engineers to lay telephone lines between the country's main cities, and permitted the establishment of an air route between Kabul and Tashkent. Above all, he was the man who compromised traditional Afghan neutrality by signing the country's first friendship treaty with the Soviet Union.

Nadir Shah leant in the opposite direction. Although described by British diplomatists who knew him as a 'fanatical patriot', he is now regarded by resistance ideologues as a British agent. Even at the time, the legitimacy of his rule was never recognised by progressive Afghan nationalists. Clandestine leaflets entitled 'The British Jackal' were distributed in Kabul, and even those who had no reason to love Amanullah indulged in malicious speculation about his successor's British connections. The leeway given to him by Delhi when he was collecting his tribal army on the southern border looked particularly suspicious. And rumours that he was no more than a pliant tool of the British spread further when it was learned that he had accepted a subsidy of 10,000 British rifles and £180,000 in cash after seizing power in Kabul.

Far from being a British stooge, though, Nadir Shah scrupulously adhered to the cardinal rule for all pragmatic Afghan rulers: a policy of active neutrality. He sent home the Russian advisers employed by Amanullah, and in their place brought in experts from countries far removed from the central Asian power struggle: Germans, French, Italians and Japanese. Even in the capital's foreign-language schools, instruction in English was given by Indian teachers, with the result that many well-educated Afghans grew up speaking French or German, but far fewer were fluent in English.

In sharp contrast to his supposedly 'pro-Soviet' predecessor, Nadir Shah bowed to pressure from Moscow to prevent bands of Basmachi rebels raiding Soviet territory from bases in northern Afghanistan. As a result of Kabul's suddenly effective border patrols, the Basmachi were virtually wiped out by the end of 1933, and Moscow was able to consolidate its control over the troublesome Muslims on its southern flank. To avoid antagonising his other powerful neighbour, the king consistently refused to give moral or material support to disaffected tribesmen living on the British side of the southern frontier, or to the left-wing Indian Pashtuns who had joined the Indian freedom struggle.

The same determined neutrality, flavoured with strong anti-British feelings and wariness of the Soviet Union, continued to dictate foreign policy after Nadir Shah's death. In an effort to escape from the stranglehold of the two regional giants, his brothers looked further afield. Diplomatic relations were established with the United States in 1936, and a joint friendship treaty was signed with Iran and Turkey. Economic assistance was sought from the Axis powers, Germany, Italy and Japan, a development which caused British officials much concern. Several prominent Afghans, including the royal uncle Shah Mahmud, attended the 1936 Berlin Olympics and were much impressed by Nazi Germany's display of efficiency and discipline.

Germany, though, was too distant to be of much practical use after the Second World War began. Resisting the temptation to seize the Pashtun borderlands ceded to British India by Abdur Rahman in 1893, Kabul maintained its neutral position. It was a wise decision, but a humiliating one. As it became clear that an Allied victory was inevitable, Britain's imperious demands for the expulsion of Germans from Afghanistan were countered by orders for *all* non-diplomatic personnel, including the British, to leave. Even so, Britain got the best of the deal, including a Bechstein grand piano which British diplomatic staff 'liberated' from the German embassy in Kabul.

The post-war period was a time of radical change. Political life in South Asia was dominated by the sudden realisation that Britain was going to quit its Indian Empire, and the winds of freedom sweeping the subcontinent generated milder gusts which penetrated even the high stony mountain passes of Afghanistan. In 1946, Mohammad Hashim stepped down as Prime Minister to enable his more liberal younger brother, Shah Mahmud, to experiment with a limited form of democracy. Previous parliaments had been tame bodies, mainly comprising royal kinsmen, conservative landlords and tribal and religious leaders. The relatively free elections of 1949 produced a different sort of legislature. Over one-third of its members were committed to the kind of liberal reforms being openly advocated at the time by a mainly middle-class, Western-educated lobby group called the Movement of Awakened Youth. Published in 1947, the Movement's manifesto demanded legal rights for women, the eradication of bribery and corruption, the promotion of industry, social justice and the diversion of national resources to projects of public welfare. In the words of the free-thinking Pakistani socialist Raja Anwar, the manifesto represented 'the flowering of the tender plant whose seeds Amir Amanullah Khan had sown against such odds twenty years earlier.'[1]

With the election of the 'Liberal Parliament' of 1949, free newspapers sprang up overnight, carrying increasingly critical comments on the way the country was run. A student union was founded at the University, where intense young men debated everything from atheism to democracy. The stultifying grip of conservative Islamic orthodoxy was a favourite target, but even the royal family started to find itself being crudely satirised in plays and articles. After two years, with calls mounting for further freedoms, increased democracy and the establishment of political parties, the ruling establishment ran out of patience. The student union was disbanded, all non-government newspapers were closed down and the regime's most radical opponents were jailed.

Fresh elections restored the status quo ante. But although the growing dissatisfaction of Kabul's educated bourgeoisie could be suppressed for a time, it couldn't be wished away altogether. After secret deliberations, a consensus emerged among the royal family that the older generation would have to make way for the new. Shah Mahmud stepped down as Prime Minister, and his place was taken by the king's energetic, strong-willed cousin, Sardar Mohammad Daoud Khan.

Prime Minister between 1953 and 1963, and later President from 1973 to 1978, Daoud has been dubbed 'The Red Prince' by resistance ideologues.[2] His policies and actions undoubtedly did contribute to the communist takeover of 1978. His commitment to rapid, centrally planned economic development drew Afghanistan into a dangerous dependency on Moscow. And the cynical alliance he forged in 1973 with the Afghan left-wing, opened up the army and administration to communist infiltration for the first time. Even so, like his uncle Nadir Shah, Daoud was a patriot and a Pashtun nationalist. Indeed, it was his obsession with Pashtun nationalism which, more than any other single

33

factor, was to push him into the uncomfortable embrace of the Russian bear.

Afghanistan's southern border with India was fixed in 1893 in an agreement between Amir Abdur Rahman and the British negotiator Sir Mortimer Durand. It was an absurdly artificial boundary, which sliced through the middle of ancient tribal territories, dividing cousin from cousin. At the time, the Afghan amir was content enough, since it put an end to the repeated British encroachments into Pashtun tribal territory of the previous fifty years. But the Second World War, which drained Britain of the resources and resolve to hold onto its restive Indian Empire, had a profound effect on Kabul's attitude towards the Durand Line. When the British quit India in 1947, Abdur Rahman's description of Afghanistan as 'a goat between two lions' no longer seemed appropriate. The southern lion, Britain, had withdrawn, licking its wounds, to its island lair. In its place were the two independent states of India and Pakistan, the latter weak and fragile.

The rulers of Afghanistan have never forgotten that, before the British came, they ruled Peshawar, Quetta and the Baluchi deserts as far south as present-day Karachi. The British withdrawal revived their dreams of restoring what Nadir Shah's brothers considered to be Afghanistan's rightful suzerainty over the frontier. In August 1947, as the Union Jack was lowered in Delhi for the last time, Kabul took the position that the Durand Line agreement had effectively lapsed, and two years later, all treaties referring to the Durand Line as an international border were unilaterally abrogated. Actions followed words. Only a fortnight later, Afridi Pashtuns gathered in strength on the Pakistani side of the Durand Line to declare the establishment of independent Pashtunistan – land of the Pashtuns.

The most prominent advocate of Pashtunistan in the 1940's was Khan Abdul Ghaffar Khan, the ascetic leader of a Pashtun social-reform movement which evolved under the batons of British policemen into a fully-fledged independence movement in the North West Frontier. During the early days of the struggle against British rule, Ghaffar Khan and his 'Redshirts' received little support from other Indian Muslims. Nationalists from places like Allahabad and Lucknow – the sophisticated urban heartland of the Muslim-minority provinces of northern India – tended to look down on Pashtuns as primitive savages, while the pro-British Muslim landlords of the Punjab regarded them as dangerous radicals. Spurned by his co-religionists, Ghaffar Khan and his politician brother Dr Khan Sahib forged an alliance with Mahatma Gandhi and his largely Hindu Indian National Congress. They may even have struck a tacit deal with Gandhi for Pashtun autonomy within a united India. But as 1947 approached, and it became increasingly clear that the subcontinent would be partitioned, they began to militate for Pashtunistan.

Pashtunistan is a concept which has the virtues and drawbacks of meaning different things to different men. To Ghaffar Khan, it may well have carried spiritual overtones. He had devoted his life, not just to independence, but to the moral regeneration of a people racked by blood feuds, bribery, family disputes and degrading social customs. Pashtunistan for him must have represented not just a political entity, but also an ideal world of moral salvation. To his fellow Pashtuns of the North West Frontier, Pashtunistan could mean anything from autonomy within Pakistan to complete independence. To the wild tribesmen straddling the Durand Line, it probably meant the splendid prospect of everlasting anarchy, without interference either from north or south. To the rulers in Kabul, who adopted the call for Pashtunistan with alacrity, it clearly implied the integration of Pakistan's North West Frontier Province into the Afghan state.

Although never clearly defined, the concept of Pashtunistan was powerful and emotive enough to inspire Pashtun nationalists like Ghaffar Khan to spend endless years in Pakistani jails, and to sour relations between Pakistan and

Afghanistan until the Soviet invasion. Even in 1988, one of the arguments advanced by General Zia ul Haq's advisers in favour of signing the UN-sponsored Geneva accords was that they would finally and formally force the Kabul government to recognise the Durand Line as the international boundary.

Diplomatic hostilities between the two countries broke out immediately after the departure of the British, when Afghanistan voted against the inclusion of Pakistan in the United Nations. Pakistan retaliated by a partial economic blockade, tying up Afghanistan's vital transit trade with bureaucratic red tape, one of the subcontinent's most intricate art forms. Tensions escalated. In the early fifties tribal war parties – described by Kabul as 'freedom fighters' – crossed the frontier to plant Pashtunistan flags on Pakistani territory. Pakistan responded by shutting down the Afghan transit trade entirely, closing the border for three months. In 1961, with the two countries on the brink of war, the border was sealed again.

The prolonged conflict with Pakistan over the Pashtunistan issue had profound consequences for the neutrality of landlocked Afghanistan, whose rulers had little option but to turn to the Soviet Union for economic and political support. The USSR's creeping influence did not go unchallenged. In 1955, Afghanistan became one of the founder members of the Non-Aligned Movement, which started out full of idealism and determination to escape the Cold-War syndrome. But unlike other founding members – among them Indonesia, India and Yugoslavia – Afghanistan was too small and too close to the Soviet Union to resist its gravitational pull. Although the United States soon replaced Britain in the post-War era as the Soviet Union's main rival in the Great Game, viewed from Kabul, the two players were no longer of equal strength.

In contrast to the solid presence of the British in India before 1947, the United States wove its circle of containment around the Soviet Union through a network of proxies. In 1955, the same year that Afghanistan joined the Non-Aligned Movement, Pakistan became the last link in the Baghdad Pact (later CENTO), an anti-communist security alliance which also included Britain, Iran, Iraq and Turkey, with the US as an ex-officio member. Afghanistan's possible inclusion in the Pact was discussed with US officials. But even if Daoud had been tempted to compromise his country's traditional neutrality, his personal commitment to 'Pashtunistan' would have made it difficult for him to join any club of which Pakistan was a member. In any case, Washington wasn't pressing too hard. In 1953, a secret US Defense Department study concluded that Afghanistan 'is of little or no strategic importance to the United States'.[3]

Even so, in the post-War period, it was to the United States that Kabul first turned in its search for a friendly and neutral source of military and economic aid. In 1946, with the help of a private American company, work started on the construction of two dams and an extensive network of canals designed to transform the Helmand valley, in south-western Afghanistan, into the country's main breadbasket. The project immediately ran into problems, but it was not until the early fifties that the US government was persuaded to intervene by extending credit, and not until 1959 – the year in which President Eisenhower visited Kabul – that the US State Department woke up to the fact that Moscow's less ambitious but more numerous economic-aid projects were winning friends, and designated Afghanistan an 'emergency action area'.

Under Stalin, Soviet economic aid to developing countries was negligible. But after his death in 1953, the Kremlin's approach to the Third World underwent a rapid change. Under Krushchev, Moscow shed its doctrinaire disparagement of the bourgeois leaderships of newly independent nations, and embarked on a new, pragmatic course, in which economic aid was recognised as a powerful tool to extend political influence. Afghanistan, desperate for rapid development, became one of the main nations on which the Krushchev government chose to shower its fraternal largesse.

The first important Soviet-Afghan agreement – a $3.5 million loan to construct silos and bakeries – came just four months after Daoud became Prime Minister in 1953. More agreements followed in the same year: $1.2 million for the construction of a gas pipeline across the Amu Darya, $2 million for road building and – to the delight of the dust-caked citizens of Kabul – $2 million for asphalting the streets of the capital, a project which had been turned down as uneconomic by United States aid officials. A visit by Bulganin and Krushchev in December 1955 produced aid on a far larger scale: a $100 million long-term development loan, for projects ranging from hydro-electric plants and fertilizer factories to a new military airport and the world's highest road tunnel. Krushchev favoured high-visibility projects which not only paid political dividends, but also – as with the airport at Bagram and the Salang Tunnel – had strategic potential. Notwithstanding official Soviet claims that its economic assistance programme sprang wholly from disinterested benevolence, Krushchev candidly admitted to a group of visiting American Congressmen that 'We value trade least for economic reasons and most for political reasons'.[4]

US aid was motivated by similar considerations. The American journalist Henry Bradsher reports being told by military and civilian sources in the US that a $15 million project to develop Qandahar airport, completed in 1962, was undertaken with its potential as an emergency US Air Force base firmly in mind; as further evidence, he cites a consistent pattern of deletions from declassified US documents on the project.[5] Krushchev certainly appears to have been concerned that US military planners had their eyes on Afghanistan. 'At the time of our visit there,' he later wrote in his memoirs, 'it was clear to us that the Americans were penetrating Afghanistan with the obvious purpose of setting up a military base.'[6] Given the extensive use of Soviet-funded facilities during the 1979 invasion, Krushchev's words reek heavily, if unintentionally, of irony. But Moscow's sense of unease at being encircled during the Dulles-dominated fifties is often overlooked by those who choose to see a sinister master-plan of Russian expansionism stretching unbroken from the days of Peter the Great to the present day.

Between the early 1950s and 1979, when it halted its aid, the United States loaned or granted a total of $532 million to Afghanistan. Soviet credits extended over the same period were more than double that sum – over $1.265 billion – and were far more effectively deployed. There were other players in the aid game too. By 1970, China was Afghanistan's fourth largest aid donor, and in 1974, the Shah of Iran, spearheading a US-inspired counter-offensive against Soviet influence, offered a massive loan of $2 billion. As the Cold War took hold, Daoud employed the time-honoured Afghan tactic of playing off one power against the other. He was, in the words of a 1975 CIA biographical report, a man who 'was happiest when he could light his American cigarettes with Soviet matches'.[7]

The sheer volume of Soviet assistance, and its concentration in specific sectors of the economy, gradually eroded the autonomy of Afghanistan's economic policy-making. The first 'Five Year Plan', launched in 1956, was based primarily on the recommendations of Soviet advisers, and, by 1978, there were about 2000 such technical and economic experts in the country. Creeping Soviet control was exerted by linking Kabul's growing indebtedness with a system of barter trade agreements. As the debt grew and rescheduling became necessary, the Afghan government found it increasingly difficult to negotiate better terms for its exports to the Soviet Union, particularly natural gas. The agricultural sector, where central planning was virtually non-existent, was almost entirely neglected by Soviet aid officials, while in the manufacturing and mining sectors,

Soviet assistance was confined mainly to projects linked directly or indirectly with the Soviet economy.

Kabul's own short-sighted foreign policy accentuated its growing economic dependence on its northern neighbour. As already noted, the dispute over 'Pashtunistan' caused Pakistan to close down its border with Afghanistan for several months in 1950, leading to immediate shortages of petrol, kerosene and other essential imports. The Soviet Union promptly stepped into the breach. For the first time since the 1930s, it concluded a barter agreement with Kabul, which also permitted Afghan exports to transit free of charge through Soviet territory. In 1961, Daoud's own decision to close the border with Pakistan had even more profound effects. Within ten days, the Afghan foreign minister was on his way to Moscow, and returned with a Soviet offer to airlift out the fruit crop plus a new agreement for a major increase in transit facilities through the Soviet Union.

Soviet military assistance to Kabul began at around the same time as its economic aid. At first, Kabul looked further afield for suppliers, particularly to the United States. But because of its new strategic alliance with Pakistan, the US was reluctant to strengthen the Afghan army at a time when Pakistan-Afghan relations were so strained. Even a face-to-face meeting between President Truman and the visiting Afghan Prime Minister Shah Mahmud in 1951 led nowhere. Two years later, when Daoud took over, the request was repeated and once again rejected. Spurned and angry, Daoud immediately opened negotiations with the USSR on its long-standing offer of military aid, and, in August 1956, contracted for $25 million in arms, including tanks, MIG 17 fighters and jet bombers from the Soviet Union and Eastern Europe.

The 1956 pact represented a decisive break from Kabul's earlier wariness about military dependence on its powerful neighbours. Over the next two decades, Soviet weapons and weapons systems valued at over $600 million were supplied to the Afghan government, and military facilities, particularly airfields, were developed. The new hardware transformed the rather primitive Afghan army and air force into relatively modern and well-equipped forces, comprising over 100,000 men at the time of the 1978 coup.

Armed forces undergoing rapid modernisation tend to develop a symbiotic relationship with their suppliers. In Pakistan, for instance, the long-standing military jargon, traditions and techniques inherited from the British began to fall into disuse in the mid-1950s, when the Americans stepped in with a massive military aid programme. In Afghanistan, the Soviets made good use of their long-awaited opportunity. Between 1956 and 1977, nearly a third of the entire Afghan officer corps was trained in the USSR, where they were also given compulsory courses in dialectical materialism and international communism. Many were influenced by the Soviet way of life, and some were recruited by the KGB or the Soviet military intelligence agency GRU.

Washington did not seem unduly concerned. The US State Department policy review report of 1972 concluded that, 'Afghanistan has a natural political, economic, commercial and cultural relationship with Russia. Any effort on the part of other nations to reduce Soviet-Afghan relations below this natural level would be contrary to the interests of both parties, and the resulting situation could not persist.'[8] A leading US authority on Afghanistan, the late Louis Dupree, begged to differ. In 1973, he warned of the dangers of Afghanistan becoming totally dependent on the USSR for replacement items, spare parts, and military instructors. 'If an anti-American coup occurs in the armed forces', he wrote, 'the inflexible American aid philosophy of the 1950s must accept a share of the responsibility.'[9] Just five years later, Dupree's prophecy was fulfilled. The military leaders of the 1978 coup had all received training in the Soviet Union.

FOUR

The Dangerous Decade:
Islam, Marxism and the Democratic Experiment 1963–1973

Daoud needed a strong army: not only to pursue his quarrel with Pakistan, but also to ensure the success of his campaign against tradition. For in spite of the imperious manner, violent temper and reliance on the secret police which marked him out as the antithesis of a liberal, Daoud was determined to achieve economic growth. And that required social reforms, in order to bring women into the work-force and break the political and social grip of religious and tribal leaders.

A calculating pragmatist rather than a romantic idealist like Amanullah, Daoud tested the waters carefully before introducing his first major reform, the abolition of *purdah*, or the seclusion of women. He began by gradually insinuating women singers and presenters onto the airwaves of Radio Afghanistan. Several state-controlled companies started to employ unveiled female staff, and women first started to wear stockings in public in 1957. Then, in 1959, Daoud repeated the dramatic gesture which had contributed to Amanullah's downfall exactly thirty years before, by putting his unveiled wife on public display.

Sensation and outrage ensued. But the manner and timing of the unveiling conveyed a powerful message to Daoud's conservative opponents. The Prime Minister's wife, accompanied by the equally bare-faced wives of other top civilian and military officials, appeared alongside their husbands on the reviewing stand during the annual celebrations of Independence Day. As the troops marched past the stand with their newly acquired Soviet equipment, it must have been clear to the spectators that dissent would not be brooked. The message was promptly rubbed in by Daoud's secret police, who arrested several dozen religious leaders found preaching against the government's un-Islamic tendencies. Women, released from the cotton prisons of their *chadors*, were soon to be found working in offices and factories, while Kabul University went co-educational.

The use of the armed forces and paramilitary police to intimidate opponents of Daoud's modernisation programmes was successful elsewhere too. When the government's road-building scheme in Paktia province was threatened in 1959 by an outbreak of tribal warfare, Kabul was able to rush its newly-mechanised army to the area with a speed which both impressed and dismayed the tribes. In the same year, a revolt in Qandahar was successfully crushed. But although ruthless, Daoud proceeded with caution against his conservative opponents, particularly the religious establishment. Each step towards the creation of a more modern and secular state was carefully vetted by his legal advisers to ensure that it did not violate the *Shariah*, Islamic law. The *ulema* were first invited to produce incontrovertible Quranic proof that a proposed reform was specifically forbidden by Islamic tenets. Only if they failed to do so, yet persisted in their objections, were more draconian measures taken.

Political reforms, however, failed to keep pace with social and economic changes. Daoud the autocrat was temperamentally unsuited to democratic politics; one formed minister likened his habitual manner with cabinet colleagues to 'a general dealing with his sergeants'. Subordinates were too frightened to question his decisions or to tell him if things were going wrong, and inefficiency and administrative incompetence were left to fester. At the same time, his efforts to promote education in the provinces, and the policy of luring the brightest provincial boys to Kabul with scholarships, brought increasing numbers of radicalised and

43

frustrated young men into contact with an insensitive government and an inert bureaucracy.

Daoud's blinkered foreign policy was the other major cause of dissatisfaction. His deliberate incitement of the Pashtun tribes on the southern side of the Durand Line had already pushed the country to the brink of war with Pakistan twice since 1953. The self-imposed economic blockade he ordered in 1961 was the last straw. It brought American aid projects grinding to a halt, forced a twenty-percent cut in the budgets of all ministries, pushed up prices – on some items by a hundred percent – and led to a dangerous dependency on the Soviet Union. Eventually, the restlessness of the educated minority and their desire for a greater say in the running of the country communicated itself to the ruling family. Even Daoud recognised that Afghanistan would have to change with the times. In a series of letters to his cousin King Zahir in 1962, he urged the introduction of a limited form of popular representation and curbs on the power of the monarchy. Possibly, in his heart, he expected to be voted back to power under the new constitution. But whatever his future plans, by early 1963 Daoud seems to have accepted that he had led the country up a diplomatic blind alley, and on 3rd March he submitted his resignation to the king.

After thirty years as an almost powerless figurehead, dominated first by his uncles and then by his cousin, Zahir Shah was now in a position to take real power into his own hands for the first time. Instead, he set about converting himself into a constitutional monarch. Having defused the crisis with Pakistan, his main priority was to ensure that the stifling thirty-five-year-old grip of the royal family on the country's political life was relaxed, and to prevent a comeback by Daoud. The king's new appointee as Prime Minister was a German-educated engineer and non-Pashtun, Dr Mohammad Yousuf, the former minister for mines and industries. From now on, the king made it known, the royal family would devolve its responsibilities to the educated Afghan middle class.

To the dismay of Daoud and other members of the royal family, that promise was converted into law in the 1964 constitution, which specifically debarred the king's relations from becoming Prime Minister, Members of Parliament or Justices of the Supreme Court. The constitution, approved after much acrimonious debate by an unusually representative Loya Jirga, provided the legal underpinning for a ten-year period of Democracy-i-Nau, or New Democracy. The constitution made Parliament the fount of power, although the king retained the right to dissolve it. The right to form political parties was conceded, at least in principle, for the first time. Secular legislation by Parliament was to take precedence over the *Shariah*, and the judiciary was separated from the executive. Human rights provisions provided for, among other things, equality before the law, freedom of expression and of worship, the abolition of banishment and forced labour, and elections by secret ballot.

The first elections under the new constitution were held in August and September 1965. Despite an intense propaganda campaign by the government to inform Afghans about their new freedoms, the rural majority reacted with their usual disdain for the bewildering goings-on in their remote capital. Even in Kabul, only about forty percent of eligible voters went to the polls, and the resulting Parliament was still dominated by rural landlords and members of the *ancien régime*. In the absence of a party structure, only they could bear the heavy burden of election expenses until the perquesites of office presented an opportunity to reimburse themselves. The most visible sign of the changing times was the election of four women MPs in a house of 216, and a sprinkling of well-to-do Marxists, headed by the student leader Babrak Karmal.

The contending factions which sprang up in the newly-elected *Wolosi Jirga* (Lower House) give a fair picture of the diverging trends of Afghan politics in 1965. Dupree

45

identifies six informal groupings: the ultra-conservatives, headed by the traditional religious leaders; a Pashtun chauvinist group, which feared the erosion of Pashtun domination; a group representing the interests of entrepreneurs, which favoured the relaxation of state controls on the economy; a centrist group which broadly supported the scope and pace of the king's progressive policies; a small group of liberals who wanted rapid development led by the public sector; and the tiny but highly vocal group on the far-left, which sought a radical utopia through the application of Marxist principles.[1]

Few of these groups had a constituency outside the main urban centres. For all the foreign-funded growth of the previous decade, most parts of Afghanistan in 1965 were still steeped in backwardness. Hundreds of thousands of nomads still criss-crossed the country in their annual migrations. Even in the settled areas, rural communities were introverted and hostile to outsiders, particularly government officials. Land, a wife, honour and clan identity were the only things which had value. The only point of contact most villagers had with the outside world, apart from a rare radio set, came during trips to the bazaar in the local town, where the tea-shops were centres of political and other gossip.

In mountainous regions, communications were even more primitive, and even neighbouring valleys might speak different dialects. In remoter areas, as late as the 1960's, some villagers believed that Amanullah, or even Habibullah, was still on the throne. Travelling in Nuristan in 1956, Eric Newby found hillmen who had to make an eighteen-day round trip to trade butter for caps. In most villages, there was no electricity. The industrial labour force was minuscule; about 14,000 workers lived in and around the capital, with a further 6,000 working elsewhere, either in the cotton-, sugar- and ghee-producing centre of Kunduz in the north, or in and around the other four main cities. Even these industrial workers tended to own a small plot of land back in their native villages. The cities themselves were no more than overgrown towns. Apart from Kabul, only Qandahar had a population exceeding a hundred thousand.

The political and educational horizons of villagers were as limited as their material possessions. By 1965, most towns had a modern government school run by a salaried teacher. Some wealthy families employed private tutors who taught secular subjects in Persian, but the bulk of teaching in the countryside was done by religious figures – *mullahs*, *maulvis* and *pirs* – and was centred on the mosque.

Mullahs were often barely literate: their main function was to teach young boys the ritual of prayer and key Quranic texts. Maulvis, religious scholars trained in private seminaries, were well-versed in subjects such as Arabic grammar and rhetoric, but were often just as prejudiced and blinkered as the mullah in their attitude to secular learning. Pirs, or hereditary saints, were supposed to initiate their disciples into the rites of Sufism, Islam's mystical tradition. But they were frequently more interested in exploiting the commercial potential of their venerated positions. One of the leading pirs in the resistance movement today is Syed Ahmad Gailani. In the 70's, he held the Kabul concession for Peugeot cars, but still allowed the water in which he washed his feet to be distributed to the sick. Other pirs in humbler circumstances did the best they could for themselves, battening off the superstition of villagers. As late as 1987, a Western traveller in Afghanistan, Bruce Wannell, noticed the 'abstracted dreamy manner and doll-like features of several pirs and sayyeds I met, as if a long tradition of accepting the adoration of the populace had fixed them in this attitude.'[2]

The education transmitted by these religious figures had, by the early twentieth century, become almost meaningless. The absurdity of the traditional 'art of disputation', as described here by a distinguished former Dean of the Faculty of Letters at Kabul University, Professor S. B.

Majrooh, would have provided perfect material for a Monty Python sketch:

> All possible questions were listed and the answers given and the student had simply to learn them by heart (if someone objects this, you answer that . . .) Opponents would come face to face; people would gather around them enjoying the confrontation like a cock fight. The defeated party was the one who failed to remember the right answer to the objection or faced a new objection not mentioned in his references. The best fight was disputation between two well-known maulvis. Each one would come with a large following of his students and donkey-loads of commentary books in Arabic. Arguments against arguments, books against books were produced. The disputation, interrupted by prayers, meals and sleep, was resumed the following morning and would continue for days. Strong emotions of anger, exchange of insults and occasionally physical fighting among the rival students were integral parts of the art of disputation. In the end, the opponents would depart without having won a clear-cut victory, promising to come soon for the next round.[3]

Kabul in 1965 presented an entirely different picture from the rest of the country. Though still in parts primitive, foul-smelling, fly-blown and decrepit, the aid boom of the fifties and sixties brought to the Afghan capital a jumble of high-rise buildings, offices, factories, cinemas, restaurants, supermarkets and garages. More important, it also brought an influx of ideas from the outside world. Foreign development projects required local people skilled in modern techniques; modern education opened the eyes of Afghan students to the huge gulf separating conditions in their country from those in the industrialised world.

Kabul had for generations been regarded by the intelligentsia as a centre of modern civilisation and attitudes. The country's only university and most of the high schools were situated there, as well as the apparatus of government and the central bureaucracy. The capital acted as a magnet for anyone whose aspirations went beyond the confines of their local community, and as a gateway to the world outside. Brewing amidst the stagnation of the countryside, it was a city in intellectual ferment. The bazaars buzzed with rumour about the goings-on in the Palace, while middle-class dissidents and dreamers conspired together in meeting places with radical chic, like the Shahi Bazaar Coffee House. The brief liberalisation of 1949 allowed political debate to move into the public arena for the first time, but even that proved too dangerous for the ruling regime. The abrupt termination of the liberal experiment in 1952 forced dissent and debate underground for another dozen years.

Throughout Asia, those were years of enormous change. The Suez Crisis of 1956, the growing military relationship between Pakistan and the United States in the mid-fifties, the abolition in 1962 of the Yemeni monarchy (perhaps the closest parallel to Afghanistan's own system), the Sino-Soviet split in the same year, and America's increasing involvement in Vietnam, all demanded intellectual assimilation and revised attitudes towards the interplay of nationalism, imperialism and development. By the time Zahir Shah's reforms eased the lid off the Kabul pot in 1964, it was already near boiling point. Newsprint provided the easiest and quickest medium through which to express the accumulated proliferation of ideas. Despite the considerable restrictions imposed on the press by the new regime, at least twenty-five newspapers sprang into existence in the capital between 1965 and 1970, as every shade of opinion between the extremes of revolution and reaction took the opportunity to expound their prescriptions for Afghanistan's political salvation.

There was a lot to criticise, and many receptive ears to listen. The lower and middle echelons of the civil service were particularly fertile ground. As bureaucrats, they were by definition part of the élite; even a humble clerk was a member of an exclusive club – the literate minority. But for those without connections, promotions and advancement could be painfully slow. In a society where clan and family ties were crucial, regulating against nepotism was next to impossible. People with the right connections – including friends and relations of the delegates elected to Parliament in 1965 – managed to secure jobs for which they were untrained and unsuited. In contrast, graduates who had gained their educational opportunities through merit and ability often found themselves unemployed, or in junior positions. Vacancies in the medical and teaching professions were not publicly advertised; jobs in the ministries were dished out as private favours, which, in a society founded on barter, had to be returned. No-one wanted to be sent out of Kabul to work in Afghanistan's benighted provincial backwaters. And, as the sixties progressed and both Soviet and American aid programmes to Afghanistan were slashed in size, the situation became even worse for young, educated males, and correspondingly better for the propagandists.

If Kabul was Afghanistan's intellectual hothouse, then Kabul University was the hothouse incubator. The first faculty – Medicine – was founded in 1932. By 1964, when USAID money paid for a new campus development on the western outskirts of Kabul, there were eleven faculties altogether, including Political Science, Theology and Engineering. Except for the Theology faculty, which was associated with Egypt's famous Al-Azhar University, each faculty was affiliated with American or European institutions and conducted its classes according to Western methods.

The University was the goal for any bright young Afghan who could not afford a foreign education. Ironically, in a capital which was semi-divorced from the rest of the country, its most élite institution became the centre of a nationwide network. By the late sixties, students from the provinces were coming to Kabul in unprecedented numbers, either to the University, or to the newly established teacher-training college attached to the Ministry of Education. Over half the students lived together in campus dormitories. They tended to be maintained by government scholarships, and were more susceptible than youths from relatively sophisticated urban backgrounds to the political cross-currents sweeping Kabul society.

Students, plucked from their small-town backgrounds and introduced to a whole set of alien ideas, were the natural recruiting ground for ideological extremists of all hues. Those who had entered the teaching profession and would be returning to the provinces were particularly suitable. Often they took back with them their newly implanted radicalism, and by the mid-seventies, urban centres throughout the country were tenuously connected by informal networks of Kabul-trained political activists.

Islamic radicalism – more often referred to in the West as fundamentalism – was one of the ideologies which took root at Kabul University. Unlike orthodox Islam, it did not repudiate Western rationalism, but instead sought to harness science to its own ends. Many of the leading recruits to the Islamic movement were engineering students, either at the University or at the Soviet-built Polytechnic. Gulbuddin Hekmatyar, later to emerge as the most powerful and feared of the resistance leaders in Peshawar, and Ahmed Shah Massoud, who would become the best-known of the mujahedin field commanders, both started adult life as engineering students in Kabul. Government secondary schools and the *madrassas*, theological seminaries run by the government, were other centres of recruitment.

The aim of the radicals was the creation of an Islamic state based on equality, brotherhood and social justice. Like true communism, it was not instantly attainable, but something which had to be worked towards. The *Shariah* was the perfect law, and was, if interpreted correctly, the source of all knowledge necessary for the correct ordering of society. The radicals were equally outraged by the inroads of secularism and Westernisation on their society, and by the supine compliance of the traditional, conservative *ulema* to the corrupt dictates of what they considered to be Kabul's un-Islamic regimes.

Extreme puritanism was the most visible hallmark of the Islamic radicals. Materialistic values and decadent activities were an abomination to be rooted out: in particular, alcohol, gambling, usury, cinema shows and sex – in short, the main pursuits of modern Western civilisation. The Society of Muslim Brothers, founded in Egypt in 1928, was the prototype organisation of the radical movement. Its goal was to create a genuine true Islamic society by positive social, political and, if necessary, military action. Members were organised into 'families', primary units in a pyramidal structure, which emphasised personal piety and group solidarity. A similar movement began to develop in Afghanistan in 1958, led by a group of religious intellectuals and Egyptian-trained professors at the Theology faculty of Kabul University. By 1965, their student disciples had organised themselves into a militant branch known as the Muslim Youth Organisation, which had strong links, at least ideologically, with the Muslim Brothers in Egypt. At first they confined themselves to the campus, where they build mosques, preached sermons and battled with the communists, but around 1970, the radicals took their preaching and Islamic reform movement into the countryside.

A certain type of student tended to be attracted to the world-view of the Islamic radicals. Different areas of Afghanistan had different religious traditions. The plain of Shomali, for instance, to the north of Kabul, had long been a bastion of fundamentalism. It was in this area that Bacha Saqao had rallied enough supporters to depose the 'godless' Amanullah in 1929. Broadly speaking, the less tribal an area was, the more influence the radicals could hope to exert. The sons of Tajik and Uzbek refugees who had fled to northern Afghanistan from the religious persecutions in Soviet central Asia in the 1920's and 30's were natural recruits. Maoism tended to attract the young, educated Shias of central Afghanistan, rebels against their own rigidly hierarchical society. For rather less clear reasons, Soviet-style Marxism was most attractive to de-tribalised Pashtuns in both Afghanistan and Pakistan.

For some provincial youngsters, who had been alienated from their religious upbringing by the ignorance and dogmatism of traditional religious teachers, socialist or Marxist philosophy seemed to offer a comprehensive answer to the dilemmas of their society. The French-educated Professor Majrooh, who watched countless students passing through his classes at Kabul University, later described the attractions Marxism had for young Asian minds on which a Western training had been superimposed:

> Having learned the new ideas about time, history and rapid development, the educated became impatient. There was in their countries the remains of the colonial time, tyrants and dictators, oppression and vast misery of the local people. They did not believe that a process of evolution would achieve anything; anyway it would have been too slow a process for them. They wished to see the changes in their own span of life. For this reason, the myth of revolution became the magical solution for all evil. In this respect, Marxism–Leninism presented the most attractive prospect: it was magic with a scientific and rational appearance, a rational dream doomed to become true.[4]

The People's Democratic Party of Afghanistan was one of the organisations formed by these educated and impatient revolutionaries. Some of them seem to have approached Marxism with the unquestioning faith which the majority of their countrymen reserved for Islam. In 1970, an ode was published to celebrate the centenary of Lenin's birth, in

53

which the 'Great Leader' was praised in terms traditionally reserved for the Prophet Mohammad. It was outrageous enough to bring the traditional clergy and the Islamic radicals together for the first time in a demonstration which was violently suppressed by the government regime inside the grounds of one of the capital's main mosques.

Some of the PDPA leaders – even the notoriously brutal Hafizullah Amin – are rumoured to have been deeply religious at some stage in their lives. When I met the present party chief, Dr Najibullah, in Kabul in March 1987, I asked him what part Islam had played in his life. Even at that time, when the regime was making strenuous efforts to establish its religious credentials, Najib could only bring himself to answer ambiguously that 'I was born in a Muslim family'. Yet Afghans, both in the government and the resistance, say that Najib was a devout teenager. 'When we were in high school, Najib was a good Muslim,' a senior official in the resistance movement told journalist James Rupert just after his former classmate was appointed head of the PDPA in May 1986. 'One day, we had gone swimming near Kabul and were riding our bicycles back and Najib made us stop on the way for prayers. He never missed his prayers'.[5]

It's impossible to know why, or exactly when, Najibullah decided that Islam could not provide remedies for the ills of his society. But by the time he enrolled in the University as a medical student, he had stopped saying his prayers five times a day and had become instead a full-time left-wing activist. Somewhere along the line, rejecting one dogma and embracing another, Afghanistan's future leader switched his allegiance from Islam to communism.

Najib joined the PDPA after leaving high school in 1965, the year of its birth. The founding fathers of the party had had a much longer involvement in left-wing politics. Nur Mohammad Taraki, who was to become Afghanistan's first communist president, claimed later that the nucleus of the PDPA 'was formed twenty years before it was established'.

54

Alone of all the party's founders, Taraki came from the exploited rural classes for whom the communists claimed to speak. His family, which belonged to the large turbulent Ghilzai Pashtun clan, had no reason to love the ruling establishment in Kabul. They were among those Ghilzais whom Abdur Rahman Khan had forcibly resettled in the Hazara areas of central Afghanistan in order to keep both communities busy fighting with each other rather than against his royal court.

Takari's father was an illiterate, semi-nomadic livestock dealer who had higher ambitions for his son, and sent him to the local village primary school. After completing his secondary schooling in Qandahar, he was hired by the Pashtun Trading Company, which sent him in 1934 to work as a clerk in the Bombay office of its fruit export business. There, he first encountered communism, meeting and mixing with members of the recently-formed Communist Party of India. Those first ties lasted for forty years, and he was still in contact with the CPI in 1976, when it played a crucial role in re-uniting the divided People's Democratic Party.

After returning to Afghanistan in 1937, Taraki got a government job and took a part-time course in law and political science. Soon he was in trouble with the authorities. Either because of his radical ideas, or, according to hostile biographers, because he was suspected of embezzlement, he was posted to the north-eastern province of Badakhshan, Afghanistan's equivalent of Siberia. Those two years of internal exile must have completed his alienation from the ruling regime. With little else to do, Taraki began to write socially-aware poetry, short stories and novels which eventually got him noticed not only by other Afghan intellectuals, but also by the Soviet embassy. But he was still regarded by the government as more of a nuisance than a threat. While the leading radicals were imprisoned after the crackdown of 1952, Taraki was given a job in Washington as an embassy press attaché. Even after publicly denouncing Daoud at a press conference and being recalled to Kabul, Taraki failed to win for himself the revolutionary laurels of arrest. No further government jobs were made available, but he worked for several years as a translator at the US aid mission in Kabul.

Anyone employed by foreigners in Kabul was automatically monitored by Daoud's political police, and it's possible that Taraki was given the opportunity of redeeming himself by acting as a government informer on US embassy activities. But by this time his real patron, and certainly his ideological mentor, was Moscow. Although there is no definitive proof that he was a paid agent of the KGB, he may have been in touch with the Soviet embassy as early as 1948, and by 1960 he is thought to have been receiving a subsidy from the embassy in the guise of royalties from translations of his novels into Russian.

Taraki was an introverted, unsophisticated, hard-drinking, impractical and rather weak man, a dreamer rather than a do-er. The man who was destined to become his chief lieutenant, disciple and murderer was just the opposite. Hafizullah Amin was described by his tutor at Columbia University, New York, where he took an M.A. in educational administration in 1957, as 'smooth and personable . . . a bright guy with lots of ability'.[6] Amin preferred to work behind the scenes, and his ideological commitment to Marxism is questionable. But he did have hard-headed organisational ability, deviousness, unbridled ambition and the ruthlessness necessary to get to the top.

The son of a low-level civil servant who died when he was still young, Amin was put through primary school by his brother before his ability was recognised. From then on, he became a scholarship boy in a series of Kabul institutions – secondary school, teacher-training school, the University (where he studied physics and maths), and later at the American universities of Columbia and Wisconsin. Teaching was the best avenue of advancement for poor provincial boys with no connections, and Amin's career took off quickly. By the time he was selected for a scholar-ship at Columbia, he was already principal of a Kabul high school, and on his return was posted to a succession of schools and training institutes.

Amin's involvement in teacher training was ideally suited for someone seeking to influence those who themselves would be influencing even younger minds. By the early 60's, he had not only met Taraki, but had also developed an extensive network of contacts in different provinces, followers who would form the communists' main power-base in the rural areas. Amin's political thinking seems to have veered sharply to the left during his first trip to the United States in 1957. A further chance to study the evils of capitalism, at Wisconsin University between 1962 and 1965, turned him into a fully-fledged communist. Returning to Kabul, he joined the newly formed PDPA and narrowly lost the Paghman seat in the 1965 elections.

Both Taraki and Amin were from modest backgrounds, and both were Pashto-speaking members of the Ghilzais clan, which has been in almost constant revolt against its Durrani overlords since Afghanistan was created. Their main rival for the leadership of the fledgeling communist movement was a man of a different stamp. Babrak Karmal's only disadvantage in life was the death of his mother when he was very young. Part of his youthful rebelliousness may have sprung from the resentment he felt towards his step-mother, but otherwise, he had all the privileges of a member of the Dari-speaking Durrani establishment. His father retired at the end of a successful military career, having attained the rank of general and the Governorship of Paktia province, and Babrak was educated at one of the best schools in Kabul.

Even before he was formally admitted to the University to study law in 1951, Babrak was beginning to earn a reputation as a firebrand and orator. In those heady days of the liberal parliament, he plunged headlong into the excitement, a rebel with only a vague cause and without

57

any coherent ideology. He wrote articles for one of the short-lived opposition newspapers of the time, and played a prominent role in demonstrations protesting against the closure of the student union. When the clampdown came and Taraki was sent away to Washington, Babrak was considered important enough to be jailed alongside other leading leftists. It was only there, behind bars, according to his own account, that he was converted to communism together with another inmate, Mir Akbar Khyber, a former police officer who became Babrak's close friend and ideological adviser. It was in jail too, experiencing for the first time some of the privations of his fellow countrymen, that Babrak assumed the name Karmal, meaning 'the workers' comrade'.

Babrak got out of jail in 1956 and then spent two years in the army doing national service before rejoining the University and completing his law degree. With the cachet of a three-year prison sentence adding to his natural flamboyance, he cut an attractive figure for younger student radicals as he set about recruiting supporters in earnest. Two of the men who came under Babrak's influence at that time – Noor Ahmed Noor, from a prosperous land-owning family, and Sultan Ali Keshtmand, a Shia from the Hazarajat – belong to the rare category of PDPA founding members who are still in high office today. Another of Babrak's most ardent supporters was a female medical student called Anahita Ratebzad, who, at the time, was married to Zahir Shah's personal physician. Like many Afghan women, Anahita was taken with Babrak's fleshy good looks, and she is reputed to have become his mistress.

In 1960, Karmal and Khyber set up a 'study circle', one of a number of ostensibly innocuous groups organised by left-wing intellectuals to exchange ideas and conspire against Daoud. Such study circles had existed since 1956, but it was only in 1963 that the idea of forming a common leftist front began to materialise. For the first time in a decade, the atmosphere seemed right for underground political activities to come into the open, and Daoud's resignation was taken as the signal to increase the pace of organisational activity. It took just five weeks after the promulgation of the 1964 constitution, which theoretically legitimised political parties, to complete discussions on the basic documents of the new party.

On New Year's Day 1965, thirty men gathered at the house of the movement's elder statesman, Nur Muhammad Taraki, to launch the People's Democratic Party of Afghanistan upon an unsuspecting Afghan public.

Even at that time, fifteen years before the Soviet invasion, communism was a dirty word in Afghanistan. Most Afghans equated it with atheism, and many in the north of the country had first-hand experience of the religious persecutions practised by Soviet communists against the Muslims of Soviet central Asia in the 1920's and 30's. The decision not to describe the PDPA as a communist party may have been taken partly to avoid its immediate suppression by the authorities. At the same time, it also suggests that the founders of the PDPA realised that the ideology to which they subscribed was unacceptable to the peasants and workers whom they claimed to represent.

Nevertheless, in spite of denials by every PDPA leader from Taraki to Najibullah that it was ever a communist party, the PDPA's constitution leaves no room for doubt. Article 1 reads: 'The PDPA is the highest political organ and the vanguard of the working class and all labourers in Afghanistan. The PDPA, whose ideology is the practical experience of Marxism-Leninism, is founded on the voluntary union of the progressive and informed people of Afghanistan: the workers, peasants, artisans, and intellectuals of the country.'[7] In fact, it was a party composed solely of male, mostly middle-class Marxist intellectuals. The workers, peasants and artisans referred to in the constitution were conspicuous by their absence from the founding congress. Women – who were guaranteed equal social and political rights in the founding charter – were represented

59

only by Taraki's wife, whose contribution was confined to serving the tea.[8]

The organisational structure adopted by the PDPA was an exact copy of the Soviet model. Its 'main principle and guideline' was 'democratic centralism', which the party constitution defined as the 'adherence of lower officials to the decisions of higher officials' (in other words, unquestioning obedience to the party). Membership was restricted, and candidates had to undergo a probationary period.

The party ideology was outlined in the first two editions of the party newspaper *Khalq* – 'The People', or 'The Masses' – which began publication in April 1966 under a blazing red masthead. What was effectively a watered-down version of the party manifesto identified the source of Afghanistan's misery and backwardness as the 'economic and political hegemony of the feudal class'. The party's immediate 'strategic objective' was therefore defined as the promotion of a 'national democratic revolution', in other words, the intermediate phase predicated by classical Marxism as the path to socialism for any pre-industrial society. The manifesto advocated sweeping reforms in virtually every area of life, including land reforms and debt relief for small farmers. Economic growth would be 'non-capitalistic', and on a scale grand enough to eliminate backwardness 'within the lifespan of one generation'. Foreign policy, as summarised by a party history published ten years later, consisted of supporting 'the world-wide national liberation movement against imperialist aggression, and friendly relations with the socialist countries, primarily with the Soviet Union'. Just in case anybody had missed the point that the new party was oriented directly to Moscow, Taraki accepted an invitation to visit the Soviet Union in 1965. He stayed for forty-two days and was quoted as saying later that he had been treated like a head of state.

The seven-member Central Committee set up by the PDPA at its founding congress represented a carefully worked-out balance of individuals drawn from different left-wing study circles. Taraki was chosen as General Secretary and Babrak Karmal as his deputy. But the subsequent elections to Parliament – in which Babrak won a seat while Taraki was defeated – made the alliance even more uneasy. The rivalry between the two men, never far from the surface, exploded the following year, when the government banned the PDPA newspaper *Khalq* as dangerously subversive. Babrak blamed the closure on the decision to adopt a red masthead, which he criticised as 'leftist adventurism', a barely veiled attack on Taraki, who was editor-in-chief.

After much bitter infighting, the PDPA split into two rival parties in July 1967, only two years after it was founded. Each had its own Central Committee, manifesto and constitution. Taraki's faction continued to be known as 'Khalq', while Babrak named his faction 'Parcham', or 'The Banner', after the newspaper he was licensed to publish in 1968. With a seat in parliament, a following among the student community and the 'Parcham' newspaper acting as his mouthpiece, Babrak clearly felt that his was the stronger position, and appeals by the Soviet embassy to both factions to unite fell on deaf ears.

The underlying reasons for the split are difficult to unravel. If it was simply a clash of personalities between Taraki and Babrak, it's unlikely that the rivalry between 'Khalq' and 'Parcham' would have lasted until the present day. Clues must be sought in the different social backgrounds of the two men, and what they represented. Although their fundamental aims were similar, judging by the almost identical manifestos of their respective parties, their motivations and tactics were very different. Taraki, in spite of his earlier compromises with the regime, was a Marxist purist of long-standing conviction. Babrak was a more recent convert to communism and the antithesis of a conviction politician. It's significant that he and his closest supporters tended to come from wealthier, urban, Dari-speaking families, which were more attuned to the ways of the establishment. Khalq supporters, on the other hand, were generally from poorer families in the rural areas, and were predominantly Pashto-speaking.

Babrak and his entourage were more rebels than revolutionaries, perhaps more attracted to Marxism by their intellects than by their emotions. While Taraki believed firmly in revolution, Babrak favoured a more pragmatic, evolutionary approach. His praise of Zahir Shah as the world's 'most progressive king' earned his faction the contempt of the Khalqis, who dubbed it the 'royal communist party'. But by the time Babrak came to power and was able to put his more cautious approach into practice, it was already too late. The Khalqi wing of the party had already antagonised the country beyond endurance with its drastic reforms. Whether or not Babrak would have done things any differently, the arrival of Soviet tanks and gunship helicopters in support of 'the revolution' did not encourage the average Afghan peasant to search for subtle differences between the rival wings of the party. Even today, after ten years of rule by Parcham, their opponents universally refer to PDPA activists as 'Khalqis'. However important it may be in Kabul, the split is completely irrelevant to the resistance; all are communist, and none must be allowed to remain in power.

Unrepresentative though they were of the majority of their countrymen, the founders of the PDPA – and of the other left-wing parties which sprang up at around the same time – found a ready audience among the student community in Kabul. The first issue of *Khalq* sold 20,000 copies and was peddled on the streets by high school and University students. Over the next ten years students turned in growing numbers to the left. 1968 was the heyday of anti-Americanism, and as US military involvement in Vietnam came to its climax, Kabul's restless youths attached themselves to the periphery of the global student community by growing their hair long and mounting demonstrations. Their influence was out of all proportion to their numbers, and demonstrated the fragility of Zahir Shah's tentative experiment with democracy. The very first manifestation of student power, beginning just ten days after the new Parliament convened on 14th October 1965, was enough to unseat the king's handpicked Prime Minister.

The atmosphere in the new Parliament was volatile from the very start. The king's decision to retain Dr Yousuf as Prime Minister, who in turn retained the services of a good number of ministers from the Daoud era, was intensely frustrating for the newly-elected delegates. In spite of the powers given to Parliament by the 1964 Constitution, it seemed as if the same old ministerial clique intended to perpetuate itself in office. At the same time, few delegates had any idea of how to conduct themselves in a parliamentary democracy. The air was thick with abuse, as member after member heaped charges of corruption, bribery and nepotism on the cabinet. Even the royal family was attacked in veiled terms.

On the day that Dr Yousuf was to seek a vote of confidence, Babrak Karmal, who had emerged as one of his most vocal parliamentary critics, played his master card. Instigated by PDPA agitators, students from the University burst into the Assembly chamber shouting angry slogans and staged a sit-in. Amidst the chaos, troops were called in to clear the chamber and Parliament was adjourned. The next day, 25th October, troops opened fire on another protest demonstration, killing two students and a bystander. The deaths provided the first martyrs for the student cause. The bloodstained shirts were turned into red banners, and demonstrations became a daily occurrence. Dr Yousuf lasted just four more days. On 29th October he resigned, and the king appointed a western-educated liberal, Hashim Maiwandwal, as the new Prime Minister.

The growing ferment, both inside and outside the Parliament, was fed by the overnight mushrooming of publications representing the views of all shades of opinion; communists, Islamic radicals, Pashtun chauvinists, social democrats and many others. Their only common feature was that they were all highly critical of the government. In 1967, one journal went so far as to name a long string of highly-placed individuals and government officials as CIA spies, while Islamic journals tended to print exposés – real or imagined – of the nefarious activities of the KGB.

More worrying still to the government was the way in which the unrest was beginning to spread beyond the capital. The sudden drop in foreign loans after 1965 was beginning to bite, and graduates increasingly found themselves unemployed, or thrust into unsuitable jobs outside Kabul which left them bitter and dissatisfied. As student activists started returning to the provinces to teach or work, stirrings of militancy began to be felt in the backwaters of Afghanistan. In 1968, student strikes which began in Kabul spread as far afield as Nimroze in the extreme south-west, Kunduz in the north and Paktia on the south-eastern border with Pakistan. Some strikes were non-political, but others were staged in support of industrial workers, who were also being swept up in the wave of unrest. Between April and June 1968 there were at least twenty strikes for better pay and conditions in industrial centres around the country, some of which turned violent. In May 1969, more deaths occurred in Kabul in a clash between police and students. Educational institutions were shut down, which only made matters worse, since the students returned to their home towns and villages and continued to organise demonstrations.

It's hard to say how much of the trouble of these years was a spontaneous reaction to unfulfilled expectations and how much was directly fomented by extremist groups. The strength of the left was undoubtedly increasing steadily, with the drive for recruitment expanding from the student community into the civil service, the police and the army. Pro-Peking Maoist organisations, like Shola-e-Javed or Eternal Flame, won a following among the Hazara Shia underclass in Kabul, and is believed to have been behind a rash of industrial strikes which erupted in the summer of

1968. Later, the PDPA claimed that it led about two thousand meetings and demonstrations throughout the country from 1965 to 1973 'and thus played a vital role in the political reawakening of the masses'.

The elections of 1969 did nothing to relieve the mounting tensions. With Parliament's influence on the increase, backwood notables and tribal elders arranged for their sons or nephews to be elected. Money-power, combined with official interference, ensured an even more deeply conservative Assembly than before, although non-Pashtuns were better represented. The left was all but eliminated. Of the four Marxist members, only Babrak Karmal retained his seat, though Hafizullah Amin managed to secure election from Paghman.

Outside Parliament the feud between communism and Islamic radicalism was beginning to spiral out of control. The University was particularly badly affected. In 1971 it was closed for six months as the authorities struggled to deal with the start of a prolonged academic dress rehearsal for the all-out civil war of the following decade. The controversial 'Ode to Lenin' printed in the pages of *Parcham* in 1970 brought the battle off the campus and onto the streets of Kabul. The tame, pro-government mullahs who organised the first protests were quickly joined by fanatics from the provinces who took the movement over and started preaching against the regime. Some were imprisoned and others deported back to the provinces, where they busied themselves with fomenting minor revolts which had to be put down by the army.

The Islamic backlash also took the form of attacks on women wearing Western dress, one of the most provocative symptoms of encroaching secularisation. By 1970 branches of the 'All-Afghanistan Women's Council' had been established in many provinces to campaign for female literacy and women's rights, and Islamic radicals were incensed. According to one senior PDPA woman activist I met in Kabul, mullahs declared in 1971 'that women should stay in the house. Reactionaries sprayed acid on women's faces when they came out in public without a veil, and when women wore stockings, they shot at their legs with guns with silencers'.[9] Such attacks provoked counter-demonstrations by women. For over a decade they had been working in factories and offices in Kabul and they were now enrolling in growing numbers at the University. They already had much to lose.

In the end, though, it was the more elemental forces of nature which put an end to the ten-year-old democratic experiment. There is little documentation in English of the drought which began in 1969 and lasted for three years, but its economic and human effects were catastrophic. The estimates of the number of deaths in the famine of 1971–2 vary wildly, from 50,000 to half a million. The isolated mountain highlands of Hazarajat were particularly badly hit. Over half the livestock there is thought to have died or been slaughtered because of lack of fodder, and countless parents were forced to sell their children into bonded labour. The lack of communications and of roads penetrating the interior made it virtually impossible to send in relief supplies.

After the failure of the second successive harvest in September 1971, with food prices already treble their 1968 level, the government predicted a further grain shortfall of half a million tons, and finally appealed for international assistance. But even when help finally arrived – including 200,000 tons of wheat from the United States – much of it was squandered through profiteering, corruption, inefficiency and maladministration. Public confidence in the regime – insofar as it existed – was badly shaken. The winter of 1971 was a harsh one, and while the king took himself off to Italy on holiday, countless peasants and nomads lost their flocks through starvation or their land to money-lenders.

Zahir Shah's last Prime Minister, Moosa Shafiq, did his best to salvage the situation. His background – educated in

Muslim theology at Al-Azhar in Cairo and in international law at Columbia University – suggests a conscious effort by the king and his advisers to placate both extremes of the increasingly vocal opposition. In his short but vigorous seven-month-long tenure, Moosa Shafiq resolved a longstanding river-waters dispute with Iran, launched anti-corruption and literacy drives and revitalised the administration. But the fate of the king and his system was already sealed. The plans of the conspirators were already laid.

On 17th July 1973, after ruling Afghanistan for exactly forty years, Zahir Shah was deposed. At his first press conference, the country's new ruler told reporters that 'whenever a nation verges on disaster, and corruption in governmental institutions reaches its highest, and hope for reform is totally lost . . . then a resort to revolutionary actions must take place.' The man promising revolution that summer's day was none other than the king's cousin and former Prime Minister, Mohammad Daoud.

FIVE

Revolution in Two Acts: Daoud's Republic and the Communist Coup 1973–1978

Daoud had been watching developments with growing unease and, no doubt, a deepening conviction that what was needed was a dose of strong leadership. Debarred from holding high office by the 1964 constitution, his only route back to power was through the military, and as Defence Minister and later as Prime Minister, he had already laid the groundwork for a future coup. The reconstruction of the armed forces had been one of his top priorities, and the $25 million arms deal he had struck with the Soviet Union in 1956 had given them the modern weaponry necessary for any army's self-respect. At the same time, he had consciously built up an officer corps loyal to himself, personally supervising the appointment of all middle-ranking and senior officers, and favouring those who had no power-base or family connections of their own.

The young army officers who started to congregate around Daoud in 1969 provided the instrument he needed to help him seize power. But he also needed political support, to run the administration after taking-over. The left-wing seemed to be the best ally. Some of the Soviet-trained army officers coming under his wing had already made contact with the growing pro-Soviet Marxist movement. And while Daoud himself was too much a product of the proud Pashtun aristocracy to embrace an alien ideology, he had never hesitated to co-opt the services of the left whenever it suited his purposes. After becoming Prime Minister in 1953 he had crushed the Awakened Youth Movement, yet three years later he released all but the most diehard of the left-wing activists from jail and rehabilitated many of them into the administration, including Babrak Karmal. A decade later, as the democratic experiment lurched towards irretrievable breakdown, Daoud once again welcomed leftists, along with liberals and restive army officers, into his political seminars, whose aim was to analyse the mistakes of his previous regime, and discuss how to do better next time.

With his Soviet links, statist policies, royal pedigree and advancing years, Daoud must have seemed to Babrak the ideal short-term figurehead for the 'national democratic' phase of the Revolution. So far as Daoud was concerned, Babrak – the son of one of his trusted former generals – provided a convenient channel of communication with the pro-Soviet left. According to the Kabul rumour-mill, Daoud helped to finance Parcham soon after its break with Khalq in 1967. Babrak became a frequent participant in Daoud's seminars, and at some stage Daoud must have recognised that, among the motley crew of malcontents, dissidents and hot-heads who constituted his political base, only Babrak and his Parchamites had the cadres, cohesion and discipline which he would need to secure control of the civil administration and implement the reforms he had in mind.

Some of the left-wing army officers who participated in the 1973 coup met Babrak for the first time at Daoud's political seminars. But by that time, realising that propagating Marxism among the masses would be a slow business, Parcham had already embarked on a deliberate policy of military recruitment. It may be that the Soviet embassy sometimes tipped Parcham off about potential recruits who had received training in the Soviet Union. Babrak was later identified as a long-standing KGB agent by Major Kuzichkin, a KGB official who defected to the West in 1982.[1] In 1973, however, communist subversion of the armed forces was still limited. It was only after Daoud seized power that many of the army's young turks became disillusioned with the slow pace of reform and gravitated towards the communist camp.

Western journalists were quick to allege that the 1973 coup was directly instigated by Moscow. But, so far, *glasnost* has not blown open the doors of the Kremlin's secret archives on Afghanistan, and the evidence remains circumstantial. Whether involved or not, Moscow had plenty of reason to welcome the replacement of a Western-oriented liberal democracy with a Moscow-friendly autocrat surrounded by a coterie of Soviet-influenced civilians and soldiers. Even better, the new regime was generally acceptable to the Afghan people. Daoud was the king's first cousin, a Durrani Pashtun of royal descent. For most Afghans, it was no more than the latest in a long series of palace coups: a development which they had no reason to oppose so long as they were left in peace.

The coup was all over before breakfast. Around dawn on 17th July 1973, several hundred rebel troops seized the royal palace, the radio station and the airport. Key royalists were arrested, including another of the king's more ambitious cousins, Major-General Abdul Wali Khan. The king himself was away in Italy for medical treatment and didn't put up even the semblance of a struggle. A few weeks later, he abdicated formally and placed himself at the service of the Republic 'as an Afghan citizen'. He must have realised from the start that he had no cards to play. Even his army chief of staff was reported to have participated in Daoud's takeover, and there was virtually no resistance. A week later, Daoud reported at his first press conference that only 'four members of the police force were killed as well as two armymen when their machinegun went off accidentally, and I very much regret to say that a dedicated and heroic tank operator was sacrificed when his tank plunged into the Kabul river.'

At 7.20 a.m. on the day of the coup, Daoud went on Kabul radio to proclaim the abolition of the monarchy and the creation of the Republic of Afghanistan. He attacked the preceding decade as a period of 'false democracy which from the beginning was founded on private and class interests', and the constitutional monarchy as a 'despotic regime'. The following day, it was announced that a 'central committee' had been formed, and that Daoud had been 'elected' President and Prime Minister.

The full membership of the committee was never revealed, but it contained a significant number of left-wingers. About half a dozen closet communists were also included in the Cabinet. Among them were Hassan Sharq (who was to make a dramatic reappearance fifteen years later when he was drafted in as Prime Minister at the tail end of the Soviet occupation), and the army's Major Faiz Mohammad, who was allotted the powerful post of Interior Minister. Other left-wing officers like Abdul Qadir and Zia Mohammad Zia were rewarded with senior military appointments. Parcham's top civilian leaders – including Babrak himself, Anahita Ratebzad and Noor Ahmad Noor – became members of the Central Committee and of Daoud's inner circle. Scores of Parcham supporters were given jobs in the middle ranks of the bureaucracy, and 160 of the party's keenest young radicals were dispatched to administrative positions in the provinces, where they tried without success to put their progressive ideas into practice.

Parcham's sudden arrival in the ante-rooms of power via the backdoor gave it cause for immense satisfaction. Khalq was out in the cold, and Babrak was determined to keep it there. According to Khalqi propaganda, he let it be known that any continuation of party activity amounted to treason, since the government was already carrying out the PDPA's goals. Indeed, some of the reforms outlined by Daoud a month after the coup could have come straight out of the PDPA manifesto. The new regime's aims were defined as the creation of a strong state sector, higher living standards and a radical administrative overhaul. Friendship with the Soviet Union was placed at the top of the foreign policy agenda – it was, according to Daoud, 'unfalterable'. He also promised minimum wages, social security insurance,

71

free primary education for both sexes, land reforms and the establishment of agricultural co-operatives.

Daoud's commitment to reform was not just a cynical ploy to consolidate his rather precarious power-base. He made an early start by distributing his own ancestral lands, and in 1976 introduced legislation which set stringent ceilings on land holdings. But his radicalism was tempered by extreme pragmatism. His main concern was revenue collection, and he recognised the limits beyond which it was dangerous to go. Landlords, for instance, were generously compensated for land expropriated by the state, and peasants who couldn't afford to buy the surplus got no help from the state. Daoud was too experienced, and too much a product of the establishment, to launch a frontal assault on the country's traditional bastions of power. Outlining his programme in a speech just one month after seizing power, he warned that the experiences of other Third World countries 'confirm the fact that haste and resorting to every possible and impossible measure for the sudden overcoming of centuries of backwardness and the immediate reforming of all affairs, is a futile and immature act.' It was a warning that the PDPA would have done well to heed when it completed the second act of the 'revolution' in 1978.

Given time, Daoud's cautious approach would almost certainly have lost him the support of the left wing. But before they could turn against him, potential opponents found themselves isolated by allegations of corruption and inefficiency spread by the wily President. By late 1974 the rift between Daoud and Parcham was so well known that Khalq sent the President a letter offering to replace 'corrupt' Parchamites with its own officials. But Daoud, now feeling far more secure, ignored the offer. He was already easing prominent leftists out of the Cabinet. The first ministers were sacked in mid-1974. The following year, Deputy Prime Minister Hassan Sharq, Interior Minister Faiz Mohammad, and several others were given the push. At the same time, Daoud completed his purge of the left by sacking from the armed forces nearly forty Soviet-trained officers, including men like Abdul Qadir who had helped him seize power two years earlier.

By 1975, it was becoming clear that Daoud was reverting to his old autocratic style of government, concentrating all power in his own hands and ruthlessly suppressing all opposition. Trusting no-one, he found it even harder to delegate than during his first period in office, and at one point in the mid-70's held no less than six Cabinet posts himself. The leftists were replaced by cronies, conservatives and hardline anti-communists. Opponents outside the government also came under attack. Alleged plots were crushed in each of the first four years of Daoud's rule. Hundreds of political prisoners were arrested and some were murdered or executed, including a former Prime Minister, Hashem Maiwandwal, a widely respected social democrat who had formed his own party in the late 1960's and who was generally considered a potential partner and eventual successor to Daoud. The extremist groups which had proliferated in the late 1960's also found themselves on Daoud's hitlist, including the Maoist parties and the Islamic radicals. Within a year of the coup, Daoud's inefficient but ubiquitous political police had penetrated the meetings of the Muslim Youth Organisation and arrested two hundred of its sympathisers. The movement's leaders escaped just in time. Led by Gulbuddin Hekmatyar and Burhanuddin Rabbani, a group of Islamic radicals fled to Pakistan where they were welcomed with open arms by Pakistan's new Prime Minister, Zulfikar Ali Bhutto, and became the nucleus of the early Islamic resistance movement.

Having rid himself of both communist and Islamic radicals, Daoud banned political activities and opposition newspapers, and set up his own National Revolutionary Party. Bankrupt of more productive political ideas, by 1977 he was moving towards institutionalised one-party rule.

Daoud's double-cross of the left was mirrored by his

betrayal of Afghanistan's 'unfalterable' friendship with the Soviet Union. His initial tilt to Moscow was at least partially intended as a trade-off for Soviet support on the Pashtunistan issue. In 1973, Daoud spotted an opportunity to strike a decisive blow for his favourite cause. The year before, Pakistan's eastern wing had broken away in a brutal civil war, and its Bengali inhabitants, with Indian help, had established the independent nation of Bangladesh. The Pakistani army was defeated and humiliated, and the country's other minority nationalities, particularly the Baluchis and the Pashtuns, were clamouring for greater autonomy, if not outright independence. When Prime Minister Bhutto engineered the dismissal of the opposition-run provincial governments of Baluchistan and the Frontier Province in 1973, Baluchi tribal leaders, supported by the Marxist students, raised the standard of revolt.

Daoud quickly arranged for training facilities to be provided near Qandahar for the Baluchi insurgents, but neither Delhi nor Moscow were prepared to help him dismember Pakistan further. In June 1974, on his first visit to Moscow as president, Daoud was told to negotiate with Pakistan, and his public attack on Pakistan's 'unlawful and stern attitude' towards its Pashtun and Baluchi minorities was censored by the Soviet media.

Daoud came away from his visit to Moscow with a moratorium on debt repayments, pledges of a further $428 million in development aid, and a warning that he should strengthen his partnership with the Parcham faction of the PDPA. His proud spirit must have rebelled. In an effort to reduce the army's dependence on the Soviet Union, he had already arranged for Afghan officers to be trained in India and Egypt. Now he began to purge the Soviet-trained officers who had helped him seize power. From that point onwards, Daoud turned increasingly to the West.

Iran spearheaded the campaign to wrest Afghanistan out of the Soviet orbit. Despite his reservations about the abolition of the next-door monarchy, the oil-crazed Shah offered

Daoud $1 billion in aid, doubling the offer in 1975 to $2 billion. It was a staggering amount, more than the sum of all foreign assistance received by Afghanistan since it first threw open its doors to the outside world. Only a fraction of the promised Iranian aid was ever disbursed: within a few years it had become clear that the Shah's grandiose plans to become the region's fairy godmother as well as its policeman were mere pipedreams. But Daoud had also started negotiating with the Saudis, Kuwaitis, Iraqis and other pro-American, oil-rich nations. By 1976, when the US Secretary of State Henry Kissinger visited Kabul, he felt able to express 'the United States' strong support for [Daoud's] initiatives, which have improved relations among the states of the region'.[2]

Iran's largesse towards Afghanistan entailed a painful *quid pro quo*: negotiations with Pakistan on the Pashtunistan issue. By mid-1976, an ageing, weary, and disheartened Daoud was finally ready to make the biggest political U-turn of his career. The Baluchi insurgency had been ruthlessly crushed, and Bhutto had paid Daoud back in his own coin, arming and financing Maoist and Islamic radical uprisings in several parts of Afghanistan in 1975. In the summer of 1976, Bhutto and Daoud paid reciprocal visits to each other's capitals and put their initials to an agreement which recognised the Durand Line as an international boundary. In return, Bhutto agreed to release imprisoned Pashtun and Baluchi leaders.[3] The agreement, however, was never sealed. The following year, Bhutto was overthrown by his army Chief of Staff, General Mohammad Zia ul Haq. And although Zia tried to finish what Bhutto had started, Daoud never again offered to recognise the Durand Line as an international border.

Moscow was incensed by Daoud's Iranian-brokered realignment with the West. During his second visit to Moscow in 1977, Daoud's talks with Soviet leaders were cool to the point of frigidity. Afghan officials let it be known later that Brezhnev criticised the composition of Daoud's new Cabinet, and angrily challenged him to 'get rid of all those imperialist advisers in your country'. Daoud's response – that when they were no longer needed, *all* foreign advisers would be asked to leave – could have done nothing to assuage Brezhnev's anger.

It was no coincidence that the schism between Kabul and Moscow was matched by a healing of the breach at home between the two wings of the PDPA. In 1973 the rivalry between Khalq and Parcham may have suited the interests of Soviet intelligence. With one of its protégés in government and the other in opposition, it was well-placed for all eventualities. But Daoud's thorough purge of the left meant that it was advisable for his communist opponents to seek safety in numbers. The first talks were held, possibly at the instigation of the Soviet embassy, in the summer of 1975. But it took another two years, plus mediation by the Communist Party of India and other go-betweens, to patch up the damage caused by a decade of poisonous propaganda directed against each other by the PDPA's rival wings.

Moscow's interest in healing the breach must have intensified considerably after Daoud's showdown with Brezhnev in June 1977. The following month, formal agreement was finally reached on a united administrative structure. In reality, though, the unity was less than skin-deep. Babrak accepted Taraki as the PDPA's General Secretary, but in return he demanded the exclusion of Hafizullah Amin from the eleven-member Politburo. Both the Politburo and the thirty-member Central Committee were divided more or less equally between supporters of the two factions, and their respective military cells were kept entirely separate. In effect, it was no more than a temporary alliance in preparation for seizing power from Daoud.

Although Parcham had been the first to look for recruits in the armed forces, by mid-1977 Khalq's influence was greater. The success of the 1973 coup opened the eyes of the Khalqis (as well as of the Islamic radicals) to what might be achieved by suborning the military. Until then,

76

Taraki had taken the classical Marxist position that social-ism could only be achieved by raising the consciousness of the rural and industrial proletariat. But by 1973, according to his official biography, Taraki had decided on the basis of a 'scientific appraisal of Afghan society' that using a military shortcut to power was acceptable, since 'the classi-cal way in which the productive forces undergo different stages to build a society based on scientific socialism would take a long time'.[4]

Amin, who had already proved himself a brilliant organ-iser and adept propagandist, was put in charge of Khalq's military recruitment programme. The results were spec-tacular. Parcham lost out on several fronts. Many of its sympathisers were ousted from the armed forces during Daoud's 1975 purge. At the same time, its collaboration with the republican regime undermined its revolutionary credibility and forced it to halt its recruiting drive. Amin was under no such constraint. At the time of the reunifi-cation of the PDPA, Khalqi army officers far outnumbered those sympathetic to Parcham. According to Taraki's biography, as early as 1976, 'Comrade Amin presented to the Great Leader his written views to the effect that the PDPA [i.e. Khalq] could with a certain number of casualt-ies on the part of the armed forces topple the Daoud govern-ment and wrest political power. However, Comrade Taraki with his profound farsightedness asked Comrade Amin to wait till the objective and subjective conditions in the coun-try were ripe and the Party had grown still stronger.'

A former CIA operative and Afghan specialist, Anthony Arnold, argues that Taraki's unusual demand for written reports from Amin on his military recruitment programme makes sense only if the reports were meant to be passed to a Soviet intelligence officer for onward transmission to Moscow. Arnold also points out with some justice that 'profound farsightedness' was not one of Taraki's strong points. His decision to delay the coup attempt may there-fore have been influenced by his Soviet mentors.[5]

Moscow had good reason to bide its time. Even combined, the total membership of both factions of the PDPA in 1978 was only about 6,000, hardly enough to sustain a communist revolution. Different branches of the Soviet executive probably had conflicting views about how to proceed. Arnold suggests that Khalq may have been under the wing of the Soviet military intelligence agency GRU, while the KGB may have favoured Parcham, with its more gradualist approach. The KGB defector Major Kuzichkin claimed that the KGB (then headed by Andropov) warned the Soviet Politburo in 1978 that an overtly communist regime in Afghanistan would present 'hair-raising problems', and provoke widespread hostility from the tribes.

Later accounts published by Taraki, Amin and Karmal all agree that the second and decisive act of the revolution was originally planned for the late summer of 1978. Moscow would have been aware of the intended date, but there is some evidence to suggest that it was taken by surprise when the coup occurred at least three months earlier than planned. The train of events which triggered the coup began on 17th April 1978. Earlier that day, Daoud told close associates that he had finally decided to broaden the base of his regime by inducting technocrats and liberals into the Cabinet. The same night, whether by coincidence or design, Parcham's leading ideologue, Mir Akbar Khyber, was led out of his house by two gunmen and shot dead in the street. The identity of the assassins has never been conclusively proved. The Daoud government laid the blame on Islamic radicals, while the PDPA accused the CIA. At the time, many people believed that the assassination was masterminded by Daoud's brutal police chief in order to gauge the strength of the communist movement, while later, leading Parchamites pointed the finger of blame at Amin – perhaps the most likely explanation.

Khyber was a well-known figure. His funeral procession whipped up by the anti-imperialist rhetoric of Taraki and Karmal, turned into an angry demonstration against the

Daoud regime. Alarmed by the unexpected show of the PDPA's militancy and crowd-pulling power, Daoud set a careful watch on the army cantonments and other potential centres of disaffection and took stock of the situation. Then, in the early hours of 27th April, his security police struck. Seven top PDPA leaders, including Taraki, were taken into custody. Unbeknownst to Daoud, Taraki's arrest was the pre-arranged signal for staging the coup.

As with most coups, the exact details of what happened are obscure. The three communist leaders who ousted each other in rapid succession over the ensuing two years – Taraki, Amin and Babrak – put out wildly conflicting 'official' versions, each designed to show themselves as the sole architects of the revolution.

Nevertheless, Amin does seem to have played an important role. For reasons never properly explained, he was not bundled straight off to jail like the other PDPA leaders. Instead, he was put under house arrest for ten hours with an extremely lax police guard posted outside. Not only were his children free to come and go with messages to other conspirators, but the police even allowed a fellow-member of the PDPA Central Committee into the house. According to the official party history, Amin used this period under house arrest to organise the revolution, writing out and dispatching detailed assignments for about two dozen key individuals including the crucial contact man in the military, a junior air-force officer called Syed Mohammad Gulabzoi, who passed on to his superiors Amin's instructions to begin the coup at 9 a.m. the following morning.

Even so, Amin undoubtedly exaggerated his own role. According to Khalq's own account, as many as ten secret rehearsals for the coup had been carried out in the preceding months. If so, why was it necessary for Amin to dispatch such detailed written instructions? The government itself announced on Kabul radio that evening that it had foiled an 'anti-Islamic plot' and arrested its leaders. Parties and entertainments were held in the cantonments to celebrate the arrest of the communist leaders, and their sympathisers in the armed forces were therefore already alerted to the urgent need to take action to forestall their own arrests.

At 9 a.m. on 27th April Daoud was still oblivious to the storm about to break around him. He was chairing a Cabinet meeting in the Arg Palace in central Kabul, where the fate of the PDPA leaders was being hotly debated. The would-be revolutionaries, now including Amin, were incarcerated in a jail only 300 yards away from the Palace. Meanwhile, at the headquarters of the 4th Armoured Corps on the eastern outskirts of the city, Major Aslam Watanjar was bamboozling his senior officer into signing an ammunition requisition order, ostensibly so as to be ready to move his tanks to the defence of the government at a moment's notice.

Watanjar had been assigned the command of the rebel ground operations. To protect his tanks, it was vital to secure control of other key establishments: Kabul airport, the military airbase at Bagram and the city's main anti-aircraft missile base. At Bagram, though, things were not going to plan. The signal for a general military uprising was supposed to be given by a squadron of aircraft from Bagram buzzing the presidential palace. But according to his Khalqi rivals, the most senior rebel officer at Bagram, Lt. Col. Abdul Qadir, had locked himself in his office and was only persuaded to co-operate after a posse of 4th Division tanks arrived at the airbase.

The first rebel fighter was brought into action at about 4 p.m. But by that time Watanjar had already launched his assault without air support. Just before midday the Arg Palace was surrounded by rebel tanks, and at noon Watanjar ordered the first shell to be fired. Daoud called his Cabinet meeting to an abrupt halt. His Defence and Interior Ministers slipped away to rally loyalist forces, while the Palace's own armour and anti-tank units engaged the rebels. The sounds of battle encouraged Khalq supporters everywhere to seize armouries and command centres. Senior officers were killed or incapacitated, and wherever possible rebel-controlled units were rushed to the scene of the fighting.

There was inevitably much confusion. No-one knew who was on which side. Even some of Parcham's sympathisers in the armed forces put up resistance, perhaps in the mistaken belief that a right-wing coup was in progress. Despite being commanded by a closet Parchamite, the élite two-thousand-strong Republican Guard continued to fight until only a few hundred were still alive. Elsewhere, units of the 7th and 8th Divisions and the 88th Artillery Battery put up spirited resistance. But there was little co-ordination between the loyalist forces. The Defence Ministry, on the south-western outskirts, fell to the rebels early on, and the Defence Minister's jeep was blown up by a shell as he was leading loyalist armour to break the siege of the Palace. By late afternoon jet fighters from Bagram were bombing and strafing government positions, and key installations were being captured. By 5.30 p.m. the jailed PDPA leaders had been found and taken to the radio station, by now in rebel hands.

At 7 p.m. an announcement was made over Kabul radio which informed the bemused citizens of Kabul (somewhat prematurely, since fighting was still going on and Daoud was still holding out in the Palace) that:

For the first time in the history of Afghanistan, the last remnants of monarchy, tyranny, despotism and power of the dynasty of the tyrant Nadir Khan has ended, and all powers of the state are in the hands of the people of Afghanistan. The power of the state rests fully with the Revolutionary Council of the Armed Forces.

In fact, the *ancien régime* held on until just before dawn on 28th April. At 4 a.m., after resisting for sixteen hours, the last survivors of the Republican Guard finally surrendered.

Daoud, over a dozen members of his immediate family and some close advisers were all gathered in one room when rebel commandos burst into the Arg Palace. The 'Red Prince' is reported to have asked, 'Who has brought about the coup?', to which the senior officer, Lt. Imamuddin, replied, 'The PDPA lays claim to the Revolution.' Daoud then began to shout abuse and, pulling out his revolver, shot Imamuddin in the arm. The commandos then opened fire, killing Daoud and his entire family, and bringing to an end the almost uninterrupted 230-year-old rule of the Durrani Pashtuns.[6]

The Great Saur Revolution – named after the Afghan month in which it occurred – was a revolution only in the sense that a fundamental change in government had come about. There was no popular participation. The citizens of Kabul barricaded themselves in their houses; the rest of the country was mostly unaware of what was going on. Essentially it was a military coup, carried out by disaffected units of the army and air force against a larger body of apathetic and ill-organised troops. Several months later, Hafizullah Amin admitted without a hint of embarrassment that the army had played 'the major role of the proletariat' in a revolution which he considered as irreversible as the Bolshevik Revolution of 1917.

In the aftermath of the coup, though, it was not immediately clear whether the soldiers or the politicians were in charge. The coup's military ringleaders, Watanjar and Qadir, made the initial radio announcements, and, in true Islamic style, the broadcast began with the words 'Bismillah Al-Rahman Al-Rahim' ('In the name of God, the most compassionate and merciful'). Later in the evening, the newly announced 'military council' broadcast a short policy statement in which neither Marxism nor socialism was mentioned. Domestic policy, it said, would be based on 'the preservation of the principles of the sacred teachings of Islam', as well as on 'the promotion of the advancement and progress of our beloved people of Afghanistan'. Amidst the confusion, Afghan exiles in Pakistan told the newspapers that 'Islam-loving elements' were now in power, while for three days, the official Soviet newsagency Tass referred to a *'coup d'état'* rather than a revolution.

It was another three days before Taraki was revealed as the leader of the new regime. During that time, intense manoeuvring for position had been going on. Khalqi army officers had played the most important role in the coup, and Amin quickly laid claim to being its main architect. Even while the coup was in progress, he and Babrak Karmal had exchanged bitter words on several occasions. The Parcham faction had been largely bypassed in the planning and execution of the coup. But, now that power had been won, Parcham's support was vital. Hundreds of its supporters were already salted away in the bureaucracy, the legacy of its short-lived partnership with Daoud. Nor could the military ringleaders be ignored. Neither Watanjar nor Qadir were members of the PDPA Politburo, though they had their sympathies with the party's rival wings. The PDPA was beholden to them as revolutionary heroes, but could it be certain of retaining their allegiance? Both men had also played prominent roles in Daoud's 1973 coup before turning against him.

A temporary solution to this delicate equation was worked out within a few days. The mysterious military council was superseded by a 'Revolutionary Council of the Democratic Republic of Afghanistan', which included five members of the armed forces in addition to most of the PDPA Central Committee. Taraki was Chairman, Babrak was his deputy. Taraki was also Prime Minister of a revolutionary Cabinet in which portfolios were allotted equally to Khalq and Parcham. The balance was held by three military officers, with the rebel army commander Watanjar holding the post of Deputy Prime Minister, alongside Amin and Karmal.

The announcement of Taraki's 'election' as President of the Republic and the composition of his Cabinet helped

83

clarify the question of who was in control. Some observers, both foreign and Afghan, were already speculating that Soviet advisers and pilots had participated directly in the coup and that Moscow had finally triumphed in the 'Great Game'. Soviet military advisers had been spotted at Kabul airport with rebel armoured units; one of the revolution's heroes, Colonel Mohammad Rafi returned abruptly from Moscow just five days before the coup, and the Soviet military attaché was rumoured to have helped plan the assault on the Palace.

Moscow was the first foreign government to recognise the new regime; Kosygin and Brezhnev sent their 'hearty congratulations' to Taraki on 3rd May. But even after the PDPA's leading role was revealed, the policy of deliberate mystification was kept up. In its first editorial after the coup, the English-language *Kabul Times* proffered reassurances that the revolution would usher in 'a future in which the faith, values, traditions and aspirations of the Afghan people will be truly and genuinely respected.' The first overt sign of the regime's ideological thrust came only on 9th May, when Taraki broadcast a new policy statement in which the original reference to preserving the 'sacred principles of Islam' was replaced by the promise of 'democratic land reforms' and the elimination of 'imperialist influences'.

Not everything that was happening in Kabul, though, was to Moscow's liking. On the few occasions that the revolutionary Politburo met in the first two months after the coup, the tensions between Babrak and Amin flared into head-on confrontations. One of the first rows demonstrated that little had changed since the PDPA split of 1967. In a scene reminiscent of Babrak's denunciation of the red masthead of the party newspaper a decade earlier, the Parcham leader objected violently to the new all-red flag with which Khalq proposed to replace the Afghan tricolour. The objection was well-founded, as the regime discovered when the public unfurling of the new flag met with wide-spread protests.

Repeated disagreements between the two factions led first to the expansion of the Revolutionary Council and then to an appeal to Brezhnev to play the role of mediator. Brezhnev declined to intervene. Finally, on 17th June, it was agreed by a majority vote of the Central Committee that state policy would be laid down by Khalq. Rumours were already circulating in Kabul that Babrak was under house arrest – his picture had disappeared from the newspapers. A week later the Central Committee decided to send him and his chief associates into diplomatic exile as ambassadors abroad. Babrak was posted to Prague, his younger brother Mohammad Baryalai to Islamabad, Noor Ahmad Noor to Washington, Anahita Ratebzad to Belgrade, Dr Najibullah to Tehran and Raz Mohammad Paktain to Moscow.

No doubt Amin would have preferred the liquidation of his Parchamite rivals, but the balance of power within the ruling coalition was too fragile for drastic action. Although Khalqis were in charge of AGSA, the newly-renamed political police, both the Defence and the Interior Ministries were in the hands of Parchamites, who had used their power to appoint loyal supporters lower down the state apparatus, including police officials and provincial governors. With the leading Parchamites now out of the way, Amin moved swiftly to consolidate his pre-eminent position. Two days before Babrak left to take up his ambassadorial assignment, Amin replaced him as Party Secretary – the most powerful position in any Leninist organisation – and was given overall responsibility for party reorganisation.

This was the start of Khalqi totalitarianism, wielded in the name of the people (literally, since the Persian word *khalq* means 'the people'). Although the party leadership began an active recruitment drive, the only members it really trusted were its original supporters – the 'children of history', as Taraki called them. Instead of fulfilling its promise to devolve power, the party began a process of rapid centralisation unequalled in Afghan history. Babrak's concept of a 'united national front' was abandoned. Instead, the party set up front organisations designed to represent different sections of society – peasants, women and youth, often headed by relatives or close associates of the PDPA's leaders. By mid-summer, party committees, often staffed by urban youngsters and the local teacher, were being set up at district level, and provincial governors and lower-ranking government officers were rapidly replaced by party card-holders.

At the same time, Khalq began to purge the administration, educational institutions, the professions and the army to root out Parchamites and other potential opponents. Hundreds were sacked, many were jailed, and some were tortured to disclose the names of other Parchamite moles. In mid-July Taraki was reported as saying that 'there was no such thing as a Parcham party in Afghanistan, and there is no such thing now.'

Moscow, anxious to restore the unity of the PDPA, advised Taraki that Parchamites should be allowed to occupy one-third of party and government posts. Amin never intended to follow that advice, but his resolve to ignore it was greatly aided by the discovery in August of a secret Parcham-led plot to overthrow the regime. The details and confessions released later by the Khalqi-controlled media are suspect, but a genuine conspiracy does seem to have been in train to topple the regime on the Eid holiday, at the beginning of September, when Muslims celebrate the end of the Ramadan fasting month by feasting themselves to the point of exhaustion.

The plot was apparently hatched by Babrak and his associates during the four weeks before he packed his ambassadorial valise and left for Prague. The plan was for the reluctant ambassadors to return secretly to Kabul a few days before Eid. Taking advantage of the holiday atmosphere, they would provoke demonstrations which would compel the army to intervene. Senior military officers, including heroes of the Saur Revolution such as Defence Minister Abdul Qadir, Col. Mohammad Rafi and the new army Chief of Staff General Shahpur, would then seize power and install a 'United National Front' government. According to Kabul radio, a number of Muslim nationalists and non-PDPA left-wingers such as Tahir Badakhshi of the anti-Pashtun Settem-i-Milli organisation were also involved.

The discovery of the plot gave Amin the perfect excuse to complete his purges against opponents, real or imagined. Qadir, Shahpur, Keshtmand and Rafi were all arrested in mid-August. The AGSA chief Asadullah Sardari, who came to be known as 'the Butcher' for his brutality, personally supervised the torture of some of the plotters, including his PDPA Central Committee colleague, Sultan Ali Keshtmand. All five confessed and were sentenced to death. Most of the remaining Parchamites were thrown off the Central Committee and expelled from the PDPA.

A general witch-hunt followed. There were renewed purges in the bureaucracy, the police, the Interior Ministry, the media and the army, where few officers over the rank of major kept their jobs. According to Raja Anwar, who was himself a long-time inmate of the newly built Pul-i-Charkhi jail just outside Kabul, at least 400 Parchamites were jailed after the exposure of the Eid conspiracy, and 250 Parcham and Settem-i-Milli workers were executed.[8] Other accounts put the toll much higher, though there are no reliable figures. In October 1978, Amnesty International estimated that there were 4000 political prisoners in Afghanistan, and executions were said to be averaging fifty a night. Political prisoners inherited from the Daoud regime had already been executed to make room for the new influx.

There is some evidence to suggest that Moscow was involved in the Eid conspiracy. Certainly, as the gap between the ambitions of the Khalq regime and the realities of Afghan society grew ever wider, Moscow's interest in seeing a government of national unity in Kabul increased. It is believed to have made discreet approaches to two former nationalist Prime Ministers, both of whom were subsequently executed by the Khalqis. Parcham's softly-softly approach to Marxism was much more to Moscow's liking, and it was put into practice immediately after the Soviet invasion. But whatever anxieties it harboured about its client regime in Kabul, Moscow appeared to the outside world to be in full control by the end of 1978. In the first few months after the Saur Revolution, over two dozen economic and aid agreements were signed between Moscow and Kabul, and, in July, an unpublicised $250 million arms deal was finalised. Western diplomats in Kabul dubbed the Soviet Ambassador, Alexander Puzanov, the 'little czar', and more Soviet advisers were drafted in to run civilian affairs, partly because of the large-scale purges of the regime's opponents in the administration. Experts from the Soviet Union and Eastern Europe – notably East Germany and Bulgaria – were also hired to advise on party organisation, intelligence, and security police operations.

In the early days, most Afghans viewed the new regime with indifference. Some felt outright relief. The latter years of the Daoud regime had inspired little other than fear and contempt. The new regime was an unknown quantity. Its leaders may have been upstarts in the eyes of the Pashtun aristocracy, but for the underprivileged and frustrated middle classes, its promises held out hope of at least some improvement. The Marxists' main rivals, the Islamic radicals, had already been cowed, imprisoned or forced into exile by Daoud. Babrak Karmal, five years later, felt able to look back with nostalgia to the revolution's early days when 'an unforgettable atmosphere full of joy and expectation reigned in the streets, roads, squares and in the common man's household.'[9]

Even allowing for hyperbole, there may be some truth in Babrak's reminiscence. Taraki encouraged his party workers to downplay ideology when talking to peasants – and play up the material benefits they could expect to receive. The journalist John Fullerton relates the story of a foreign-educated Khalqi sympathiser who took a group of elders from his Pashtun tribe to Kabul to meet Taraki. Even seven months after the coup had occurred, they still knew nothing about the PDPA, let alone its rival wings. But when they met Taraki, 'they were very surprised. They turned to me and exclaimed, "Why, the man speaks Pushtu. He speaks our language. And what's more, he tells very good jokes!" The government encouraged them in the belief that they would get what they wanted from the PDPA regime: good roads, medical care, schools for their children and jobs aplenty.'[10]

In late 1978, Taraki and Amin started an intensive campaign to woo the border tribes, in order to neutralise opposition which was already coming from Pakistan. If tribal elders could be lured to Kabul for a brief visit, it was relatively easy to impress them. They were fed well, housed well, they marvelled at the television network recently installed by the Japanese, and met senior members of the new government. For Kabul's permanent residents, though, illusions were short-lived. According to the British ambassador of the time, one joke which went the rounds shortly after the coup told of 'an officer who saw a man at 10.30 and shot him; when asked why he had killed the man when the curfew wasn't until 11 o'clock, the officer replied, "I know where that man lives, he would never have made it." '[11]

More sinister were the attentions of the revamped political police, AGSA. Western residents soon found their Afghan friends too scared to talk to them. Revolutionary courts, set up soon after the coup, were empowered to try dissidents for a wide variety of vaguely defined 'crimes against the state'. Most political prisoners, though, were held without any kind of trial, and were cut off from all contact with the outside world. Many simply disappeared. Parcham sympathisers were not the only ones at risk.

89

Among the first detainees of the new regime were seventy-four women and children belonging to the royal family. As the weeks went by, they were joined in jail by religious leaders, civil servants, doctors, professors and any member of the intelligentsia too outspoken for his own good. Interrogation centres were set up all over Kabul, and even party militants still at high school were reportedly allowed to join in torture sessions, which, according to Amnesty International, included electric shocks, whipping, beating and pulling-out of fingernails.[12]

By the summer of 1978, thousands of professional Afghans – doctors, engineers, civil servants and others – were starting to leave the country, fleeing either to Pakistan, Europe or the United States. But it was not only the educated middle classes who were offended by the new regime. As the Khalqi revolutionaries grew more secure in their possession of power, the promises to honour the values and traditions of Afghan society were forgotten. In October 1978, Khalq's new red flag was unfurled, on the occasion of the first big government-orchestrated demonstration. Such 'people's rallies' became increasingly common thereafter; by the spring of 1979 up to three a week were being held. Needless to say, they were not voluntary. Government offices, schools, and even hospitals were told to close down. Children only just old enough to learn to shake their clenched fists were hustled onto the streets to demonstrate in favour of the party. As business and tourism slumped, private businesses were forced to make contributions to the party coffers and an hour a day of 'voluntary' work was demanded from government employees, a practice which was deeply resented. Not even the private lives of the people were safe from the intrusions of the regime's frenzied activists. On the first anniversary of the Saur Revolution, posses of soldiers and party activists armed with machine guns circulated through Kabul forcing householders to paint their properties red until supplies of red paint were exhausted.

The regime's excess of ideological fervour was at its most disastrous when applied to the holy religion of Islam. The invocation to God with which the coup leaders had been careful to preface the premature announcement of their victory was dropped from the broadcasts of Kabul radio within a few weeks. The Justice Minister, Abdul Hakim Jowzjani, horrified his audiences by offering public prayers for the souls of Marx and Lenin. Amin threatened to crush those 'who, in the name of Islam, plot against the April Revolution', while Taraki inveighed against leading mullahs as 'the brothers of Satan'. From the safety of exile, traditional religious leaders wasted no time in declaring *jehad*, or holy war, against the regime. In the rural areas, mullahs had to be more circumspect; but it was not long before they started denouncing the regime's egalitarian reforms as unIslamic. The most outspoken were sought out by the regime's 'security groups' and joined the growing list of those who simply disappeared.

None too subtly, the Khalqi regime sought to replace faith in God with the cult of its own leaders. Amin was the arch culprit. It was he who flattered Taraki from the beginning with names such as 'the Great Teacher' and 'the star of the East'. As time went by, Taraki began to believe his own propaganda, even if no-one else did. Portraits of Taraki – always smartly dressed in a three-piece Western suit – were put on obligatory display in government offices, businesses and shops. Taraki's doings filled the front pages of newspapers; whole paragraphs were taken up with the ever-expanding string of his ridiculous titles. His portrait was even painted into press photographs of other ministers, and as time went by the figures in the foreground became fuzzy and indistinct while Taraki's face loomed ever larger.

In spite of the deepening hostility the regime was provoking in Kabul and other towns, the rural areas of Afghanistan might have remained generally indifferent had it not been for the economic and social reforms which were introduced in the latter half of 1978. Before Babrak's departure for Prague, Taraki seemed to have accepted the need to proceed with relative caution. 'I believe it will be a year or two before we can go through with our plans for land reform', he declared at the start of June. 'We do not want to over-hasten our reforms; we want to implement them step by step.' Yet the very next month, the PDPA promulgated the first of three revolutionary decrees which were intended to overturn at a stroke the traditional pattern of economic and social relationships in the rural areas.

Even today, Afghans have heated arguments about land conditions in their country prior to the revolution. There were no proper land records, and mortgage contracts and debts were rarely put in writing. The first-ever census of the Afghan population, undertaken by the Khalq regime, was little more than a rough estimate. The number of nomads was particularly baffling, with official estimates varying anywhere between one and three million. Although debt-bondage, semi-slavery and landlessness were fairly common, and land around the main towns tended to be owned by a small number of absentee landlords, agrarian conditions varied enormously from place to place. In tribal areas, land was often held collectively, and self-regulating mechanisms such as the jirga system, in which decisions were taken by consensus, restrained the power of the village headmen, or maliks.

Ignoring all these imponderables, the Marxists crafted their reforms on the mistaken premise that all Afghanistan's woes stemmed from the dominance of a class of exploitative feudal landlords. In July 1978, they abolished certain categories of rural debt; small plots of land which had been mortgaged for five years or more were automatically returned to their original owners. In November, a fifteen-acre limit was imposed on land-holdings, a measure which the government believed would free fifty percent of arable land for redistribution to the poor. At the same time, irrigation systems were nationalised. Another decree published in the same year sought to regulate marriage contracts. An upper limit was set to the traditional 'bride-price', paid by the groom's parents, in order to curb indebtedness and protect the dignity of women. The decree also set a minimum age for marriage – sixteen for girls, eighteen for boys – and insisted that no-one should be forced to marry against their will.

The reforms may have been admirable in intent, but they were almost tailor-made to provoke widespread opposition. The decree on marriage struck at the very heart of an ultra-conservative social system in which women were, legally speaking, no more than chattels. If Pashtun poets are to be believed, romantic love was traditionally reserved for young boys rather than women; marriages were typically arranged by parents or tribal elders in order to reinforce or extend kinship ties. The land reforms were equally insensitive to prevailing customs. In its haste, the regime forgot that land by itself was of little value. To produce his crops, a peasant needed access to water, seeds, manure, ox-power and other services, inputs which were normally provided by money-lenders and landlords. But by cancelling debts and redistributing excess land, the regime took away the incentives of landlords and moneylenders to help their dependents, without providing any alternative system of credit and agricultural services.

The result was the destruction of the fragile equilibrium of a rural economy where subsistence was already the norm. Those with sufficient means and cunning had bogus documents drawn up which converted their private debts into unrepayable agrarian mortgages. Dispossessed khans harried any peasants who had the temerity to try farming their newly-acquired land. Peasants who were transported to vacant lands hundreds of miles away, found on arrival that not even the most basic of facilities had been laid on, and had to return home, poorer than ever. Local party officials exploited the reforms to reward their own families or tribes with lands confiscated from their rivals.

It's hard to say whether the Khalqis were naive agrarian reformers who genuinely thought that their edicts would win the majority of the population over to the side of the revolution at one fell swoop; or, as has been argued, whether they realised that their reforms were unworkable, and intended them to be the first step towards a fully-fledged system of collectivisation.[13] Whatever their motives, they overlooked the power of Islam, in which property ownership is considered to be sacred. Mullahs, many of whom owned land of their own, quickly condemned the reforms as unIslamic, and even peasants who stood to benefit were outraged by the insensitive manner in which the decrees were enforced.

The regime's roving land-reform commissions were staffed by zealous urban youngsters, protected by soldiers. They would arrive in a village, gather the inhabitants together, chant slogans and make speeches in praise of the Great Leader, beat up any landlord or mullah who dared to protest, then re-distribute the land title deeds before disappearing again in a cloud of dust. It was not a good way to make friends. Landlords and tenants were frequently of the same tribe, and although Pashtun tribes in particular are riven with rivalries, they always tend to unite to defend their kinsmen against outsiders. Moreover, anything to do with the government in Afghanistan has always aroused deep suspicions.

Even when peasants were ready to pocket the land title-deeds, they were frequently shocked by the disrespect shown to their elders or to local landlords. Both the conservatism of the peasantry and the brashness of the reformers is nicely illustrated by a story told by a Khalqi army officer at a wedding party in Balkh. His unit had recently ambushed and killed a 'gang of counter-revolutionaries', and when they went over to examine the bodies, two-thirds of them had land ownership deeds in their pockets. The Khalqi officer's comment was, 'look at these ignorant people, we give them land and they fight against us.'[14]

The same brash disregard for traditional customs and sensibilities also aroused widespread popular opposition to the regime's other major programme, mass literacy. Party planners reckoned they could teach nearly half the population to read and write within a mere three years. Literacy was considered the only way to break the mullahs' grip on the rural areas, and it was also the easiest and quickest way to promote socialism. The literacy manual prepared by the Education Ministry was indistinguishable from party propaganda; a third of it was devoted to slogans praising the regime, and one whole page was taken up with a description of the tank as a symbol of popular liberation.

Taking their cue from the party leadership, local PDPA officials, many of whom were teachers, outdid each other in their literacy enrolment drives. Every week, villagers were herded into their local squares to hear their first 'A for Amin' from the thousands of volunteers who fanned out into the coutryside. Even women were forced to attend, which deeply shocked their menfolk. The first lethal clash between the government and ordinary villagers is reported to have broken out after soldiers forcibly dragged women out of their homes to attend a literacy class, violating every accepted norm of Afghan behaviour. Hundreds of other incidents throughout the country sealed the fate of the regime and its reforms. Tradition was being blatantly trampled on, and instead of directing their wrath against their class enemies, as the Khalqis hoped, the Afghan peasantry turned against the state itself.

So far as the Khalqi leadership was concerned, by November 1979 the 'revolution' was almost complete. In the space of seven months, it had seized power, purged and banished its political rivals and promulgated basic reforms designed to wed Muslim Afghanistan to socialism. Yet it had also sown the seeds of its own destruction. As the reforms gathered pace, so did the reaction against them. At first, Taraki seemed almost gratified by what he called the 'sharpening of class struggle', but as the months went by it became increasingly evident that the rural population, far from being divided along class lines, was uniting against the regime under the potent green banner of Islam.

SIX

Prelude to Invasion:
Hafizullah Amin and his Downfall

Moscow was aware of the Khalqi regime's growing unpopularity, and disliked its claim to have invented an entirely new Third World formula for Marxist revolution. It was unhappy about the factionalism in the party, contemptuous of the personality cult being built around Taraki, and viewed Amin's ruthlessness in jailing and executing thousands of suspected opponents as damaging to the regime's chances of survival.[1] But among the Soviet Union's southern neighbours, Kabul was its sole ally; the upheaval of the Iranian revolution of 1978–79 made it all the more imperative that it should not fall into the hands of Muslim reactionaries. There was no doubt that Moscow would come to the regime's rescue; the price Kabul had to pay in return was its independence.

In the months after the coup, Soviet military and civilian advisers flooded into Afghanistan. Young communists who were appointed to senior government positions found by the end of 1978 that their advisers had become their masters, whose peremptory instructions they were expected to obey. Dozens more economic agreements were signed, including a huge loan of $1000 million to finance the Five Year Plan, and a permanent joint commission was set up which extended Soviet control over Kabul's economic decision-making.

Military aid also cut both ways. In December 1978, Taraki went to Moscow to sign a treaty of friendship and co-operation which empowered Kabul to call on the USSR, if necessary, for direct military assistance. Amin, who was chief negotiator, wanted to insert amendments putting Soviet troops under the command of Afghan officers, and giving Kabul the sole right to decide when they should leave. He was overruled, but his reservations proved more than justified when, twelve months later, the December treaty provided Moscow with the legal pretext for its invasion.

It was not long before the Khalqi regime began to contemplate the necessity of invoking the treaty. The first major rebellion against its authority occurred in the spring of 1979 in the western city of Herat. Set in a fertile oasis at the edge of the arid Iranian plateau, Herat was once the intellectual and artistic capital of Afghanistan. Before the devastation of the war, the turquoise tombs of centuries of scholars, poets and holy men shimmered amidst the surrounding pomegranate gardens. Persian civilisation had always influenced the city's intellectual life, and the Islamic revolution in neighbouring Iran had a profound impact on its substantial Shia population. Thousands of them had migrated to Iran to work as labourers in the oil-rich days of the Shah, and many had participated enthusiastically in Khomeini's revolution. Now they were back home, restless and out of work.

Kabul alleged that the March uprising was the work of disguised Iranian soldiers, but most authorities believe that it was essentially a popular rebellion, provoked by the regime's reforms, fomented by Islamic radicals and the traditional clergy, and quickly joined by dissident army officers, ordinary townspeople and peasants from the surrounding plains. Bastions of the regime's power – the Governor's house, the prison, police stations and the cantonment – were the first targets of the mob. Later they raged through the streets, butchering not only Khalqis but also Soviet advisers and their families. For more than a week all communications between Herat and the rest of the country were severed, and exaggerated rumours swept

Kabul that up to 400 Soviet citizens had been massacred and horribly mutilated.

The retribution of the regime was belated, but massive. A year later, an Indian visitor found Heratis still shuddering at the memory of the bombardment carried out from the nearby airbase of Shindand, in which thousands are believed to have been killed. According to some reports, Soviet pilots may have participated. Troop reinforcements were sent from Kabul and Qandahar, and after three days of fierce fighting the city was recaptured. For Herat it was the beginning of ten years of savage war which have earned the city its reputation as Afghanistan's Hiroshima.

The most ominous aspect of the Herat uprising from the Soviet point of view was the participation of the local army garrison. As long as the regime could bank on the loyalty of its troops, the growing armed resistance to the regime in the remoter provinces had seemed tolerable. But Herat, which provided the spark for rebellions throughout western Afghanistan, showed that those loyalties were under strain. Most of the soldiers stationed there either deserted or joined in the uprising after murdering their Khalqi officers. Ismael Khan, then a junior army officer, and later to become the area's most famous mujahedin commander, was one of the mutineers: like the communists, Islamic radicals had also begun to infiltrate the armed forces in the 70's. The only real resistance offered to the Herat rebels came from PDPA officials, who knew they could expect no mercy.

In contrast to the Khalqi-dominated officer corps, the army rank and file were poorly paid conscripts who were as unsympathetic to the regime as the rest of the civilian population. As spring turned to summer, desertions from the army mounted steadily. Whole units joined the resistance or simply returned home to their villages. As early as June, Western intelligence estimated that over 2000 Afghan soldiers had defected, while the guerillas claimed that they had been joined by 10,000 troops, including an entire mechanised brigade.[2] Further purges in the army only exacerbated the discontent, and repeated army mutinies punctuated the last months of the Khalqi regime's existence.

Aghast at the slaughter of several dozen of its citizens in Herat, and at the unreliability of the Afghan army, Moscow began to reassess its position. Its immediate priority was to strengthen the regime against further rebellions. Just one week after the Herat rebellion was suppressed, Soviet cargo planes loaded with tanks, armoured personnel carriers and the latest helicopter gunships were flown into the Afghan capital. The next step was to ensure that the new equipment would be effectively used. The officer responsible for political affairs in the Soviet armed forces, General Alexei Yepishev, arrived in Kabul with six other generals to assess morale and discipline in the Afghan army. He found the first low and the second lax, and, after his visit, more military advisers were drafted in to replace the Soviet dependents now being sent home to safety.

Diplomatically, Moscow backed Kabul's allegation that foreign interference was responsible for the growing unrest, and issued warnings to Pakistan, China and unnamed Western countries. But it was aware that the Khalqi regime's own policies were partly responsible for its security problems. A senior official, Vassily Safronchuk, moved into an office in the presidential palace to persuade Taraki to moderate his hardline policies and broaden the base of the government. His advice fell on deaf ears. The PDPA was about to splinter into even smaller factions, wrecked on the colossal ambitions of Hafizullah Amin.

When the first reports of a rift between Taraki and Amin surfaced in the Western press, Taraki told journalists that they were as 'inseparable as a flesh-embedded nail' – an unfortunate analogy in view of the ingenious tortures being practised by Amin's henchmen in Kabul's interrogation centres. But Taraki must have been well aware that the young army officers who had led the revolution, like Watanjar, were gunning for his chief lieutenant. For months, they had been trying to loosen Amin's grip on military affairs. The Defence Ministry's belated response to the Herat rebellion, plus the fact that the garrison commander was Amin's own appointee, strengthened their hand. In a government reshuffle on 17th March, Watanjar was appointed Defence Minister, and Amin was kicked upstairs to the largely ceremonial position of Prime Minister.

Amin was a born conspirator, however. He had already installed his relations and close associates in key positions, and his disassociation from formal decision-making over the next few months may have increased his support within the Politburo. For the regime was in deepening trouble. Party officials in the provinces had started to carry automatic weapons around to protect themselves, and by April 1979 it was dangerous to leave the main road between Herat and Kabul. Foreign development projects throughout the country were being wound up for security reasons; agricultural production fell rapidly, down by one-third in the spring of 1979. Even town suburbs were becoming unsafe, and in late June open disaffection spread for the first time to Kabul itself. Light tanks and armoured personnel carriers rolled onto the streets of the capital to quell violent demonstrations by thousands of Hazara Shias, and in the next few weeks, thousands of Shias were rounded up, never to be seen again.

The situation was so dire that a scapegoat had to be found. The ineffective Taraki, whose cult had been inflated to preposterous proportions, was the only suitable candidate. A Politburo meeting on 28th July decided that 'collective leadership' was necessary, which, in effect, meant that Amin was back in charge. Watanjar was demoted back to the Interior Ministry, and Amin ensured that his own supporters were appointed as deputies in ministries still officially controlled by his rivals. He also had his elder brother and nephew appointed to influential positions, an act of nepotism so blatant that Taraki accused him of tarnishing the fair name of Marxism. Taraki's wife later told

Raja Anwar that Amin's reaction was to leap from his seat and demand angrily, 'So, should I murder my family?'[3]

Amin's new ascendancy did not go unchallenged. One week after Watanjar was stripped of the Defence Ministry, tanks from an army brigade stationed at the Bala Hissar, Kabul's great fortress, started to roll towards the city centre and were only turned back after a four-hour battle with loyalist forces. Soon afterwards clandestine leaflets began circulating in Kabul which called on all Khalqis to join hands against 'the treachery of the corrupted band of Amin'. The frustrated young army officers who staged the April 1978 coup – Watanjar, Gulabzoi, Sarwari and Mazdooryar (later dubbed the 'gang of four') had already emerged as Amin's leading political rivals. Now they began to plot his downfall.

The power-struggle came to a head in early September, when Taraki left Kabul for a meeting of the Non-Aligned Movement in Havana. Raja Anwar, who later met and talked with many of the key actors in jail, has recently published an insider's account of the drama which is unlikely to be bettered. According to Anwar, the head of the political police, Asadullah Sarwari, phoned Taraki shortly after he arrived in Havana to tell him that Amin planned to murder the gang of four and seize power while Taraki was abroad. Sarwari also informed Moscow of the supposed conspiracy, and Brezhnev later confirmed that he had passed the warning on to Taraki. Sarwari's information was enough to convince Moscow that Amin, a man it already viewed with suspicion, had to be neutralised. The exiled leader of Parcham, Babrak Karmal, was told to be at hand when Taraki stopped over in Moscow on his way home from Havana, and secret talks were held between the two Afghan leaders, Brezhnev and the Soviet Foreign Minister Andrei Gromyko.

From Moscow's point of view, the parleys were a great success. It was agreed that the unity of the PDPA should be restored, and that Karmal would replace Amin as Prime

Minister and number two in the party. Gromyko advised Taraki to send Amin and his chief supporters into diplomatic exile. In pursuit of Moscow's long-standing aim of a 'national democratic government' in Kabul, half the Cabinet ministers would be taken from outside the party. After the meeting was over, Taraki told a group of Afghan students who met him at the airport that 'it will be necessary to get rid of the mosquito which has made it impossible for the party to sleep peacefully at night.'

Back in Kabul, Sarwari was preparing the insecticide. Amin was to be assassinated by a team of specially trained sharpshooters on his way to meet Taraki at the airport. What Sarwari didn't know was that his nephew had betrayed the plan to Amin. Taraki's plane entered Kabul airspace on schedule, only to find itself ordered by ground control to circle for another sixty minutes. At the end of the hour, Amin drove up to the airport at a leisurely pace. He had changed his car and his route, and in the process had signalled to the conspirators that he knew all their plans and was firmly in control. Only after he arrived was the presidential plane allowed to land.

A pregnant stalemate followed. When they met that evening, Amin demanded that Taraki should dismiss the gang of four, but instead, Taraki offered him an ambassadorship. Next day, Sarwari persuaded Taraki to invite Amin to lunch at the presidential palace to 'talk things over', apparently intending to shoot him as soon as he arrived. But Amin was suspicious, and only agreed to come after the Soviet ambassador had offered his services as a mediator. This time, the ingenious Sarwari devised a new plan to kill Amin: a time bomb hidden in a toilet. But, again, Amin seems to have been forewarned. He turned up for the meeting two hours early, expecting trouble. The chief conspirators had not yet arrived, but Taraki's guards had been ordered to shoot anyone approaching the President's quarters. Amin's bodyguard was killed in a gun battle which left the Cabinet room and the palace staircase riddled with bullets, but Amin himself escaped. He hurried back to the Defence Ministry where he put the armed forces on full-scale alert, and ordered a complete round-up of his opponents. At 8 p.m., Kabul radio announced that 'four rebel officers' had been dismissed. No announcement was made about Taraki. He had been confined to the palace on Amin's orders.

Next day, the PDPA Central Committee accepted Taraki's resignation on the grounds of 'ill health', and elected Amin his successor. Secretly, it adopted a resolution accusing Taraki of 'a terror attempt . . . against our scholarly principled Comrade Hafizullah Amin'. Three weeks later, Amin decided to get rid of Taraki altogether. The earthy, emotional boozer, who had dreamed of a socialist utopia and was elevated by a military coup into the 'Great Genius Leader', died ignominiously, suffocating under a pillow held over his mouth by Amin's henchmen.

The whole affair seems to have been badly botched by Moscow. There's no doubt that the Soviets wanted to get rid of Amin in one way or another. Ambassador Puzanov helped lure him into the trap set for him at the Palace, and as soon as their intrigues were foiled, the gang of four were given sanctuary in the Soviet embassy. Yet, according to Raja Anwar, Amin was repeatedly warned of the dangers he faced by Soviet intelligence, acting through Sarwari's nephew. Further muddles were to come. A month later the gang of four, still hiding in the Soviet embassy, organised another military coup against Amin. They must have had the green light from Ambassador Puzanov, yet Soviet military advisers attached to the rebel units reportedly refused to co-operate, and the coup was bloodily suppressed.

The most likely explanation for the inconsistency of Soviet actions in the autumn of 1979 is that senior officials in Moscow were divided over how Afghan policy should be handled. By late 1979, Brezhnev – never the most decisive of leaders – was in a state of physical and mental decrepitude. Four years earlier he had suffered a massive stroke and had narrowly escaped being pronounced clinically dead. His hopeful heirs-apparent – including Foreign Minister Gromyko, KGB chief Andropov and Defence Minister Ustinov – all seem to have been pursuing their own independent foreign policies, and it may be that Soviet military intelligence decided unilaterally to tip Amin off about the plots against him.

The KGB certainly wanted to get rid of him. Its assessment was that Amin was a 'smooth-talking fascist'[4], and in July 1979 the US chargé in Kabul Bruce Amstutz was informed by the East German ambassador that Moscow considered 'the key ingredient' in a political solution of the regime's growing problems to be 'the departure of Prime Minister Hafizullah Amin'.[5]

Moscow's displeasure was provoked to some extent by Amin's independent-mindedness. A leading American analyst of south-west Asian affairs, Selig Harrison, met Amin twice in 1978 and found him to be 'a formidable, strongly nationalistic figure who was clearly not prepared to play the role of supine puppet. His confident attitude, reflected in numerous off-the-record comments, was that he knew how to handle the Russians, who needed him as much or more than he needed them.'[6] A similar assessment was made by Bruce Amstutz in July 1979, when he commented in a cable to Washington that Amin was probably clever enough to outsmart the Russians.[7]

Like all Afghan leaders, Amin had always tried to keep his foreign options open. As Foreign Minister and then Prime Minister, he had avoided Taraki's sycophantic praise of the Soviet Union and had always used his speeches to stress Afghanistan's 'independence'. But whatever hopes he may have had of winning international legitimacy and Western economic assistance for the Khalqi regime were dashed early on by the unfortunate death of the US ambassador to Kabul, 'Spike' Dubs.

In February 1979, a few months after taking up his assignment in Kabul, Dubs was kidnapped by activists of the Maoist group Settem-i-Milli and shot dead during a bungled and premature assault on the hotel room where he was being held hostage. The regime's handling of the affair, including the contradictory statements it made about the identity and demands of the kidnappers, left Washington convinced that there was a sinister design behind its ambassador's death. Amin got a large share of the blame, along with his Soviet advisers. American aid programmes were slashed, and in August President Carter signed a law which prohibited all further aid until the regime accepted official responsibility and apologised.

Soon after seizing power Amin tried to re-open a dialogue with Washington. In late September, after a series of meetings, he appealed to the US chargé d'affaires in Kabul for improved relations and the restoration of economic aid, and his Foreign Minister, Shah Wali, did the same during a visit to New York. The Americans were not uninterested. They knew of the tensions between Amin and Moscow, and sent a senior diplomat from Delhi to hold preliminary negotiations. But Amin was neither ready nor able to make the concessions Washington wanted, and the disappointed US envoy commented later that Amin 'wanted American aid all right. But he was not prepared to offer anything in return.'

Washington, however, may have misread the signals. The Afghan economy was already saturated with aid from the Soviet bloc. What Amin wanted was some way of loosening Moscow's suffocating embrace. The following month, as his position became more precarious, he appealed publicly for aid from the United States, begging Washington to study the regional situation 'in a realistic manner'. Shortly afterwards, his attitude towards Pakistan underwent a seachange, and the Pakistani President General Zia later claimed that he had received 'frantic messages' from Amin in December to send his Foreign Minister to Kabul for talks.[8]

It's intriguing to speculate that Amin might have been

contemplating a radical shift away from Moscow in late 1979. The Egyptian leader Anwar Sadat got away with it in 1972, expelling Soviet advisers *en masse* and turning to the United States for aid. But for Afghanistan, it was not a realistic proposition. Unlike Egypt, Afghanistan shared a common border with the USSR, and Amin is unlikely to have forgotten the fate which befell Daoud after he had turned his back on Afghanistan's great northern neighbour. Yet Moscow must have been alarmed by signs that Kabul was still capable of conducting an independent foreign policy. The preposterous allegations made subsequently by both Soviet and Afghan officials, that Amin had been a CIA agent all along, were mainly intended to justify his overthrow; but they also reflect a genuine uncertainty in Moscow about where the Afghan dictator's loyalties really lay.

Either to placate Moscow after the murder of Taraki, or because he realised that he could only hope to survive by winning a measure of popular acceptance, Amin began his 100 days in office by implementing some of the recommendations which Moscow had long been urging. His strategy was simple: Taraki could take the blame for all the regime's mistakes to date. The former leader's posters were torn down from walls, his portraits were removed from offices, and Amin pointedly promised an end to one-man dictatorship. His words were matched with suitable actions. Representatives from outside the party were co-opted onto a committee to draft a new constitution. A national front was established, known as the National Organisation for the Defence of the Revolution, which was designed to draw non-communists into cooperation with the regime at a local level. Lip service was also paid to Islam, with Amin demonstrating his newly rediscovered piety by undertaking to have the capital's mosques repainted at state expense.

'Security, Legality and Justice' were the official catchwords of the Amin regime. The much-feared political police (which he renamed KAM, the 'Workers' Intelligence

Bureau') would 'never perform any unjust act and will not put anyone in jail without reason,' he said in his first nationwide radio broadcast. Arrests continued, but the wholesale purges stopped, possibly because there weren't enough dissidents left to purge. Prominent coverage was given by the government-controlled media to the daily release of 'political' prisoners, although many of them turned out to be common criminals.

No-one was fooled by Amin's apparent change of heart. By early December, despite his softer policies, the regime's collapse seemed only a matter of time. A scorched-earth policy adopted by Soviet advisers in the summer had contributed to a huge refugee exodus to Pakistan and Iran. Military operations in Paktia, the home province of many of the regime's top leaders, temporarily halted a rebel push towards the city of Jalalabad in the autumn, but armed resistance was still spreading along the Pakistan border, and in November the commander of the border garrison at Asmar defected to the rebels after executing party officials and Soviet advisers. The Shia areas of central Afghanistan were already quite free from government control, and as the icy breath of winter touched Kabul, urban guerilla activities came to the capital for the first time, with sporadic assassination attempts against Khalqi and Soviet officials. Time was running out for Hafizullah Amin.

Why did Soviet troops invade Afghanistan? In October 1989, almost exactly ten years later, the Soviet Foreign Minister Eduard Shevardnadze admitted to the Supreme Soviet that 'we went against general human values. We committed the most serious violations of our own legislation, our party and civilian norms. . . . The decision, with such serious consequences for our country, was taken behind the backs of the party and the people.'[9] Despite Gorbachev and glasnost, however, the reasons for the invasion are still a matter for conjecture, lying buried in the Kremlin's secret archives. The leading culprit is clearly

Brezhnev. But even he was a victim, as well as a perpetrator, of forty years of Cold-War thinking which led both Washington and Moscow to misunderstand each other's actions and motives.

When the Khalqi regime first took power in April 1978, the US State Department was aware that 'we need to take into account the mix of nationalism and communism in the new leadership and seek to avoid driving the regime into a closer embrace with the Soviet Union than it might wish.'[10] American actions, though, particularly after the murder of Ambassador Dubs, had precisely that effect. By August 1979, the US embassy in Kabul had cynically concluded that 'the United States' larger interests . . . would be served by the demise of the Taraki-Amin regime, despite whatever setbacks this might mean for future social and economic reforms in Afghanistan.'[11] Overruling the doves at the State Department, US hawks, led by the National Security Adviser Zbigniew Brzezinski, concluded that Afghanistan presented an opportunity to give the Russians a bloody nose at minimal risk.

Although the overall level of foreign backing for the rebels was far smaller in 1979 than Kabul and Moscow alleged (see chapter 9), the impact it had on Soviet thinking should not be underestimated. The degree of paranoia traditionally felt by Moscow about military encirclement has rarely been appreciated in the West. The occupants of the Kremlin have tended to see themselves and their country as victims of historical circumstance, fearing not only military attack, but also the subversion of their political and economic system. The huge military build-up of the Brezhnev years has been interpreted by some commentators as stemming from a sense of nervous inadequacy rather than aggressive intent.[12]

In the late seventies, Soviet policy-makers were increasingly preoccupied with the growing Chinese threat on their eastern borders, and with the rapidly improving relations between Beijing and Washington. In the eighteen months prior to the Soviet invasion, several rounds of talks on mutual security were held between US leaders and China's paramount leader Deng Xiaoping, with Afghanistan high on the agenda. Moscow's concerns about what it perceived as the aggressive intentions of its rivals were also heightened by American actions after the Iranian revolution. Moscow had no cause to mourn the fall of the Shah in January 1979, but it was highly sensitive to the resulting regional instability, and it was worried by what a humiliated Washington might do to repair the damage done to its interests. The American naval build-up in the Persian Gulf during the hostage crisis, and the creation of a mobile Rapid Deployment Force to police south-west Asia after the Shah's fall, were bad enough. But could it be that Washington was also seeking a more permanent alternative to the military facilities which Iran had previously provided? That at least was the justification which Brezhnev advanced shortly after the invasion. There had been 'a real threat', he told *Pravda*, 'that Afghanistan would lose its independence and be turned into an imperialist military bridgehead on our southern border.'[13]

The Islamic revivalism spawned by the Iranian revolution added to Moscow's unease. There were about fifty million Muslims in the Soviet Union, and their numbers were steadily increasing. Throughout the 1970s, there were occasional reports of illegal Muslim brotherhoods being revived in some parts of Soviet central Asia, and after the triumph of the ayatollahs in Iran, there were signs of an upsurge of fundamentalism in Soviet Turkmenistan. Even the West – without a significant Muslim population – was hypnotised by the spectre of Islamic fundamentalism. Ayatollah Khomeini provided an extraordinarily powerful symbol of Muslim identity and anti-colonialism, and if predominantly Sunni Afghanistan went the way of Shia Iran, the Kremlin must have reasoned, the repercussions in Soviet central Asia could be immense.

Moscow's twin fears of Islamic revivalism and military

encirclement, together with the growing foreign patronage of the Afghan rebels, tended to be overlooked as contributory causes of the Soviet invasion. At the time, the Cold War-warriors of the West stressed more sinister motives: age-old Soviet expansionism, the onward drive to the warm water ports of the Gulf and the Indian Ocean, and the severing of the West's vital oil arteries. Cables from the US embassy in Kabul, though, had been warning Washington for months that Moscow was contemplating action against its wayward client in Kabul. Yet the only signal Moscow got back was that the US intended to take full advantage of its growing difficulties in Afghanistan. Washington was banking on the assumption that the Kremlin would consider direct military intervention to be too costly to risk. It was an assumption which was to have disastrous consequences.

Preparations for limited military operations in support of the Khalqi regime had been going on since early 1979; by the end of November the Soviet armed forces were in a state of readiness for full-scale intervention; an aerial bridgehead had been made ready in June, at Bagram airbase, forty miles north of Kabul. Amin himself may have approached Moscow for military assistance as early as October; by late November, according to his former ministers, he had requested Moscow to send 10,000 troops, who would be used to secure the capital while the Afghan army took on the rebels in the provinces. At that stage, though, Moscow still seems to have been undecided about what form the intervention should take: outright invasion, or a more limited deployment of troops to contain the spreading resistance?

Soviet leaders, both military and civilian, were deeply divided over this question. Shortly after the Soviets completed their withdrawal from Afghanistan in February 1989, the commander of Soviet land forces, General Valentin Varenninkov, revealed that the top generals of the Soviet general staff had been opposed to full-scale invasion, and had proposed instead a far more limited role for Soviet forces. According to their plan, Soviet military personnel would be stationed in garrisons around Afghanistan, but would not be used in offensive operations. However, the Defence Minister Ustinov, KGB chief Andropov and Leonid Brezhnev overruled the warnings of their generals.[14] At some point – nobody knows exactly when – the decision was made to kill two birds with one stone: in other words, to dispatch Soviet troops to crush the resistance as well as to install a more moderate and compliant regime in Kabul.

Amin seems to have believed that the two heavily equipped Soviet battalions which started arriving at Bagram airbase in mid-December were the advance guard of the force he himself had requested. He may still have believed it when, on Christmas Eve 1979, an élite Soviet battalion flew into Kabul airport from Bagram to secure it for the massive airlift of Soviet infantry and armour which followed over the next few days. To neutralise potential opposition, Soviet advisers told their Afghan army units to prepare for a training exercise by trading in their live ammunition for blanks.

On the evening of 27th December, Kabul's main communications centre was blown up. It was the pre-arranged signal for which the Soviet troops who'd arrived over the previous three days had been waiting. The first tank shell hit Amin's headquarters on the outskirts of the city at 6 p.m. Pul-i-Charki prison was captured at the same time, and key installations like the Kabul radio and television station came under fierce attack. Within the space of a few hours, most resistance had been overwhelmed. Three hundred miles to the north, Soviet tanks and troop columns were crossing the Amu Darya river and pouring into Afghanistan.

The official version of that night's events is that Hafizullah Amin was overthrown by Afghan troops. Moscow's propaganda machine was quickly set in motion to try to establish that the 'limited contingent' of Soviet troops as invited into Afghanistan only after Amin had been killed in an internal coup, and took no part in the fighting. The truth is quite different. Around 200 Soviet soldiers were killed in the operation, and the resistance put up by the 4th Afghan Armoured Corps continued until next morning. The KGB defector Vladimir Kuzichkin revealed in 1982 that the attack on Amin's headquarters was carried by a KGB assassination squad dressed in Afghan army uniforms, a story partially confirmed in May 1989 by a leading Soviet historian.[15]

The web of lies woven by Moscow and Kabul during and after the invasion, designed to minimise the inevitable international outcry, was made necessary by the failure of a plan to get rid of Amin without firing a shot. According to his widow, KGB agents posing as Russian cooks doctored Amin's food at lunch on 27th December. Everybody at the meal fell unconscious, except for Mrs Amin herself, who had not eaten. Help was summoned, and Soviet doctors immediately proposed that the President should be transferred to the headquarters of the Soviet Medical Corps. Once Amin had recovered and found himself in Soviet hands, the plan was that he would be given the option either to resign as President or stand trial for Taraki's murder. The new President – Babrak Karmal – would then issue a legal invitation to Soviet troops to enter Afghanistan to help defend its borders.

Amin, though, had eaten only sparingly at lunch, and since he showed signs of making an early recovery Afghan doctors and the commander of the Presidential Guard insisted that he should remain in their care. The failure of the plan meant that KGB commandos and crack Soviet army units had to be sent into action a few hours later. If only his appetite had been better, Amin might still have been alive today.[16]

At 8.45 p.m., Radio Termez came on the air, transmitting on the same frequency used by Radio Kabul, and broadcast a speech by Babrak Karmal. It made no mention of Soviet involvement, but informed the people of Afghanistan that 'the day of freedom and rebirth . . . has arrived. Today the torture machine of Amin . . . has been broken . . . the Central Committee of the united PDPA . . . proclaims true people's power.'[17] A few days later, in his first official statement, Babrak made the implausible claim that he had returned secretly to Afghanistan in mid-October, and had convened a secret meeting of the PDPA Central Committee at which Amin had unanimously been dismissed as president.

In fact, Karmal was either in Termez, or still in Moscow, when Soviet troops invaded his country. Afghanistan's new leader was far more of a Soviet prisoner than either Taraki or Amin had been, and because of the failure of the KGB's dirty tricks department, it was impossible to hide it from the rest of the world. Moscow's claim that it sent troops to the aid of a legitimate Afghan government was automatically discredited. The stage was set for a proxy war between the superpowers in which the Afghan people themselves were the only certain losers.

SEVEN

The Bearded Warriors:
Resistance Inside Afghanistan
1978–1988

In New York, where I spent the Christmas of 1979, the news of the Soviet invasion shattered the usual seasonal lethargy. Incensed Americans levered themselves out of their armchairs, went out to their local liquor stores, bought bottles of Russian vodka and smashed them on the sidewalks. The fear and outrage was spurred on by political leaders. Jimmy Carter pronounced the invasion 'the greatest threat to peace since World War Two', and immediately announced a series of sanctions, including the non-ratification of the SALT II arms control treaty, a ban on exports of wheat and high technology to the Soviet Union, and a boycott of the 1980 Moscow Olympics.

The West's fear of Soviet aggression transformed a little-understood conflict in a remote part of the world into a *cause célèbre*. Half-forgotten imperial memories of the valorous tribesmen of the North West Frontier were resurrected. Retired army officers nostalgically recalled the ignominious defeats suffered by nineteenth-century British armies in Afghanistan – a sentiment neatly caught by the cartoonist Giles with the caption, 'I see your old treacherous tribal riff-raff, enemies of the British Raj, are now your glorious allies, Colonel!' Expectations that the Red Army would have a rough ride were summed up by the last British Governor of the North West Frontier, Sir Olaf Caroe. In a post-invasion epilogue to his exhaustive study of the Pathans, Sir Olaf quoted an old Persian couplet: 'You can swallow a rough bone; but once it is embedded in your bowels, it cuts them up.'[1]

For the first two months after the invasion, Soviet troops encountered little armed resistance in the countryside. Because of the snows, winter has never been a good time for fighting in Afghanistan, and Moscow's first priority was to consolidate its control over the Kabul government and the army. But the intrepid shock troops of Western journalism who hastened to the new 'frontline against communism' were undeterred by the lack of action. Stories of incredible courage against unbelievable odds were telexed back home by reporters who had ventured no further than a few hours' rickety bus ride from Peshawar to the Afghan border. Even ITN News was infected by the tabloid myths of heroic tribesmen when they reported shortly after the invasion that Afghan guerillas were dousing themselves in petrol, setting themselves alight and diving into the open hatches of passing Soviet tanks. The Afghans might be primitive, badly armed and even slightly mad, we were told, but they were rugged individualists, lovers of freedom. Although the image of the resistance received some dents in the years that followed, as late as 1988 Mrs Thatcher still felt able to assert: 'Let us be clear about what is happening in Afghanistan. Virtually the whole Afghan nation is engaged in a war of liberation against a Soviet occupation army.'[2]

There can be no doubt that the Soviet invasion did provoke many Afghans not already engaged in civil war to join the armed opposition. The Pashtun tribes still cherished memories of their defeat of the British armies of the nineteenth century; Soviet troops were even more unwelcome, because of their communist ideology. The humiliation of being invaded by atheists was particularly acute. Several areas which had until then remained generally passive, like Qandahar in the south-west and the Shomali plains north of Kabul, now became some of the most active resistance strongholds. The invasion also dismayed educated nationalists living in the towns and cities. Those who had not already escaped fled abroad to start new lives or join the resistance, including nationalist army officers unable to bear the prospect of serving under Soviet officers. By 1982 there were an estimated 2,500 army officers fighting with the guerillas, providing them with the bulk of their trained manpower.

Peasants, too, were stunned and enraged by the invasion. Abdul Hai, a forty-year-old farmer, had ignored the communist coup and continued to mind his own business, which was cultivating wheat and fruit on his few acres near the Soviet border. But when Russian trucks started rolling down the road near his village, he was enraged. Taking up his rifle, he started shooting at the convoy, and as word of his bravery spread, so did his following. Within a few years he had become the commander of his own local band of several hundred guerilla fighters.

The sight of Soviet aircraft flying through the December skies, and of columns of Soviet tanks passing through towns and villages on their way to Kabul provoked a horrible sense of *déjà vu* in northern Afghanistan. Many settlers there had migrated to Afghanistan only fifty years earlier, in order to escape the persecution of Muslims in Soviet central Asia. Now it looked as if history was about to repeat itself. While some young men prepared themselves to fight, many more families got ready to leave the country.[3] If protecting their religion meant leaving their new homeland, so be it: the Prophet Mohammad himself, by fleeing from Mecca to Medina under threat of persecution by unbelievers, had shown the way. The Quran specifically singles out for future rewards 'those that emigrated in God's cause after they were wronged'.

Popular resistance to the Soviet invasion added a new dimension to the *jehad*, the holy war in defence of Islam, which had already been proclaimed by religious leaders within weeks of the communist coup of April 1978. The term 'mujahedin', which has now been universally adopted to denote the Afghan guerillas, literally means soldiers of the jehad. In the West, after the Soviet invasion, it came to be used almost as a synonym for 'freedom fighter', but for Afghans, the religious connotations are all-important. Islam shapes and patterns the experience of everyday life in Afghanistan. Government buildings, schools and dispensaries stand on the outskirts of an Afghan village, while the mosque stands at its heart. Communal prayers are held five times each day, and for one month every year, Afghan Muslims fast between sunrise and sunset. *Jehad* – war against an unIslamic regime – is an integral part of the Muslim's religious duty.

The proclamation of *jehad* by accepted religious leaders confers on a warrior a religious certainty which strengthens his determination to fight and his willingness to die. Unlike some Muslims, such as Iranian Shias, most Afghans do not go out of their way to seek martyrdom. The readiness to walk through minefields displayed by Arab volunteers fighting in Afghanistan is a source of caustic amusement to the more pragmatic Afghan mujahedin. Yet there is a profound belief that those who kill an enemy, or are themselves killed in *jehad*, will go straight to Paradise. Whatever their private sorrows, Afghan women tell visitors to refugee camps that they have nothing to grieve for, since their husbands, fathers, brothers and sons died as martyrs. For ordinary Afghans, religious superstition was one of the few potent weapons they had to counter the Soviet hardware used to raze their villages. During a three-month inspection tour of foreign aid projects inside Afghanistan in 1987, Bruce Wannell, a British scholar and aid-worker, was on many occasions 'entertained with accounts of the corpses of true mujahedin, who were free of sin and therefore had not rotted, even though they were buried weeks after their death; or of flights of pigeons stopping bombing raids.'[4]

Afghans follow a wide variety of Islamic traditions. There is little in common between the pirs, or leaders of mystical Sufi brotherhoods, the maulvis with their piles of Arabic commentary books, the ignorant and bigoted village mullahs, and the modern Islamic radicals who seek to restructure society strictly according to the Quran. Among Pash-

118

tuns, Islam has even been adapted to accommodate the sometimes contrary dictates of their pre-Islamic tribal code, the Pashtunwali, based on honour, revenge and hospitality.

Among Pashtuns, firm religious convictions co-exist with an earthy pragmatism. A folktale quoted by the anthropologist Frederik Barth neatly illustrates the point: 'A mullah came to our village and started upbraiding us for our ignorance and laxness in observing Islam. We didn't like the disrespectful way he spoke to us, so we shot him – and now we have a fine holy grave where we can pray!'[5] Nevertheless, irreligious though their behaviour sometimes seems, Islam is an integral part of the Afghan identity and culture. As Barth puts it, 'atheism not only represents a ridiculous denial of the existence of God, and thereby of the world and His creation: atheism is also a dangerous and amoral denial of the basic preconditions of all human and social standards.'[6]

Instead of trying to enlist Islam's egalitarian ideals in support of its social reforms, the Khalqi regime sought to replace Allah with the party, and Islamic justice with the abstract notion of class warfare. Even though the Khalqi leadership made sporadic attempts to disguise its socialism as Islamic, party activists – often drunk and always abusive – did not bother to conceal their contempt for Islam. A pious shopkeeper from Kunduz tells how, soon after the revolution, the Secretary of the local youth organisation came into his house, knocked the Holy Quran onto the floor with his bayonet and shouted 'how long is this old book going to govern you bloody fools!'[7] With such outrageous behaviour commonplace, it's not surprising that mullahs everywhere came out in opposition to the PDPA and its reforms, making the Khalqis even more determined to stamp out their influence over the peasantry and replace it with the authority of the communist state. Within a few months of the communist takeover, thousands of members of the clergy were rounded up by government forces and led away to jail or execution. The effect on the local population could be dramatic. The anthropologist Audrey Shalinsky describes how an Uzbek township in northern Afghanistan was galvanised into supporting the resistance by the execution of a young mosque official, whose discreet Friday sermons against the regime had been secretly tape-recorded by the Khalqi governor of the province.[8]

The Afghan view of their struggle against the Soviet occupation as an Islamic crusade, and the Western view of it as a war of national liberation, both contributed to the strength of the resistance offered first to the Khalqis and then to the Soviet army over the past ten years. But there was also another important motive for resistance, particularly at the local level: resentment against the erosion of traditional tribal autonomy by a brutal and intrusive state machine.

By the time I arrived in Pakistan for the BBC, the war in Afghanistan had already been going on for six years. The bitterness of a conflict in which hundreds of thousands of lives had been lost and five million people had fled as refugees was sufficient to explain the motivations of the mujahedin I met. It seemed pointless to ask why they were fighting. Most Afghans had lost at least one family member in the war. Like Hameed Gul, an embittered guerilla commander I met in Peshawar, who had lost twenty-two members of his family, some were the sole survivors. 'If we can get hold of those who actually killed our relatives,' he said, 'we'll squeeze them until their cries can be heard even in London.' Simple revenge, which for Pashtuns is a moral duty, and the personal loathing they felt for a regime which was waging war on its own people, was inextricably entwined with their hatred of the communist government and its Soviet backers.

It took a trip into Pakistan's own Pashtun tribal belt to get a clearer insight into one of the reasons why some Afghans began their *jehad*: to defend their own patch of land, and their own way of life. In February 1988, I joined the party of a junior British Foreign Office minister who was visiting a poppy-eradication scheme in Dir, a former princely state of about one million people. Poppy, which for the past forty years had been the main cash crop for Dir's impoverished peasants, is now being stamped out by the Pakistani government with the active encouragement of Western aid donors, including Britain. By building irrigation works, small industrial enterprises, electricity generators, roads, schools and dispensaries, the government hopes to persuade the peasantry that a better life awaits those who agree to grow alternative crops such as wheat, maize and rice.

In principle, the project is admirable. But the local tribesmen, whose territory straddles the Pakistan-Afghan border, deeply resent being told to change their ways and halt their lively cross-border trade in opium and weapons. In 1988 the local administration was forced to borrow nearly 8000 paramilitary troops from various parts of the North West Frontier Province to support its annual campaign of forcible poppy-slashing, but even so, they encountered fierce resistance, and poppy was still being grown in the remoter valleys. The British minister was suitably impressed, and expressed support for Islamabad's use of force to stop them growing poppy. Ironically, though, a few hours before, he had visited a nearby Afghan refugee camp to pledge continued British support and admiration for their struggle against Kabul. What struck me at the time was that, in essence, there was little to distinguish the rebellious, poppy-growing tribesmen of Dir from their Afghan cousins across the border. Both were engaged in a similar struggle: the preservation of their traditional autonomy in the face of the encroachments of an alien government.

It would be grossly misleading to compare the present-day government of Pakistan with the Khalqi regime which seized power in Afghanistan in 1978. But it could be said that many of the spontaneous popular uprisings which occurred in Afghanistan prior to the Soviet invasion were at least as much anti-state as anti-communist. Typically, they began with a visit from over-enthusiastic party activists intent on implementing the regime's land or literacy reforms, or on arresting potential opponents. Led by the local mullah or village headman, and often armed with primitive weapons such as rusty swords and ancient rifles, the incensed villagers would attack and massacre the delegation before overrunning the nearest government post.

Once underway, the revolt was likely to spread to the limits of the territory occupied by a particular tribe or ethnic group, and then come to a halt. Co-operation beyond ethnic or tribal boundaries was extremely rare. In 1979 there was little sense of a united Afghan 'nation'. Even today, few Tajiks or Uzbeks describe themselves as Afghans, and even Pashtuns, when asked to identify themselves, refer first to their father and grandfather, then to their village, clan and tribe. Most Pashtuns find the idea of being ruled by a Tajik preposterous, even one so illustrious as Ahmed Shah Massoud, the guerilla commander who has extended his authority from the Panjshir Valley to most of the north-east of Afghanistan over the past five years. Although pictures of Massoud can now be found in some Pashtun areas, many Pashtuns discount the reports of his battlefield successes. Bruce Wannell reports his Pashtun guide as grumbling, 'Those Panjshiris were mere pimps for the court, waiters in Kabul hotels, toadies to foreigners, how can they fight? It's all a concoction of French journalists and nurses!'[9]

Significantly, the first genuine popular uprisings against the Khalqi government took place among non-Pashtun tribes. The Hazaras of the central highlands and the Nuristanis of the east had suffered the most oppression and discrimination at the hands of the Durrani Pashtun establishment. Neither community had to look far back into their history to remember a time when they were independent of Kabul: both regions were invaded and annexed by Amir Abdur Rahman at the end of the nineteenth century. The advent of the Khalqi regime, perceived as illegitimate

122

throughout Afghanistan, provided them with an opportunity to regain their lost autonomy.

In the eyes of the Nuristanis, the Khalqi regime was doubly hateful. Converted to Islam at swordpoint by Abdur Rahman only seventy years earlier, they suffer from the fanaticism of recent religious converts. A British journalist who travelled through the area after the 1973 coup recalls hearing great concern being voiced about the supposed 'communist' Daoud. The communism of the Khalqi regime was clear to all. To make matters worse, Khalq was seen as an aggressively pro-Pashtun party, and despite the pledges of equal rights which Taraki and Amin made to minority nationalities, the actions of local party officials seemed to presage a further strengthening of Pashtun domination.

The rebellion in Nuristan began after communist party militants abducted and executed a group of tribal elders suspected of remaining loyal to Daoud's Interior Minister, himself a Nuristani. The first government outpost was overrun just three months after the communist coup, and by the spring of 1979, after fierce fighting in which the provincial capital changed hands several times, virtually the whole of Nuristan was 'liberated'. In the Hazarajat, the rebellion took rather longer to get off the ground. It was provoked by the slaughter of large numbers of Shia mullahs in Kabul and elsewhere during the first year of communist rule. In late September 1979, hundreds of local Hazara notables and clerics gathered to elect a ruling council; the whole of Hazarajat rose in revolt, and all government posts were seized. A number of different Shi'ite groups have operated there ever since, fighting with each other in lieu of government troops, and exercising a strict control over their respective territories.

Travelling with a guerilla arms convoy through Hazarajat in 1984, two British doctors found that each populated area they passed through was controlled by a different armed group. Instead of hastening their fellow mujahedin on their way, each local commander insisted on taking control of the weapons as they passed through his territory, demanding a large premium each time. The process took so long that after six weeks' travelling, with a thousand miles still to go to their destination, the two doctors abandoned their escort, and headed back to Pakistan.[10] Hasan Latif, a Pakistani journalist who travelled through central Afghanistan in 1987–88, had a different problem: he was imprisoned by one guerilla group until he agreed to deliver a letter to the BBC office in Islamabad. Making good his promise, he told me that many Hazaras were openly declaring their neutrality between the Kabul regime and the Peshawar-based resistance. Even if the present regime in Kabul is eventually overthrown, neither Hazarajat nor Nuristan will be keen to surrender their newly regained autonomy.

Generally speaking, the rebellion against the Khalqi regime spread more rapidly in the Persian-speaking regions of the west and north than in the Pashtun-dominated zones of the south. Alongside the Nuristanis and the Hazaras, the Tajiks of Badakhshan were among the first to raise the standard of revolt. Both Islamic radical and Maoist groups were already active in the north-east, and by the summer of 1979 the rebellion had spread to the Tajiks of the Panjshir Valley and the province of Takhar. In the north-west, where non-Pashtun groups also predominate, uprisings began with the Herat rebellion of March 1979, and quickly spread through the provinces of Farah, Baghdis and Faryab.

The brutality of the regime in suppressing these revolts swelled the ranks of the rebels. Mualem Gran was teaching in a Kabul secondary school when Daoud was overthrown. He was already well acquainted with the communist leaders and their methods, and his outspoken views got him exiled to a village school in the far north of Afghanistan. Even there, local party officials considered him too dangerous, and he was conscripted into the army. Within a fortnight, he slipped away into the mountains with his Kalashnikov and made his way back up north, only to find himself a wanted man. His village, in the northern province of Kunduz, was raided by government troops, his friends were arrested and his wife and five cousins were killed. Meeting up by chance with other dissidents, Mualem Gran helped form an armed group, which later affiliated itself to one of the guerilla parties in Peshawar.

The Pashtuns in the border areas were slower to take up the armed struggle. The Khalqi regime was initially wary of the power of the great Pashtun tribes; its roving land reform commissions and literacy campaigners were ordered to stay away from their territories. It was not until after the autumn harvest of 1979 that the Zadran tribe of Paktia province revolted, followed by the Pashtun tribes in Kunar, Ghazni and Zabul. Other tribes supported the regime insofar as it suited their own interests. Old vendettas have frequently enabled the PDPA to turn one clan into a pro-government militia by arming it against its main rival. Hafizullah Amin, who was a Ghilzai Pashtun, had no trouble in recruiting thousands of Ghilzai volunteers to fight against the Hazaras of Wardak province in the summer of 1979. Dr Najibullah, who has an extensive knowledge of the border tribes, has been even more skilful in playing off different clans against each other by distributing weapons and money in exchange for temporary allegiance. Pashtun clan rivalries are so strong that even when a whole region has gone over to the resistance, neighbouring khans often refuse to join the same party, and spend their time harrying each other instead of government outposts.

Even in the north, where tribal identities are weaker, Bruce Wannell found in 1987 'a chess-board of alliances and rivalries, often predating the jehad, whereby between each active and popular commander stood either a government militia or a rival party waiting to attack in the rear if any effort was made to fight the jehad.' Often riding for sixteen hours at a stretch through the wilderness, Wannell realised that 'not only were settlements too far-scattered, and ethnic groups too diverse to allow large-scale cooperation, but that political rivalries and fragmentation made up a picture more complex than eighteenth-century Germany'.[11]

Armchair analysts in the West have laid particular stress on the intense rivalries within the Afghan resistance since the Soviet withdrawal of 1989, but it is worth emphasising that the resistance has never been monolithic. The dramatically deteriorating image of the mujahedin since the Soviet pull-out says more about the West's self-serving interpretation of the nature of the Afghan war than about the guerillas themselves.

Slight doubts about the mujahedin began to surface in the mid-1980's, by which time enough foreign journalists had travelled inside Afghanistan for a rather different picture to start emerging of the valiant anti-Soviet freedomfighter of 1980. Occasional reports described them as disorganised, lazy, fractious, intolerant, deceitful and bloodthirsty. Their most prominent leaders were rabid Islamic fanatics who wanted to return Afghanistan to the Dark Ages, shroud their women in veils and chop off the hands and feet of criminals.

Writing in the *Sunday Times* in 1985, film producer Jeff Harmon described an incident he witnessed at the headquarters of Haji Abdul Latif, a guerilla leader operating just outside Qandahar. Twelve Afghan army prisoners were lined up in chains, waiting to be sentenced by a notorious Islamic judge called Maulvi Abdul Bari. 'The judge told me: "I have personally slit the throats of 1000 Khalqis. I have sent 500 Russian infidels to the gallows." Other prisoners, he said, were shot, decapitated or stoned to death. This information was given in front of the twelve prisoners, whose own fate seemed certain. They listened impassively, while the judge's chief executioner, Muhammad Juma, fondled an axe and grinned. "This is no ordinary axe," he said. "This is for halal [ritual throat-cutting]." '

In spite of such sensational reports, the presence of Soviet troops in Afghanistan assured the mujahedin of overwhelmingly Western sympathy and support throughout the nine years of occupation. By 1987, though, the reporting of the war was starting to become less one-sided. After six years in which only a few select journalists had been allowed to visit the Afghan capital, Kabul started issuing visas again, as part of its Soviet-inspired policy of 'national reconciliation'. Visiting reporters got an impression of life in the Afghan capital which was in sharp contrast to the weekly propaganda briefings given by American and British diplomats in Islamabad and Delhi. The regime seemed far more stable and tolerated than they had been led to believe. The citizens of Kabul didn't much appreciate being killed and maimed by guerilla rockets fired indiscriminately into the city from the surrounding mountains. The young Kabuli women, in their knee-length skirts and high heels, were appalled by the prospect of having to trade in their Western-style clothes and freedoms for the medieval restrictions which an Islamic fundamentalist government would certainly impose.

As it became increasingly clear that Moscow was committed to withdrawing its troops, the tendency to view the mujahedin through ideologically-tinted spectacles began to wane. Even American journalists started to harbour doubts. In early 1988, a visiting *New York Times* reporter voiced the changing mood of the outside world by asking the US ambassador to Pakistan whether Washington might not be 'backing the wrong guys'. Today, with Soviet troops gone, that view has gained steadily in currency. The West's exasperation with the continuing civil war is beginning to transform Afghanistan's brave freedom fighters back into 'treacherous tribal riff-raff'.

There has always been an element of truth in that description. In a country where anarchy has reigned for more than ten years and where every adult male carries a gun, it is often difficult to distinguish bandits, murderers, looters, smugglers, heroin traders and other criminals from genuine

127

mujahedin. Sometimes they are one and the same, at least from the point of view of poor peasants like Abdul Qahar, a smallholder arrested by KHAD for helping 'counter-revolutionaries'. Informed by the government prosecutor that the PDPA government was an Islamic one, he replied: 'You are quite right, and no doubt so are the mujahedin. The only infidels in this country are we poor people, they come from the mountains and force us to provide wheat and fodder, and you arrest us for co-operating with them.'[12]

Inevitably, the war threw up a new leadership in many areas. A large number of the big tribal chiefs, or khans, went into exile in Pakistan, and others joined forces with the regime. Their successors are a mixed lot. The better mujahedin commanders have created their own administrations, setting up committees to deal with matters such as health, education, justice, finance and culture. But other petty warlords, often far removed from the main zones of conflict, have antagonised the local civilian population. Each local guerilla base regulates trade and civilian movement in its area, and collects Islamic taxes from the peasants. Sometimes the taxes can be heavy, and tyrannical commanders have been known to levy arbitrary fines on wealthier residents, or demand free straw and barley for their horses. With the arrogance of armed men everywhere, ill-disciplined youngsters who have given up farming for fighting sometimes behave more like teenage delinquents than warriors of the faith, misbehaving with local women or failing to say their prayers.

Clashes between rival groups have taken a heavy toll on civilian life and property over the years. In the autumn of 1986 hundreds of people were killed in the south-western province of Helmand in an eighteen-day battle between guerillas belonging to two different parties, Hezb and Harakat. Islam had nothing to do with it. The local Harakat commander, a mullah called Naseem Akhunzada, had ambitions to be the dictator of the whole upper Helmand valley; originally involved in the anti-Soviet struggle, his main business was now the control of Helmand's extensive poppy cultivation and the smuggling of hundreds of tons of opium annually to Pakistan and Iran. On orders from Peshawar, local Hezb guerillas tried, not for the first time, to assert their control over the region. Weapons and ammunition were rushed to both sides from their respective party headquarters in Quetta, emptying out the arms warehouses on the Pakistani border. The fighting was so fierce that when Soviet tanks rumbled in to take advantage of the chaos, they were garlanded by grateful villagers.

Despite such incidents, the resistance commanded the overwhelming support of the majority of Afghans throughout the nine years of the Soviet occupation. 'Karimullah', a Westerner who embraced Islam and fought with the mujahedin for several years, told me of a typical example of the hospitality given to guerillas engaged in a major attack on a government garrison in Nangrahar province. 'The commanders involved in the operation would break down their men into platoon size. Every twenty families in a village have a mosque, and some villages have three or four. The platoon commander would go to the mosque and send for the local men, who organised their households into providing sugar, tea, flour, meat, vegetables and so on. Everything was given for free, and little boys would scurry away for three miles to get fruit and mulberries.' The Pashtun tribal code demands unstinting hospitality, and on another occasion, Karimullah recalls the typically crude welcome given to a band of passing guerillas by an elderly Pashtun, who told his unexpected and unknown guests that 'an old pussy is never afraid of an old dick!'

Distinctions between the mujahedin and the civilians cannot easily be drawn. According to (probably exaggerated) Pakistani military intelligence estimates, there were up to 400,000 mujahedin guerillas active in Afghanistan on the eve of the Soviet withdrawal. The majority were illiterate and untrained – part-time peasants, part-time fighters. Their commanders come from all walks of life: men who were formerly farmers, cooks, university graduates, land-lords, camel-drivers, mullahs, army officers, doctors, mathematics professors and gardeners can all be found commanding mujahedin fighting 'fronts'. Now that Soviet troops have left Afghanistan, the fervour of the jehad is beginning to die away in many places. But even when they are abused or exploited by the local guerilla leadership, most Afghans seem to prefer being mis-governed by members of their own community, rather than by an alien government in Kabul.

EIGHT

The Bearded Politicians:
the Resistance in Exile 1975–1989

The revolt of the Pashtun tribes in the autumn of 1979 marked the start of a new phase in the Afghan civil war. It was the opposition of the tribes of which the Khalqi regime was most afraid. Not only had they played an historical role as kingmakers, but they lived close to the Pakistani border, where refugees were already congregating and guerilla organisations were being nurtured by the pro-Islamic military government of General Zia ul Haq.

The Khalqi regime decided that the trouble had to be nipped in the bud, and launched a major offensive against the tribes of Paktia province. Casualties were high on both sides, but militarily it was ineffective. The rebels simply melted away into the hills, to return when the regime's armoured columns had returned to their bases. Its only lasting effect was to swell further the number of refugees fleeing to Pakistan. In January 1979 an estimated 30,000 refugees had already crossed the Pakistani border, many of them expecting to take only temporary refuge. Within a few weeks of the Soviet invasion, the number of refugees in Pakistan had shot up to around 400,000, a tenth of whom had fled from Paktia. Able-bodied men were either left behind to fight, or joined the expanding resistance parties based in Pakistan.

It was from Pakistan, and with Pakistani support, that the first phase of the *jehad* had been launched four years earlier. As the PDPA grew in strength, the rival Islamic movement which had grown up at Kabul University and in other educational institutions in the capital during the sixties started preparing itself for armed struggle. In 1972, what had hitherto been an informal grouping of like-minded intellectuals with a militant student wing, adopted a formal structure, a secret constitution and the name Jamiat-i-Islami, the Society of Islam.

After the 1973 coup, the movement's president, Burhanuddin Rabbani, then a thirty-five-year-old theology lecturer, offered Daoud the support of the Islamic movement if he would break with his communist partners. Daoud refused, arrests were made, and Rabbani, Gulbuddin Hekmatyar, Ahmed Shah Massoud and about a dozen other leading Islamic radicals fled to the safety of Pakistan. The fugitives were welcomed with open arms by the Pakistani Prime Minister, Zulfikar Ali Bhutto. Bhutto feared that Daoud's return to power in Afghanistan would lead to the resumption of his old aggressive policy on Pashtunistan, and blamed Kabul for a spate of terrorist attacks which rocked Pakistan's North West Frontier Province in 1974, culminating in the assassination of the provincial chief of Bhutto's Pakistan People's Party the following year.

Counter-measures were called for, and Bhutto was ready. Since late 1973 he had given financial and logistical assistance to the Afghan exiles, so as to be in a better position to destabilise Daoud if need be. They were permitted to set up headquarters in Peshawar and, gradually, financed and trained by Pakistan, a secret network of revolutionary Islamic cells was established throughout Afghanistan.

In the summer of 1975, to quote General Nasirullah Babar, a former governor of the Frontier Province, Bhutto conveyed 'a message' to Daoud, by giving the green light for armed insurrections to be staged in several Afghan provinces. Most of them fizzled out for lack of support. Only in Panjshir, where Massoud was in command, and in Badakhshan, where the left-wing Settem-i-Milli was involved, did they have any noticeable impact. As yet the general population was not ready for rebellion.

The failure of the uprisings provoked an open rift in the

1 and 2: Changing styles of Pashtun warfare:
top with locally-made jezails in the 1860s;
bottom with US-supplied Stinger in the 1980s.

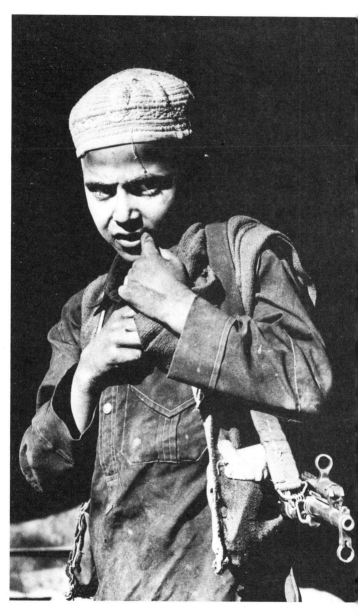

3 Young mujahed.

4 Foreign
weaponry
arriving in
Afghanistan.

5 Burned-out
Soviet
hardware litters
the Panjshir
Valley.

6 Mujahedin at prayer.
7 Tradition and modernity in Kabul

8, 9 and 10: *top* Refugees in the Frontier Province;
bottom Fleeing from Jalalabad, spring 1989.

11. A casualty of the battle for Jalalabad.

12. Dr Najibullah. 13 Gulbuddin Hekmatyar.

14 Ahmed Shah Massoud planning an attack.

15 The Soviet withdrawal begins: Jalalabad, summer 1988.

exiled Islamic movement. Professor Rabbani, the movement's leader, had argued in favour of delaying the start of an armed struggle against Daoud until a broad opposition coalition could be built up which enjoyed widespread popular support. The friction between the cautious Rabbani and the movement's hotheads, particularly Gulbuddin Hekmatyar, may have been exacerbated by the revenge exacted by Daoud for the failed insurrections. Hundreds of Islamic radicals were rounded up and executed, including Ghulam Mohammad Niazi, Rabbani's mentor and the founder of the Islamic movement.

Shortly afterwards, the movement split in two, one group headed by Rabbani, the other by Hekmatyar. Frequent attempts to re-unite after the communist coup simply caused further fragmentation. To settle the issue of leadership, a neutral figure was inducted each time to head the new alliance. But instead of behaving as a compliant figurehead, the new leader would set about exploiting his authority to build up his own following. The alliance would then dissolve amidst intense recriminations, leaving behind a rump which developed into the nucleus of yet another party. Three of the main Peshawar leaders came to head their own parties in this way – Sibghatullah Mojadedi, Nabi Mohammadi, and Rasul Sayyaf.

In spite of these splits, the original members of the Islamic movement were well placed to win themselves a mass following after the civil war began in earnest. They had access to a limited flow of funds and weapons, and their leaders were well known to Pakistan's new military administration under General Zia ul Haq. Once refugees started flooding into Pakistan, the overwhelmed Pakistani authorities turned to the Afghan leaders already in exile for help in managing the influx. Since refugees had to be recommended by one of the parties in order to become eligible for rations, their membership swelled dramatically.

What started out as small, unrepresentative, ideologically motivated parties were converted almost overnight into mass refugee organisations. At the same time, because of the special relationship they had developed over the previous few years with both the military authorities and sympathetic fundamentalist groups in Pakistan, they became the main recipients of the foreign money and weapons which started being channelled through Pakistan to the Afghan resistance. Local guerilla groups inside Afghanistan, desperately in need of weapons and ammunition, were left with little choice but to affiliate themselves with one of the Peshawar parties.

After the summer of 1979, as the fighting in the south of Afghanistan intensified, a plethora of new 'parties' appeared in Pakistan. Tribal groups which fled *en masse* across the border had no wish to surrender their autonomy to the upstart leaders in Peshawar. As one exiled tribal leader in Quetta aptly put it, 'there is a Zahir Shah in every village'. Initially these proud local leaders kept themselves and their followers aloof from the resistance parties in Peshawar, and hunted around for funds to help keep their own private *jehads* going. By the end of 1980, though, in an attempt to simplify and control the situation, Pakistan quietly delivered an ultimatum to the independent chieftains: either merge with the main Peshawar parties, or lose our military and financial support. The outcome was the creation of seven organisational monopolies, claiming to represent the entire Afghan resistance.

Manufactured largely in Pakistan, the future of these seven parties is uncertain once foreign support is withdrawn. Some of their leaders may return to the semi-obscurity from which they sprang. Those with the best chance of surviving in their present form, albeit with reduced support, are the parties whose existence pre-dates the communist takeover and which are committed to a specific goal: the establishment of a revolutionary Islamic republic.

Of these, the most important are the Jamiat-i-Islami, or Society of Islam, headed by Burhanuddin Rabbani and the Hezb-i-Islami, or Party of Islam, led by Gulbuddin

Hekmatyar. Hezb and Jamiat are committed to a radical restructuring of all aspects of life in Afghanistan – political, judicial, social, economic and educational – according to Islamic laws and principles. Along with two of the other seven Peshawar parties, they are generally referred to in the West as 'fundamentalist', but the image which that word tends to conjure up – a return to a sort of medieval obscurantism – is misleading.

Hezb, in particular, is run along modern lines. It attracts the support of earnest young men with a better-than-average education. Many of them have received a technical training and Gulbuddin himself studied engineering at Kabul University in the early seventies. Unlike the traditional clergy (some still refuse to believe that man has set foot on the moon), the Islamic radicals borrow Western scientific rationalism while utterly rejecting Western values (or the lack of them). As a result, Hezb is in some ways the most progressive of the seven resistance organisations. In Peshawar, it has set up the best medical clinics and the best schools. Co-education is as abhorrent to Hezb puritans as drinking and gambling, but the right of women to be educated is upheld, and Hezb runs high schools for girls in both Peshawar and Karachi. In the same way that the Khalqis saw literacy as an instant way of spreading communism, Hezb views education as a major vehicle for spreading its version of Islam.

Despite their diametrically opposed ideologies, the parallels between Khalq and Hezb are striking. Both seek to destroy the traditional structures of Afghan society and replace them with an entirely new order. Both are impatient of opposition, and believe themselves beset by global conspiracies. Both have an egalitarian ethos in theory, but in practice are rigidly hierarchical. Hezb's secretive organisational structure consists of different tiers, with strict vetting and a probationary period for those aspiring to full membership. Party activists even have their own Marxist-style jargon, with Gulbuddin, sitting at the apex of the party's organisational pyramid, known to his comrades-in-arms as 'Brother Hekmatyar'. Both Khalq and Hezb have extensive intelligence networks, and use terror tactics to silence and intimidate their opponents. The tendency of each is towards totalitarianism.

Meeting Gulbuddin for the first time is an unnerving experience. Because of his reputation for murderous ruthlessness, I was prepared for the worst. But the man I encountered was dressed in drab brown pyjamas, with a full black beard, and long, delicate fingers. His English was imperfect, but he talked rationally, at times even with humour, inviting sympathy and understanding. He didn't seem like a fanatic. Only something slightly reptilian about his eyes, and the soft, honeyed voice with its slightly hypnotic edge kept me on guard. I sensed enormous energy reined in by absolute self-control. Alone of the seven Peshawar leaders, Gulbuddin possesses genuine charisma, but when I left the charmed circle of his presence, I always felt somehow tainted.

Gulbuddin was brought up on the margins of traditional Afghan society. Although a Pashtun, he was born in the northern province of Kunduz, in a village only about eight miles from the Soviet border. Tribal customs and traditional values are anathema to him. 'Many Pashtuns have lost Islam,' he says. 'The old traditions of Afghanistan were the treacherous ways of the old rulers to fool the people.'[1] Hezb has no time for the old values, such as respect for age and consensus decision-making. Even after leading his party for nearly fifteen years, Gulbuddin is still only in his early forties. The greybeards who congregate in the offices of other Peshawar parties, endlessly debating and sipping tea, are absent from the headquarters of Hezb. Unorthodox spiritual leaders, such as *pirs*, are considered to be part of a conspiracy on the part of the *ancien régime* to keep the general population in ignorance of 'true' Islam.

In terms of their commitment to radical Islam, there's little to choose between Hezb and its main rival, Jamiat-i-

Islami. But the methods pursued by the two parties to achieve their goals differ considerably. Unlike Hezb, Jamiat recognises the complex reality of Afghan society. It accepts that the Afghan mosaic of tribal customs, ethnic rivalries and unorthodox religious traditions cannot be transformed overnight, and proceeds by consultation and consensus. 'Those who are Muslims, even though they have different economic or other ideas, can live comfortably in a free Afghanistan,' the Jamiat leader Burhanuddin Rabbani once told me. It's impossible to imagine those words being spoken by Gulbuddin Hekmatyar.

Jamiat's tolerant attitude stems partly from its ethnic composition. Unlike the other six Peshawar parties, which primarily represent the Pashtuns, Jamiat is supported mainly by the Persian-speaking Tajiks, and to a lesser extent the Uzbeks, of northern Afghanistan. After centuries of subjugation and second-class citizenship, they tend to recognise the importance of creating broad, popular fronts in order to sustain their strength. Ahmed Shah Massoud, who stayed with Jamiat after the 1976 split, has had more success than any other guerilla commander in creating a unified military and civilian command structure in north-eastern Afghanistan and, to some extent, he has broken down the barriers of party, tribe and ethnic group.

Unlike their Hezb counterparts, who generally wear a glazed expression when talking to foreigners, as if carefully hiding their hostility behind a mask of bonhomie, Jamiat officials are direct, open and honest. Burhanuddin Rabbani is an appropriate symbol of his party's more moderate style. He's a slight, mild-mannered man with curiously vulnerable eyes and a shy smile, whose obligatory mujahed beard doesn't disguise his academic grounding. You can't help feeling that he would be more at home in a book-lined study, smoking a pipe and handing out glasses of sherry to his students, than presiding over one of the most effective guerilla organisations in Afghanistan.

Maulvi Yunis Khalis, who heads another of the so-called

'fundamentalist' parties, a faction of Hezb-i-Islami, is a man of an entirely different stamp. A seventy-year-old mullah, with a long, henna-dyed beard and thick tufts of black hair sprouting from his ears, he embodies the earthiness and lack of sophistication of the tribal Pashtun. Khalis represents a mixture of traditions. Born in the village of Gandamak where the ill-fated British Army of the Indus made its last desperate stand in 1842, his childhood was spent listening to heroic tales of Pashtun valour. His religious training, at Deoband in India, was orthodox and included memorising the entire Quran. But he also had connections with the Islamic radical movement, and in 1975, after spending several years writing polemical verses and newspaper articles against the Daoud regime, he fled to the safety of Peshawar.

Khalis is a man of action rather than an ideologue. When he arrived in Peshawar, according to his own account, he was asked to take charge of the Afghan resistance movement in order to forestall an open rupture between Hekmatyar and Rabbani. When the arrangement broke down, he sided with Hekmatyar, but soon became disillusioned with the political machinations of his fellow Pashtun. Despite his age, he returned to his native Nangrahar province to fight against the communist regime, and in 1980 he was recognised by Pakistan as the leader of his own faction of Hezb-i-Islami.

Khalis runs his party along semi-tribal lines. If you belong to it, you are treated as a member of an extended family, over which Khalis himself presides like a benign but eagle-eyed patriarch. According to one of his supporters, he 'literally knows the registration number of every Kalashnikov issued to the fighting fronts in Afghanistan.' He rules the party with an iron hand, and everyone is slightly afraid of him. Yet unlike some of the Peshawar leaders, he commands the genuine respect and affection of his supporters, who know him as 'Khalis Baba', Grandpa Khalis.

Despite his antipathy towards the old Durrani Pashtun

establishment and his commitment to an Islamic order, Khalis lacks the sophisticated political vision of the true Islamic radicals. His party is refreshingly lacking in the dogma which characterises Gulbuddin's faction of Hezb. It attracts few intellectuals, but the guerilla commanders who join Khalis, mainly from provincial Pashtun land-owning families in south-eastern Afghanistan, or tribal mullahs who have established their leadership through their fighting skills, know that they will receive the respect and weapons they deserve.

The last of the 'fundamentalist' leaders in Peshawar – and the only one whom the label really fits – is Abdul Rasul Sayyaf, a Pashtun from Paghman who is related by marriage to Hafizullah Amin. Their kinship may well have saved his life. Sayyaf, who taught theology at Kabul University and was deputy to Rabbani in the early days of the Islamic movement, was imprisoned by the Khalqi regime but escaped execution. Released from jail by Babrak Karmal after the Soviet invasion, Sayyaf came straight to Peshawar, where he was asked by the feuding resistance leaders to resolve their differences by heading a new alliance. As usual, the arrangement soon collapsed under the weight of rival ambitions, leaving Sayyaf in charge of his own party, the Ittehad-i-Islami, or Islamic Alliance.

Sayyaf is a large, roguish-looking man with fleshy lips and a long crinkly beard. In the words of a Pakistani general who has had dealings with him over many years, he is a 'genuine religious fanatic'[2] and he was the only one of the seven Peshawar leaders to invite me to convert to Islam. Sayyaf's vision of an Islamic state is close to the Wahhabis, an austere Saudi-Arabian school of thought which renounces everything not explicitly sanctioned by the Quran and the sayings of the Prophet. Wahhabi Arab volunteers fighting inside Afghanistan infuriate their mujahedin hosts by denouncing them as infidels for taking intoxicants like *naswar*, a powdered tobacco which helps keep them going over long distances, and for praying at the graves of saints and martyrs.

Sayyaf denies that he is a Wahhabi, knowing that Wahhabism is generally unpopular amongst his unorthodox countrymen. But his sympathy towards that school, combined with his oratorical skills and fluent Arabic, have helped make him the darling of the Arab world. Arab money has paid for 'Sayyafabad', a guerilla camp and township for about 6,000 refugee families some thirty miles outside Peshawar. In contrast to the rather more spartan headquarters of other guerilla organisations, Sayyafabad contains every sort of facility – except, significantly, a school for girls.

The millions of dollars which Sayyaf has raised from princes, businessmen and Islamic charities in Saudi Arabia, Kuwait and the United Arab Emirates have enabled him to entice thousands of guerillas to join his party. To keep the money rolling in, Sayyaf has an impressive publicity machine geared to the Arab world, with newsletters and magazines in Arabic and videos of crack mujahedin units undergoing intensive training exercises in full battledress. But in Afghanistan, money can only buy temporary allegiance. Sayyaf's election as Prime Minister in the interim government set up by the mujahedin in March 1989 is less a sign of his strength than of weakness; he's only been entrusted with that position because he represents the least serious threat to the ambitions of his colleagues.

In the early eighties, despite the personal animosities between their leaders, the four 'fundamentalist' parties remained loosely united in a series of alliances which constantly split and re-formed. In May 1985 they joined forces with the three moderate, or traditionalist, parties in Peshawar to form a seven-party alliance which survived, albeit shakily, until the Soviet withdrawal and the creation of the interim mujahedin government.

The convenient distinction which is often drawn between 'fundamentalists' and 'moderates', is to some extent an artificial one. With the possible exception of Hekmatyar's Hezb, all seven parties contain members who would feel equally at home elsewhere, were it not for the ties of blood or money which dictate their present allegiances. All three 'moderate' parties were already established in Peshawar by the time of the Soviet invasion, and their opposition to communism is as strong as that of the 'fundamentalists'. What distinguishes them from Hezb and Jamiat is that they are in no sense radical; they are conservative, looking back either to the good old days of the *ancien régime*, or to an idealised past when Muslim Afghanistan was untroubled by disturbing modern ideologies.

The largest of the three is Harakat-i-Inqilab-i-Islami, or Movement for the Islamic Revolution, led by Maulvi Mohammad Nabi, a dignified cleric and former Member of Parliament with a taste for snuff and English worsted cloth. Despite its revolutionary name, Harakat draws its strength from the traditional clergy, the village mullahs and scholars from the private theological schools. It was these men who provided much of the early leadership for the armed revolt, and as their need for money and weapons grew, they tended to gravitate, along with their followers, towards a party which was solidly religious without being politically or socially radical.

In the first year after the invasion, Harakat was able to claim far more supporters than any of the other Peshawar-based organisations. Mohammad Nabi, who's as prone to exaggeration as most other Pashtuns, still maintains that sixty percent of all mujahedin are affiliated with Harakat, at least in their hearts. In reality, though, the party's support dwindled rapidly after 1980. Initially, its lack of political ideology and organisation, together with its weak leadership and its staunchly Muslim credentials were plus points, attracting hundreds of local leaders who wanted to retain as much autonomy as possible. But these characteristics also went against it. It was easily infiltrated by opportunists, Maoists and government agents. It was incompetent and corrupt (its treasurer disappeared with a large part of the party funds a few years ago). The best mujahedin commanders quickly became disillusioned and attached themselves to better-organised parties like Jamiat and the Hezb of Khalis, which were able to provide for their needs.

The most secular of all the seven Peshawar parties is the Mahaz-i-Milli Islami, otherwise known as the National Islamic Front of Afghanistan (NIFA), led by Syed Ahmad Gailani. Gailani is a different kind of traditional religious leader, a *pir*, or hereditary Sufi saint. To the casual eye, though, it's hard to discern his saint-like qualities. A short, stout man, who clearly likes his creature comforts, he always looks slightly ill at ease when wearing his traditional white robes and turban, and is more comfortable in a smart blue blazer. His family are equally well-heeled, their designer clothes coming from Italy and their powerful landcruisers from Japan.

Gailani's party is mainly a family concern, and most senior positions are occupied by his kinsmen. The easygoing informality which is a trade-mark of the 'fundamentalist' parties is noticeably lacking when you enter NIFA's headquarters. The retainers who guard the gate or bring tea don't quite tug their forelocks, but the class divisions are evident.

Like the other moderate parties, NIFA's military effectiveness has been limited. Its military chief, Rahim Wardak, was a colonel in the Afghan army before the Soviet invasion. Trained at West Point, the US equivalent of Sandhurst, he's since promoted himself to the rank of general, and his conversation is peppered with phrases which seem to come from some elementary military manual. 'Surprise,' he once informed me, 'is one of the nine main principles of war.' But General Wardak is at least fifty percent bluster, and many of his military operations, planned meticulously on paper and given titles like 'Operation Avalanche', seem mainly designed to impress the Western film cameramen he likes to take along with him to record his prowess.

Because of his moderate, Westernised outlook, Gailani attracts the support of the minority of educated nationalists who have stayed in Pakistan rather than settling in the West. But his real strength stems from his inherited spiritual position. Although his claim to have forty million disciples from Malaysia to North Africa is a wild exaggeration, he is venerated by some of the Pashtun tribes of southern Afghanistan, a large proportion of whom are now living in Pakistan as refugees. In addition to the *pir*'s disciples, NIFA is also backed by the Durrani establishment, the sort of men who were ministers and provincial governors in the days before the communist takeover. Gailani married into the royal family in the 1950's, and frequently flies to Italy to consult with Zahir Shah. Mujahedin from other parties consider NIFA to be the party of the tribal aristocracy, and tend to view it with contempt. Yet despite the luxurious life-style which separates him from ordinary Afghans, Pir Gailani's secular outlook makes him far more representative of traditional Afghan thinking than the hardline fundamentalism of Hekmatyar's Hezb. 'Our Islam is moderate. The fabric of our country is based on moderation', Gailani once told me, an assessment shared by many Western experts who remember the gentle humanism of Afghan life before the radicalisation of the past ten years.

Professor Sibghatullah Mojadedi, head of the Afghan National Liberation Front and President of the mujahedin interim government formed in March 1989, completes the trio of moderate leaders. The ANLF is the smallest of the seven Peshawar parties, though Mojadedi claims that it has been deliberately starved of military support, and that he is constantly being approached by mujahedin from rival parties who would join him if he could finance their military operations. The hubbub of guerilla commanders who can be found on the front lawn of the party offices on the outskirts of Peshawar lends some credence to the claim, although some seem to be curiously reluctant to fight: one commander told me he had been waiting to receive weapons in Peshawar for the previous three years.

Although not himself a *pir*, Mojadedi's family heads one of the branches of the Naqshbandiyya sufi order in southern Afghanistan, from where he derives most of his support. He's a difficult man to define. The family is a prestigious one, and claims descent from the second Caliph. It is conservative, and has in the past maintained close links with the former ruling establishment. Yet it also has a reformist tradition, and Mojadedi was on the fringes of the Islamic radical movement in the 1950's and 1960's. He forged connections with the Muslim Brotherhood in Egypt, and in 1959, accused of campaigning against the visit of Krushchev, he was jailed by Daoud for four and a half years. Yet he's also one of the most vocal advocates of the return of Zahir Shah, who, he says, is the only symbol of national unity.

Mojadedi is a small, intense, fastidious man who speaks five languages and sees himself as the champion of Afghanistan's intellectual élite. In private, he can be hysterically funny, and is always cracking jokes, some of them quite smutty. But he also has a volatile temper; on one occasion, he and Gulbuddin Hekmatyar are rumoured to have pulled pistols on each other at a regular meeting of the Supreme Council of the Peshawar alliance. Hekmatyar is Mojadedi's *bête noire*. At times, when his temper has got the better of him, he has publicly and passionately denounced the Hezb leader, whose hands, he says, are 'dirty with the blood of thousands of innocent Afghans'.

Despite the bitter feuding of their leaders, the claim of the seven Peshawar parties, to represent the whole Afghan resistance, was until recently more or less accepted by the outside world. Although the seven-party alliance was never able to speak with one voice, its leaders were at least visible and audible: they held meetings, issued press statements, travelled abroad, published party newspapers and, most importantly, received and distributed money and weapons.

Inside Afghanistan, though, dozens more mujahedin groups have always operated independently of Pakistani and US support. During the time I spent in Pakistan, my office in Islamabad was more than once invaded by Afghan delegations claiming to represent parties with massive support in central Afghanistan of which no-one else ever seemed to have heard.

The Shias, in particular, have only recently made their presence felt, mainly through the patronage of Iran. After the Hazarajat rose in revolt against the Kabul regime in September 1979, a ruling council – or Shura – was elected under the leadership of Sheikh Sayyed Beheshti. The Shura, dominated by clerics and conservative tribal elders, organised an autonomous government with a standing army of conscript soldiers. Later its authority was challenged by far more radical, pro-Khomeini parties like Nasr and Sepah-e-Pasdaran, which had links with Iran and received some weapons from the Iranian Revolutionary Guards. Another important Shia party, not exclusively confined to the Hazarajat, is the Harakat-i-Islami of Sheikh Mohsini, which has a strong following among urban educated Shias, including many sympathisers in Kabul itself. Mohsini, who claims to be Afghanistan's only ayatollah, controls a number of well-trained, active fighting fronts. Yet until these groups were welded into a rival eight-party alliance by Iran in 1987, the power-hungry leaders in Peshawar simply ignored their existence and their claim to a share in the future government of a liberated Afghanistan.

Even amongst Pashtuns, attitudes to the Peshawar seven are ambivalent. Although they have earned a certain amount of respect as the official purveyors of jehad, everyone is aware that their support has been built on artifical foundations. A controversial survey conducted among Afghan refugees in 1987 (whose organiser, Professor S. B. Majrooh, was later shot dead on his own doorstep in Peshawar) found that less than half a percent of those polled would choose one of the seven main Peshawar leaders to rule a free Afghanistan. Even Pakistan's long-serving Refugee Commissioner, Brigadier Fahimullah Khattak, once admitted to me that 'these seven leaders have been built up and have their tentacles, their small organisations, in virtually every refugee camp. They have great influence now, but their status in tomorrow's Afghanistan could be anything.'[4]

NINE

Uncle Sam and the Grinning General: US and Pakistani Involvement in the Resistance

For General Zia ul Haq, Pakistan's military dictator since September 1977, the Soviet invasion of Afghanistan represented both a threat and an opportunity. The threat was to Pakistan's own survival. Zia had warned, six months earlier, that to all intents and purposes Pakistan now shared a common border with the Soviet Union. The invasion underlined the point with dramatic emphasis. Now the question was, would the border be respected? If Moscow was intent on breaking through to the warm waters of the Persian Gulf, as some analysts believed, then the easiest route would be through the deserts of Baluchistan, still seething with discontent from the abortive tribal rebellion of the mid-1970's. If not, there was still a danger of destabilisation. The Baluchis, and to a lesser extent the Pashtuns, felt they had little stake in a united Pakistan, particularly after the imposition of martial law by the Punjabi-dominated army. The Bengalis had already seceded from the union in the 1971 war, after military intervention by India which had Moscow's full backing. Since then, Pakistan had lived with the ever-present spectre of further dismemberment.

Islamabad's biggest nightmare was the forging of a hostile axis joining Moscow, Kabul and Delhi; and in the space of just two weeks – during which Soviet troops invaded Afghanistan and Mrs Gandhi swept back to power in the Indian general elections – its worst fears seemed to be coming true. Within a month, the Soviet Foreign Minister Andrei Gromyko was publicly underlining the possibility of combined Soviet–Indian action by warning, during a visit to Delhi, that 'if Pakistan continues to serve as a puppet of imperialism in the future, it will jeopardise its existence and its integrity as an independent state.'[1]

The opportunity presented to General Zia by the Soviet invasion was the chance it gave him to shore up his shaky regime both at home and abroad. The judicial murder of the former Prime Minister Zulfikar Ali Bhutto in April 1979 had been a risky move which had threatened to unite the entire opposition against him. In October 1979 Zia felt compelled to cancel the elections he had promised to hold in November and ban all political activities. The crisis of the Soviet invasion provided a splendid diversion which enabled him to put Pakistan's own pressing domestic problems on hold. It also rescued Zia from international isolation. Bhutto's execution had turned him into something of an international outcast. It sent shock waves through the Islamic world, where Bhutto had many friends, and Pakistan's two most powerful allies, the United States and China, had joined in the world-wide appeal for clemency. When Zia ignored the appeals and had Bhutto hanged, Washington promptly suspended all aid to Pakistan. Further damage to the relationship was done in November 1979 when the American embassy in Islamabad was burned down by an irate mob.

The invasion changed everything. US intelligence immediately concluded that if the Soviet Union consolidated its control over Afghanistan, it would represent 'a major step toward overland access to the Indian Ocean and to domination of the Asian subcontinent.'[2] Washington's medium-term counter-strategy was to build up its own military capability in the region; but at the same time it needed to strengthen Pakistan, its only remaining ally there after the fall of the Shah of Iran, as a bulwark against 'Soviet expansionism'. Almost overnight, General Zia was transformed from a tinpot dictator with blood on his hands to an indispensable ally. On 31st December 1979, President

Carter's hardline National Security Adviser, Zbigniew Brzezinski, publicly affirmed that Washington would use military force in support of Pakistan in case of armed aggression. On 4th January 1980, President Carter announced that, 'along with other countries, we will provide military equipment, food and other assistance to help Pakistan defend its independence', and by March he had offered $400 million in military and economic aid spread over two years.[3]

Coolly and contemptuously, Zia rejected the offer as 'peanuts'. He was aiming for a massive injection of US military aid to secure Pakistan's all-important eastern border with India; once the threat from India had been neutralised, he argued, he would feel more confident about playing an active role in the US plan to contain Soviet aggression. It would also take more than a couple of hundred million dollars to keep the armed forces happy – and they, as he himself admitted, were his only political constituency.

The Reagan administration was far more responsive to Zia's reasoning than President Carter had been, and in September 1981, agreement was finally reached on a $3.2 billion economic and military aid package spread over six years, plus the option to buy forty advanced F-16 fighter jets. The package made Pakistan the biggest recipient of American aid after Israel and Egypt.

Zia's best bargaining chip in the high-stakes poker game he was playing with Washington was his crucial role as a link man between the Americans and the Afghan mujahedin. The CIA had already begun to extend a limited amount of help to the mujahedin before the invasion. In March 1979, Brzezinski pushed a decision through the Special Co-ordinating Committee of the National Security Council to 'be more sympathetic to those Afghans who are determined to preserve their country's independence'.[4] The precise extent of that 'sympathy' is still unclear, but by April 1979 regular meetings were being held in Pakistan between US officials and Afghan rebel leaders, and classified

CIA reports indicate that covert funds were transferred into Afghan rebel accounts as early as September 1979.[5] On the whole, though, before the invasion the CIA confined itself to financing anti-Soviet demonstrations by Afghan exiles, and beaming radio propaganda into Afghanistan itself. General Zia appears to have been wary about allowing the US to get too involved. According to CIA field reports, Washington had to put the Pakistani Director of Military Operations on its payroll in order to ensure Pakistani co-operation for its activities, and to keep tabs on what Pakistan was up to.[6]

Pakistan's own involvement in rebel activity prior to the invasion was rather more extensive. General Zia was naturally sympathetic to the Afghan resistance, particularly the Islamic radical organisations. It fitted well with the new mission he had discovered for himself in Pakistan, where, in October 1979, he announced a strict new Islamic regime, including compulsory Islamic taxes, the phasing out of interest in banks and sterner punishments for those violating the sanctity of Islam. Although not above exploiting Islam for political ends, Zia was a devout Muslim, and, like many Pakistani generals, a devout anti-communist as well. In addition, important allies like China, Saudi Arabia and Iran were all encouraging him to support the mujahedin, and were providing aid on their own account.

Nevertheless, Zia had to tread with extreme caution. Because of the danger of retaliation by Moscow, and of destabilisation within Pakistan, he could not risk giving too much material support to the resistance. What little was given had to be kept completely secret. Already, by March 1979, Moscow and Kabul were alleging that the spreading insurrection in Afghanistan was being fomented, armed and directed primarily by Pakistan. Zia reacted by flatly denying that Pakistan was supporting the mujahedin in any way, a pretence which he maintained until the day of his death. In later years, as the level of foreign aid increased, Zia's claim became increasingly threadbare. But in the months before the invasion, Pakistani aid to the Afghan leadership in Peshawar was of little consequence compared to the upsurge of spontaneous guerilla activity inside Afghanistan. What weapons the mujahedin groups based in Peshawar received at that stage seem to have been mainly outdated equipment from Pakistan's own armouries. Pakistan replenished its own stock with more modern Chinese weapons, using funds donated by Saudi Arabia, and the United Arab Emirates to buy them from Beijing.

After Soviet troops invaded Afghanistan, no-one believed that the mujahedin would be able to force them to retreat. Even General Zia was sceptical; but opinion in the United States demanded a substantial increase in US aid to the guerillas. At worst, they might be able to tie up some of the 85,000 Soviet troops deployed there while the US strengthened its own military capability in the region and launched a diplomatic offensive to secure a Soviet withdrawal. Moderates like President Carter believed that the US had a 'moral obligation' to help the resistance, while hardliners saw it as a cheap but effective way of teaching Moscow a lesson. Either way, when the CIA unveiled its plans to send covert military aid to the guerillas on 9th January 1980, there were no objections from Congress.

Pakistan's delicate position, plus Washington's own desire to maintain the fiction that the resistance was a purely Afghan affair, meant that American-made weapons could not be supplied to the mujahedin. Instead, an increasingly complex series of third-party deals had to be fixed up. Egypt was one of the first contributors to the CIA's arms pipeline. Because Moscow had been its main arms supplier until 1972, it had just what was wanted: large stockpiles of Soviet-made automatic weapons, land mines, grenade launchers and anti-aircraft missiles. Just before his assassination in 1981, the Egyptian President Anwar Sadat disclosed that he was contacted immediately after the invasion and was asked, 'please open your stores for us so that we can give the Afghanis the armaments they need to fight.'

In return, Washington offered to equip Egypt with new US weapons. Sadat agreed, and 'the transport of armaments to the Afghanis started from Cairo on US planes.'[7]

Because of Sadat's indiscreet remarks, the Egyptian deal is the best known of the CIA's early operations in support of the Afghan resistance. But there were many others. Until 1985, when Congress first authorised the dispatch of US-made Stinger anti-aircraft missiles to the mujahedin, the CIA had to exercise great ingenuity to prevent military aid being traced back to the United States. China was one of the earliest suppliers of weapons. A senior Pakistani foreign ministry official admitted to me in 1988 that 'China has always maintained a supply line to the mujahedin which the US has not always been able to because of the long distances involved.' But although, in the official's words, China's own military support for the guerillas had been 'considerable', the CIA helped to reimburse Beijing by funnelling hard currency and new equipment to China, usually through dummy corporations. The bulk of the weaponry supplied to the mujahedin through Pakistan in later years had Chinese markings.

In deals with a variety of other countries, the CIA either acted as middleman, or purchased weapons directly. Israel, for example, sold to the CIA Soviet weapons which it had captured from Syrian troops in the 1982 war in Lebanon.[8] In 1986 weapons were even bought in Poland and shipped directly to Pakistan.[9] To circumvent Congressional restrictions on the supply of US weaponry, Iran was persuaded to pass on TOW anti-tank missiles to the Afghan resistance as part of the secret arms-for-Iran deal negotiated in 1986 by Oliver North and his superiors.[10]

When there were not enough Soviet-style weapons available, the CIA arranged for them to be manufactured. According to US intelligence sources, some of the weapons acquired from Egypt in 1980 were taken off to a CIA-controlled factory near Cairo which then began making copies. Another CIA factory in the mid-West of the United

States duplicated Soviet-bloc recoil-less rifles and surface-to-surface missiles, while the Hughes Aircraft Corporation was given a classified contract to upgrade Soviet SAM-7 anti-aircraft missiles.[11] The CIA also counterfeited millions of dollars worth of Afghan currency which was distributed to guerilla commanders to help pay transport and other costs.[12]

Aiding the mujahedin was not high on President Carter's list of priorities. He still had hopes of negotiating a settlement of the crisis, and in the first year after the Soviet invasion the administration only requested Congress to authorise $30 million in covert aid for Afghanistan. Pakistan was also worried about letting the mujahedin get their hands on sophisticated weapons which might provoke retaliation. Few of the SAM-7 missiles acquired from Egypt, for instance, were allowed to get through to the guerillas, and Pakistan refused to allow mortars and machine guns of more than a certain calibre to be donated to the resistance.[13]

The humiliations suffered by the United States under Carter, including the invasion of Afghanistan, the fall of the Shah and the Iranian hostage crisis, drove him from office in November 1980. The new incumbent of the White House, Ronald Reagan, had a far more belligerent foreign policy. The Soviet Union, he announced in his most memorable phrase, was the 'evil empire' and Reagan's mission was to roll back its frontiers. For south-west Asia that meant two things: the strengthening of Pakistan by integrating it into a system of emergency bases stretching throughout the Middle East supervised by CENTCOM; and a substantial increase in aid to the Afghan mujahedin.

Between 1981 to 1985, annual US military aid to the mujahedin leapt from $30 million to about $280 million, making it the biggest single covert CIA operation anywhere in the world since the Vietnam war.[14] Congress took the lead in an extraordinary display of bi-partisan solidarity. Led by hardliners like the Texan Congressman Charles Wilson, it began in 1983 to vote more money for the Afghan resistance than the administration asked for, by diverting Defense Department money to the CIA. Meanwhile the CIA Director, William Casey, used his influence to persuade other sympathetic governments to contribute to a reserve fund for the mujahedin which could be kept secret from Congress and the US State Department. Saudi Arabia was the biggest contributor. In late 1981 Riyadh agreed to join the CIA's world-wide anti-communist crusade in exchange for permission to buy five AWAC surveillance planes, against Congressional opposition. Thereafter, according to some accounts, the Saudis matched the CIA dollar for dollar in funding for the mujahedin, funnelling more than half a billion dollars to CIA bank accounts in Switzerland and the Cayman Islands in 1984 and '85 alone.[15]

Secrecy was essential. Despite bi-partisan support for the Afghan resistance in Congress, the policy had its critics. Some felt there was a danger of repeating the mistakes of Vietnam, and 'over-technologising primitive people'.[16] Others worried that supplying more effective weaponry to the mujahedin would provoke even more massive retaliation by Soviet forces against unarmed villagers, while not substantially improving the guerillas' chances of success. At a different level, there was concern about the CIA's failure to ensure that the aid was being properly absorbed. Mounting evidence showed that the CIA arms pipeline had sprung numerous leaks which were beginning to have far-reaching consequences in Pakistan itself. The Federation for American Afghan Action alleged in 1987 that less than forty percent of the $1.1 billion appropriated by Congress for the mujahedin up to 1986 had actually reached them. Some funds, according to the FAAA's chairman, Andy Eiva, had been illegally siphoned off to support the Nicaraguan Contras, while millions more dollars had been stolen by the Pakistani generals overseeing the distribution of military aid to the guerillas. At least two generals, Eiva alleged, had 'become overnight millionaires . . . off US aid to the Afghans.'[17]

Personal corruption aside, the Pakistani army routinely misappropriated military equipment intended for the mujahedin and replaced it with its own outdated stock. Some weapons may even have been sold off by Pakistan to third countries. In April 1988, a vast ammunition storage depot situated at Ojheri, halfway between the twin cities of Islamabad and Rawalpindi, exploded in a gigantic fireball. For several hours, $80 million dollars-worth of mortars, rockets, anti-aircraft missiles and other heavy-duty weapons intended for the mujahedin rained down on the terrified citizens, killing hundreds. At the time, the explosion was put down to sabotage by agents of KHAD, the Afghan version of the KGB. But later, after the death of General Zia, it was widely rumoured that Pakistan's own military intelligence agency, the ISI, had deliberately sabotaged Ojheri Camp in order to prevent a US audit team from discovering that Stinger missiles for the mujahedin had been sold off to Iran by Pakistan.

Whatever the truth of such allegations, the CIA arms pipeline which passed through Pakistan undoubtedly created havoc in many other ways. A large proportion of the foreign weaponry which eventually reached the resistance leaders and guerilla commanders in Peshawar was sold off in the thriving arms bazaars in Pakistan's own tribal belt along the Afghan border. Sometimes, the cash was simply pocketed by guerilla officials who had developed expensive tastes during their exile in Pakistan. Genuine guerilla commanders used the proceeds to procure other essential but less glamorous supplies for the *jehad*, and to pay the exorbitant fees charged by entrepreneurial mule drivers for transporting what weaponry remained to the battle zones.

The consequences were alarming. The weapons flooded back into Pakistan in huge numbers, creating what gradually became known as the 'Kalashnikov culture'. AK-47s became an indispensible item of household equipment throughout the country, nearly as common on university campuses as among the drug-running mafias. In Karachi automatic weapons could be rented out for the day, boosting the firepower of rival ethnic groups and periodically turning the whole city into a gigantic slaughterhouse. The bandit gangs which infested Sind and Baluchistan equipped themselves with RPG-7 grenade launchers and ground-to-ground missiles, and dissident Pakistani tribesmen traded in their ancient Lee-Enfield rifles for 107mm Chinese rockets which they occasionally fired into the centre of Peshawar. Opponents of Zia's Afghan policy pointed out with vehemence that Pakistan was fast becoming another Beirut.

None of these drawbacks carried much weight with the Reagan administration. Enough weapons were getting through to the guerillas to enmesh the Soviet Union in a costly, and what soon started to seem like an unwinnable, war. As a military dictator, General Zia could afford to ignore Pakistani public opinion, and he was willing to let his country pay the price so long as he could bank on solid backing from the US. As early as 1983, Zia himself suggested to visiting US Congressmen Clarence Long that Swiss-made Oerlikon anti-aircraft cannon should be shipped to the mujahedin to protect them from the menace of Soviet helicopter gunships. 'He was perfectly willing to take a chance if it couldn't be traced back to him,' Long revealed later.[18]

The first batch of Oerlikon cannon, with their special armour-piercing shells and 1000-rounds-per-minute firerate, were eventually shipped to the mujahedin in 1985. Congressional enthusiasts who believed they would turn the tide of the war were mistaken: they were too heavy and cumbersome for guerilla warfare. But they did represent a significant escalation of the proxy war. For the first time, the US had supplied the mujahedin with weapons of Western manufacture, thereby breaching its own rules of 'plausible deniability', which were designed to preserve the fiction that Washington was not involved in the war. Scenting possible victory, President Reagan signed a directive in April 1985 which called for efforts to drive Soviet forces out of Afghanistan 'by all means available'.[19] Restrictions on foreign-made high-technology equipment were removed. British-made Blowpipe anti-aircraft missiles were first used to bring down Soviet aircraft in the spring of 1986; but far more popular, and far more effective, were the US-made heat-seeking Stinger missiles, which arrived around the same time.

Stingers enabled the mujahedin to challenge Soviet supremacy of the skies for the first time, and with isolated Afghan army garrisons no longer able to count on air support, long-range mortars, mine-clearing equipment and TOW anti-tank missiles were soon required and supplied. After 1985 the CIA was effectively issued with a blank cheque. In 1987, Congress appropriated $660 million for the mujahedin, and in 1988 they were estimated to be receiving $100 million worth of arms each month – a 4,000 percent increase since the first year of the war.

Even after President Reagan took office, debate continued within the administration over the advisability of continually raising the stakes in Afghanistan. By 1983, however, the hardliners had won the day. In time, they came to be known as 'bleeders', committed to a cynical policy of 'fighting to the last Afghan'. Lip service continued to be paid to UN-sponsored efforts for a negotiated settlement; but the private feelings of many Americans in public office were voiced by Congressman Charles Wilson, the most persistent of pro-mujahedin lobbyists, who candidly admitted, 'I viewed this as an opportunity to defeat the Soviets in the battlefield. We lost 58,000 men in Vietnam. The Russians have lost maybe 25,000 dead in Afghanistan. I figure they owe us 33,000 dead.'[20]

The Reagan administration's quest to inflict a humiliating defeat on the Soviet Union, combined with General Zia's insistence that the Americans should keep a low profile, meant that Washington left the actual distribution of US-funded weaponry to Pakistan's own military intelligence agency, the Inter-Services Intelligence Directorate (ISI).

Most of the weaponry was shipped to Pakistan's main port, Karachi, where it was exempted from normal customs procedures. After a cursory inspection of receipts by CIA station officers, the consignment was handed over to the ISI's own trucking company, the National Logistics Cell (NLC) whose giant container lorries transported them to Pakistani warehouses and military compounds in the Frontier Province or Baluchistan. More sophisticated equipment, such as long-range mortars and anti-aircraft missiles, was flown directly to airforce bases in Rawalpindi and Peshawar, and then transferred to ISI-run depots such as Ojheri Camp on the outskirts of Islamabad.

Meanwhile, in regular meetings with ISI officers, senior officials of the seven mujahedin parties would be lobbying for military supplies. Their requests, backed up by details of military operations planned in the coming months, would be made in regular face-to-face meetings with senior ISI officers. According to mujahedin sources, it was General Akhtar Abdul Rehman, Director-General of the ISI until March 1987, who always made the final decision about the quantity and type of weapons to be allotted to each guerilla party. Once the decisions had been taken, ISI- or Afghan-owned vehicles transported the weapons to arms depots run by each individual party just outside Peshawar and Quetta, or to one of the dozens of dumps near the Afghan border.

From the outside, the dumps looked innocuous enough: the usual large, mud-walled compounds common in tribal territory. Inside, though, huge mounds of machine-gun bullets, mortar bombs and rocket tubes were stacked under tarpaulins. Each dump was presided over by a quartermaster and a couple of clerks who would wait for authorisation from party headquarters in Peshawar before releasing supplies to guerilla commanders crossing into Afghanistan.

The control exercised by General Zia's military intelligence chief over the distribution of weapons to the mujahedin gave him and the ISI enormous powers of patronage. Although moderate guerilla leaders like Pir Gailani made use of their own contacts on Capitol Hill to lobby for increased US support, Washington was generally indifferent to how its secret aid programme affected the balance of power within the resistance. All that mattered was that it should achieve the most lethal results, or, as the US ambassador to Pakistan, Arnie Raphel, bluntly put it in 1988, 'we tended to help those who killed the most Russians.'[21]

General Zia, however, had his own strategic objective. Even before the communist takeover, Islamabad's relations with Kabul had been uneasy. Although Zahir Shah remained neutral during Pakistan's two wars with India in 1965 and 1971, he had kept up excellent relations with Delhi, and the Indians maintained one of the biggest and most influential embassies in the Afghan capital. Daoud had brought the two countries to the brink of war in his campaign for Pashtunistan. Now Zia glimpsed an historic opportunity to solve the problem of Pashtunistan for ever and reshape the map of south-west Asia. His ultimate dream was not just the overthrow of the Kabul regime but the installation of a mujahedin-led government which would express its gratitude by joining Pakistan in an Islamic confederation, strong enough to deal with India on equal terms and eventually, perhaps, even to regain Kashmir.

To pursue that dream, Zia needed to promote a compliant guerilla leadership with a similar outlook to his own. He had little interest in helping minority nationalities like the Tajiks and Hazara Shias who had few historical or cultural ties with the people of Pakistan. But not even the Pashtuns could be armed indiscriminately. The restoration of Afghanistan's traditional power structure would bring only very limited gains to Pakistan. The old Durrani establishment and its former collaborators (including Westernised bureaucrats and military officers, Sufi *pirs* and tribal *maliks*) were bound to resist closer integration with Pakistan once Afghanistan had regained its independence.

As a result, General Zia's regime consistently sabotaged

attempts by pro-royalists elements in the resistance to bring back the former king. A bid to unite the resistance under moderate leadership by holding a *jirga* in Quetta in the autumn of 1981 was foiled when Pakistan denied permission for it to be held. Abdul Wali, the king's cousin, and other members of the Afghan royal family, were repeatedly refused visas to visit Pakistan.

The only groups likely to benefit from a permanent linkage between the destinies of Afghanistan and Pakistan were those which were opposed to the old Afghan power structure, which drew their strength more from foreign support than from traditional society, and which were ideologically sympathetic to Zia's pan-Islamic vision. In short, Zia's ultimate objective depended not simply on the overthrow of the Kabul regime, but on the capture of power by the Islamic radicals, and preferably by his most favoured instrument, Gulbuddin Hekmatyar.

There is no categorical proof for this, but there is circumstantial evidence. Although it is denied by Pakistani foreign ministry officials who have since looked at the ISI's records, European diplomats and moderate guerilla officials consistently alleged during General Zia's regime that the 'fundamentalist' parties were receiving the lion's share of military aid from the ISI. One particularly well-informed diplomat estimated in early 1988 that Gulbuddin Hekmatyar alone was receiving twenty-seven percent of all military supplies being distributed. The diplomat couldn't understand it. Gulbuddin had never hidden his loathing of the US. 'Death to America' is nearly as common a slogan in schools run by his party inside Afghanistan as 'Death to Russia'. 'The Americans are all impressed with him,' the diplomat said. 'The more he kicks them, the more they tend to enthuse.'

Information received around the same time from key aides to General Zia provided an insight into the way the President was thinking in 1988. Sahabzada Yaqub Khan, a retired general who had been Pakistan's foreign minister for most of the eighties, admitted during a brief period out of office in 1988 that 'Gulbuddin Hekmatyar is the card we are playing.' Around the same time, General Fazle Haq, Zia's military governor in the North West Frontier Province until 1985, told me after holding a long discussion with Zia that the President 'is thinking in the long term, and may even be thinking of a confederation.'[22] Not long afterwards, and surely not by coincidence, Hakmatyar himself floated the idea of a confederation between Pakistan and Afghanistan during a press conference in Lahore. When both General Zia and his right-hand man, General Akhtar, died in a mysterious plane crash in August 1988, the general feeling among the other mujahedin parties was that Gulbuddin had been 'orphaned'.

Accountable solely to General Zia, the ISI gradually took on the role of big brother to the Peshawar leadership. Not only did it provide weapons, it also set up training facilities, provided logistics support and intelligence, used Afghanistan as a testing ground for the Pakistan army's own newly acquired weapons, escorted Pakistani generals over the border, and, increasingly, took the lead in planning military strategy on behalf of the mujahedin. When Stinger missiles were first sent to the resistance, it was the ISI which arranged the necessary training, given in Pakistani military installations by Pakistani officers and ex-US army instructors. The first guerilla commanders to be issued with Stingers were always accompanied over the border by an ISI officer, and, later on, proof had to be presented to the ISI that Stingers had been put to good use before replacements were issued.

Training of the mujahedin by Pakistan was nowhere near as extensive as Moscow and Kabul alleged. The ISI did run some training camps in Pakistan, where instruction was given in handling new weapons, as well as in skills like camouflage and mine disposal. Stinger training was given near Islamabad, and most of the mujahedin parties had their own training facilities, where Pakistani officers might be on hand as advisers. Nevertheless, even after ten years of warfare, the majority of guerillas had received little or no training. Journalists who crossed the Afghan border came away with the impression that they had been travelling with a dedicated rabble. Radio operators constantly gave away their positions by using their sets for two-way chit-chat; mortars would be loaded the wrong way round; and over-enthusiastic onlookers were occasionally fried alive by standing too close to the heat stream given out by an RPG-7 being fired. Commanders could not rely on their subordinates to remember even the most elementary details. Even someone as senior as NIFA's 'General' Rahim Wardak had to carry his own horseshoes when leading military operations. 'You can't rely on anybody knowing his job,' he grumbled on one occasion. 'You have to do everything yourself, from NCO level up to your own level.'[23]

Traditional Pashtun warfare was notoriously disorganised, often involving little more than a heavy barrage of artillery fired at a government outpost from a safe distance. But even the relatively disciplined forces of Ahmed Shah Massoud in north-eastern Afghanistan lacked basic training. During his occasional trips to visit Massoud, Sandy Gall of ITN once came across Afghanistan's most powerful guerilla commander personally adjusting the sights of newly captured weapons for his men.[24] A Jamiat official in Peshawar, pointing out how difficult the guerilla's new phase of offensive warfare would be after the Soviet withdrawal, said that although Massoud's guerillas received intensive coaching for several weeks before attacking even a small government garrison, 'they still mess it up'.[25]

In order to encourage more efficient operations and greater co-operation between different guerilla commanders, the ISI involved itself increasingly in military planning in the border areas during the last few years of the Soviet occupation. The ISI began to single out specific commanders for support, at first directing their party headquarters to send them military supplies, and later channelling aid to them directly. The ISI also began to co-ordinate joint operations between its favourite commanders. During an attack on the Afghan army's 71st Brigade headquarters in Nangrahar province in April 1988, the mujahedin of three different parties were provided with instructions typed in English and first-rate maps showing every gun emplacement. 'Nobody should ever underestimate the degree of control Pakistan exercises over such border operations,' said one participant in the attack. Later that year, the ISI was blamed by many mujahedin for planning an abortive offensive against Jalalabad which eventually had to be called off because local commanders were reluctant to participate.

As Soviet troops started withdrawing from Afghanistan in the summer of 1988, the ISI threw caution to the winds and virtually took over the planning of the *jehad*. General Zia's death in August 1988 only added to the impetus: the danger that an elected civilian government might favour a negotiated settlement of the war rather than a military solution was intensely worrying to the ISI. 'Since the death of Zia,' an Afghan source told me, 'the Pakistanis are giving specific attack plans to the military committees of individual parties. ISI people are going inside, planning operations and issuing orders. It's a pity to see they're interfering so much in Afghanistan. It could ruin relations between the two countries.'[26]

During the two and a half years I spent in Pakistan, that was a refrain which grew ever louder: Pakistan's growing interference in the war was beginning to dissipate the goodwill it had built up by sheltering three million refugees. The mutterings were loudest among officials of the moderate guerilla parties. 'We are being drip-fed with money and weapons,' one complained to me, 'so how can we plan anything?' 'Pakistan's aim is to push Gulbuddin down the throats of the resistance as their leader,' said another. 'A prisoner is more at liberty.'

The consequence of Pakistan's growing influence was to tarnish the image of the party leaders among many rank-

and-file guerillas and refugees. During trips to Quetta, where the Peshawar parties exercised less control, many of the guerilla commanders I met explained that money was the only reason for their temporary loyalty to the parties to which they were affiliated. In a memorable phrase which got me into trouble back in Peshawar when I reported it on the BBC, one commander said: 'These leaders are like an oily bone to which a lot of ants are attracted. When the oil is finished, the ants leave.' An Afghan doctor in Quetta complained that the CIA and the ISI were turning the *jehad* into a business, and the mujahedin into businessmen. 'When we examine these people,' he said of the Peshawar leaders, 'we see they are rubbish.'

In Peshawar itself, and in the refugee camps, such views tended to be voiced more surreptitiously. Western journalists visiting refugee camps heard the same pledges of loyal support to the Peshawar leaders over and over again. To some extent, that was the result of intensive propaganda. But it was also the result of fear. Hezb-i-Islami, in particular, has an extensive intelligence network, a computerised record system and a ruthless security apparatus. 'Give us any Afghan name,' Gulbuddin Hekmatyar claimed, the first time I met him, 'and after two hours we will know all his background.' Hezb co-operates closely with the Pakistani Special Branch to keep tabs on the refugee population and potential saboteurs, and, according to Dr Zabi Mojadedi of the ANLF, 'Hezb even arrests people in Pakistan, it has prison chambers here, it has executed people here.'[27] Refugees have to guard their tongues. 'In the camps,' explained a senior official in Pakistan's Refugee Commissionerate who asked to remain anonymous, 'these fundamentalist leaders have very strong agents. People are afraid to speak out against them.'

Even the political decisions of the resistance leadership seemed to be dictated by the ISI. According to one insider, an ISI officer of the rank of major or above sat in on nearly every meeting of the seven-party alliance's Supreme

Council. It was the ISI which forced the Supreme Council to come up with a proposal for a fundamentalist-led mujahedin interim government just before the final round of Geneva negotiations in early 1988. When Sibghatullah Mojadedi subsequently resigned from the Alliance in a fit of disgust with Pakistani meddling, it was the Director-General of the ISI, General Hamed Gul, who personally prevailed on him to withdraw his resignation. Yet any mention of ISI meddling on the BBC led immediately to a discreet warning from a friendly British diplomat.

In the spring of 1988, shortly before the Geneva accords were signed, a mujahedin 'alternative government' was suddenly announced in Peshawar. Neither the refugees nor the guerilla commanders had been consulted, and disillusionment was at its height. One of Pir Gailani's chief lieutenants, Mohammad Saljookie, probably spoke for many Afghans when he complained bitterly, 'we're facing two sets of puppets, one in Kabul and one here in Peshawar. The people of Afghanistan are going to lose their right of self-determination.'[28]

TEN

Postcard from Peshawar

September 1987

Not so long ago, Peshawar was still a small town. The journalist Edward Behr, who was posted there in 1947, remembers the British cantonment as 'spick and span as an English country village', with its central boulevard, the Mall, 'a somewhat narrow street, with hedges and trees on either side and shops set back behind the trees.' Across the railway tracks was the other Peshawar: an old walled city, pierced by eleven massive gates, jam-packed with winding alleys and box-like shops, streets thronged with bicycles, bullock-carts and camels, shopkeepers, smugglers, outlaws, merchants, adventurers, travellers, story-tellers, soldiers of fortune.

Change began soon after partition. A new residential area grew up further to the west, known as University Town. The walls of the old city were torn down, and Bhutto turned the Mall into a two-lane highway. But it's only since the Afghan war began that the old Peshawar has become unrecognisable. The old city and the cantonment are still there, but now they're just small suburbs of a huge, ugly, sprawling metropolis, overhung by a pall of filthy smog belched out from exhausts of the traffic which hurls itself maniacally along the city's highways.

A garrison was first built here over two thousand years ago, to keep out the wild tribesmen of the hills, just an hour or so away over the Khyber Pass. But now the tribesmen have reclaimed their own. Since 1979, the inhabitants of Peshawar and its surrounding district have been submerged in a tidal wave from across the Afghan border consisting of nearly half a million refugees.

Peshawar is now Afghanistan's alternative capital. Afghans are everywhere. They sell fruit, rugs, lapis lazuli and surplus US army boots; they run hotels, video parlours and petrol pumps; they've taken over the timber and transport industries. Afghans drive the fabulously decorated trucks which lumber, untaxed and unlicenced, on potholed highways from Peshawar to Karachi; smart fleets of Afghan-owned Mercedes buses ferry hordes of young refugees into the city every morning to work as construction site workers, and back again in the evening to the huge camps ringing the city. Expensive Japanese land-cruisers flash by, carrying a wealthy guerilla leader with his posse of bandoliered bodyguards.

University Town is the pulsating headquarters of the Afghan jehad. Most of the resistance parties have their separate political offices here, as do the countless Western and Islamic charities which help provide everything needed to keep the jehad going, from schools and medical clinics to tractors and seeds, and even ambulances to ferry back wounded guerillas from the war-front.

At the heart of University Town is the combined headquarters of the seven guerilla parties, the Islamic Unity of Afghan Mujahedin. It's a huge new complex, not yet quite finished, surrounded by a fifteen-foot wall topped with barbed wire. Inside the compound, a dozen élite guerillas are standing in full US camouflage uniforms, AK-47s at the ready. All of them are officially refugees. There are no armed guerillas, Islamabad has always insisted, on Pakistani soil.

Add your shoes to the pile outside the door, and go inside. Someone is sitting at a telex machine in one of the offices, punching out a semi-fictional battle report for onward transmission to Western news agencies in Islamabad. Perched uncomfortably on the plushly upholstered sofas in the ante-rooms, a handful of guerillas are sipping sweet green tea.

All over Peshawar tea is being sipped by commanders who are idling away their time in gossip while they wait for weapons and supplies to be issued by the party bureaucrats. In the offices of better-organised parties, the atmosphere is still chaotic, but with a purposeful briskness. Abdul Haq, who says he commands about 4,000 guerillas, has US intelligence satellite maps lining the walls of his office, and framed photographs of the ammunition dump he blew up just outside Kabul. He hasn't much time to spare. Ten minutes for a visiting journalist, then prayers. Scores of petitioners, supporters and hangers-on are still waiting outside to see him.

Sweltering in the late summer sun, the nearby refugee camps seem deserted. Most able-bodied males spend about three months at the front each year, before being replaced by a brother or cousin. Women have a much harder time. Confined to their tents or mud-brick compounds all day to escape the prying eyes of strange men, they suffer from skin diseases, dysentery and listlessness. They are locked inside their tents with only their memories of relatives and friends killed and maimed to keep them company. The psychological scars appear in unexpected places, like the Kalashnikovs and MIG fighter jets which the refugees now weave into rugs in place of more traditional motifs. Kalashnikovs are one of the facts of life in Peshawar. Just outside the city limits, in lawless tribal territory, hand-made guns have always been made; but now, in the poky shops of Darra, a one-street town half an hour away, automatic rifles hang in endless racks. Rocket-launchers are round the back. An anti-tank mine? Twenty-five rupees only.

At night, a burst of automatic fire cuts through the silence. A wedding? A blood feud being settled? You can't be sure. The unruly tribesmen living outside the city limits thrive on the chaotic conditions caused by the war on their doorstep. The money they've made from trading in smuggled weapons, opium, Russian caviar and air-conditioners can be seen in the new mansions being built on Peshawar's outskirts. For some, the war has been a bonanza. Landlords have gleefully pushed their rents to London levels, fleecing thousands of well-to-do refugees and foreign aid workers. Drug-money lines pockets from the most senior ranks of government downwards; the local newspaper, set up by a pair of Pashtun businessmen, is popularly known as the 'Heroin Post'.

For less fortunate Peshawaris, the refugee influx has been a disaster. Forests have been chopped down for firewood, hillsides have been grazed bare by the flocks of sheep and goats they brought with them. Strong young Afghans straight from the hills saturate the labour market. The man on the Peshawar omnibus is unhappy, and tells his Afghan driver 'You've taken our land, you've taken our jobs, and now we're even riding in your bus'. Down at the local newspaper office, Pakistani journalists are muttering furtively about Gulbuddin's latest threat, or about the expensive new house he's rumoured to have bought.

And then there are the bombs. They explode in the streets, in restaurants, in crowded marketplaces. There are more bombs in Peshawar than in any other city in the world, except perhaps Beirut. Everyone knows it's not the refugees, but they still get the blame. Occasionally, Afghan-owned shops are attacked and burned down by irate mobs . . . or is it by left-wing activists? No-one is surprised by the terror campaign. 'If you send bullets, you can't expect bouquets in return' is the stock phrase of General Zia's opponents. Even the Home Secretary, Shamsher Ali Khan, is pessimistic. 'One of the great historical migrations has taken place', he ruminates from behind his big polished desk in Peshawar cantonment. 'For better or worse, the Frontier Province has become the base camp of the jehad.' Outside, another jeep-load of bandoliered guerillas whizzes past.

ELEVEN

Postcard from Kabul

February 1987

I slipped away from my minder this afternoon, a few hours after flying into the Afghan capital from Delhi. It's good to wander around alone, and it's always useful to get your bearings in a new town by climbing up to some high spot and looking around. One of the best places to do it in Kabul is the Asmai Hill, a great rocky outcrop about a thousand feet high in the centre of the city. Built around its lower flanks is a timeless Afghan village. Mud-and-stone-walled houses, flat roofs, all jumbled together in a great dung-coloured cascade which seems to grow organically out of the mountainside itself. As I climb, the bustle of the city with its honking yellow-and-black taxis fades away, replaced by the quiet of the muddy medieval alleys zigzagging upwards. Heavy wooden doors shield the privacy of family compounds from the passer-by; but, here and there, an open door reveals a glimpse of veiled women washing clothes amidst the rocks and trees which form part of their courtyard furniture.

Where the flat roofs peter out and the great boulders take over, small boys with dirty faces, tattered trousers and mischievous urchin grins, are flying kites. Time to use the phrase which may have saved my life earlier today when the barber reached for his cut-throat razor and the other clients waiting to be shaved fell silent: 'Russ nistum, Inglisi astum' – 'I'm English, not Russian'. The boys don't seem to understand, but I obviously look harmless enough. You shouldn't go up the hill, they mime for me. There are mines planted near the top and a small boy was shot dead there once. They giggle happily as I clutch my chest, re-enacting the scene.

From where I stand, I can see half the city. The Kabul river, still unfed by snows, meanders below, criss-crossed by bridges. Along its banks, the centuries merge into one another. Big official-looking bungalows give way to the old town and the bazaars. In the distance is Kabul's ancient citadel, the Bala Hissar, where an unwelcome British delegation was massacred in 1879. Nearby, a multi-storied office block is under construction. Ringing most of the city, snow-peaked mountains – Kabul's 'ragged mountain skirt', as a Persian poet once called it.

For eight months I've been hearing about Kabul at weekly diplomatic briefings in Islamabad. Tanks turn down Blue Mosque street. Flares dropped by jet ignite grass-fire in embassy compound. Bombs, rockets, military convoys, pressgangs. Under the bright winter sunshine, can this be the same town? A lone helicopter, probably piloted by a Soviet airman, circles against the Paghman skyline like a faraway eagle.

At the foot of the Asmai Hill is a row of shops selling Hungarian television sets and rusty junk. There's a dark and seedy-looking pool parlour – two tables, a few wooden chairs and a small picture of Mecca are its only furniture. At one table a soldier in uniform is shooting pool with a weasel-faced man in a blue pin-striped suit and polo-neck sweater. They play with concentration. Words are few, and after each game the loser throws a pile of grubby notes onto the torn baize. Young boys crowd around the other table, re-assembling the balls with a rough, professional ease. In a small curtained-off broom cupboard, young men are smoking hashish, blowing the tell-tale smoke out through a hole in the roof. One of them, a broad-featured Hazara, is studying engineering at the Soviet Polytechnic. He refers to the mujahedin as 'basmachi' – bandits – and tells me that the hill I've just climbed is dangerous for foreigners.

The mujahedin say that the communists are the enemies of Islam, but the mosque just around the corner from here is humming with activity. Inside, small boys rock backwards and forwards as they recite from their Qurans, glancing out of the corners of their eyes as I sit and watch them. Uniformed policeman in bare feet mingle with crowds of women at the shrine of a local saint, pressing their lips to the tomb as they pray. Outside, a soldier walks the streets, fingering the prayer beads which dangle behind his back.

The old town is crowded with faces from all over central Asia. Uzbeks with their high cheekbones and wide-set eyes, Turkomen with wispy beards, Pashtuns with haughty noses. But after living for eight months in Pakistan, it's the women who catch my eye. Some are covered from head to toe in burqas – rusty yellow or light blue rather than the funereal black of Peshawar; but lots of younger women have abandoned them altogether. High heels, lipstick, knee-length skirts, hip-hugging jeans, long black hair flowing free over leather-jacketed shoulders. In the bazaars the women mix freely with traders in turbans and shawls, sitting comfortably in the dusty light behind their huge sacks of grain, pulses, dried fruit and oranges. The clothes bazaar is overflowing with last year's European and American fashions, smuggled in from Pakistan.

The merchants who trade with Pakistan are subject to heavy tolls from the guerilla groups whose territory they have to pass through on their journeys from Peshawar to Kabul. That's why you have to bring a suitcase to take away your Afghan currency: the merchants buy up all the high-denomination notes. They're easier to hide when travelling. Kabul has a thriving money bazaar as well, where you can get excellent rates for dollars, deutschmarks, sterling, rupees, even roubles. No traveller's cheques? No problem! The Hindu and Sikh money-traders, whose families left India a hundred years ago or more, will even accept a personal cheque on a British bank.

The closer you get to the centre of Kabul, the more modern and Soviet-looking it becomes, even though the Soviet library is empty. More women in short skirts, more traffic. The shops begin to fill up with Soviet goods; stainless-steel teapots, samovars, hairspray, dolls, clocks, vacuum flasks, meat mincers, plastic flowers and chandeliers. No Russian is on the streets. In an immaculate subway under one of the busiest intersections of the city, the shops are brightly illuminated. An old Pathan selling East European television sets and electrical fittings clasps my hand. Pakistan, Iran, America, all friends, he informs me. And Russia? He snorts and flicks his hand away contemptuously.

In the city centre, Afghan soldiers are body-searching at the telegraph office, and checking taxis for explosives. It is done courteously enough, but behind the façade of normality, there's menace and fear. 'I don't like socialism,' hisses a taxi-driver, 'this is a Muslim country.' A man in the bazaar, who says he's a retired government official, draws me quickly into a store. One of his cousins has just been executed in jail, one brother is in the army and another is in Pakistan. He wants to say more, but he's afraid of spies and informers. A man in the nearby shop is keeping a close eye on us.

As the light begins to fade, the tempo of the street speeds up. The crowd moves faster, and from within its anonymity, more hostile and suspicious eyes glare out. Police and soldiers, guns at their backs, seem to be everywhere. Taxis are queuing up to be searched at the road blocks. I get lost and a youth hurriedly escorts me back to my hotel, thinking I'm Russian. Better not to be out of doors after dark.

At three o'clock in the morning I'm woken by a convoy of heavy armoured vehicles passing somewhere near my hotel. The rumbling goes on for half an hour, then fades away into the silence of the city.

TWELVE

The Puppet Regime:
War and National Reconciliation
1979–1988

I was surprised by what I saw during my visit to Kabul in the spring of 1987. I was expecting to find a city sullen, grey and lifeless under the jackboots of Soviet troops. Instead it was throbbing with life. Along the Kabul river goods trucks were lined up waiting to travel back to the Soviet Union and Pakistan, and rickety coaches were touting for passengers to make the long, uncomfortable journey along the pot-holed main highway to Qandahar. The hotel in Pashtunistan Square where I stayed was packed with delegates and favour-seekers from far afield: officials from state-run co-operative farms in the northern province of Jowzjan, businessmen from Ghazni, even tribal elders from Khurram, on the Pakistani side of the border, come to bargain with the regime. At the gates of the University, the guards waved me through with a polite 'pojalysta', reluctant to body-search a foreigner who was doubtless Russian. Inside students loitered in groups, chatting, carrying books, holding hands and making rendezvous. It could have been a campus anywhere in the world. In the centre of the city no Soviet troops were to be seen.

The appearance of normality was deceptive though. Most Kabulis hadn't been able to go outside the city limits since 1980. Only fifteen miles to the west the royal summer resort of Paghman, with its triumphal arch, luxury hotels, cinemas and pleasure gardens, was a devastated ruin. The mud fortresses along the road to Paghman were riddled with bullet- and shell-holes, like Gruyere cheese, and tanks were dug in at regular intervals. At Charasiab, a rural district on the southern outskirts of Kabul, life was just as insecure. A kindergarten teacher said she had joined the local militia two years previously, 'to defend my village, the district and the country'. Her husband had been killed by the mujahedin because he worked as a government storekeeper, and her son, a high school student, had been gunned down while irrigating an orchard at night.

The only other traffic on the road south from Kabul was a convoy of dusty olive trucks, interspersed with armoured personnel carriers, heading out warily into the uncertain countryside beyond. Anyone associated with the government had to be careful. I might safely take one of the buses to Qandahar, I was assured, but no government official would dare. Air travel was safer, but still had its hazards. Civilian and military aircraft using Kabul airport spiralled upwards in tight corkscrews, dropping dozens of flares to deflect heat-seeking missiles until they reached a safe altitude. The day before I flew in to Kabul an AN-12 transport plane ferrying both military and civilian passengers was shot down by a mujahedin Stinger. It was an uncomfortable feeling reading the details in my newspaper as my Indian Airlines plane flew over southern Afghanistan.

Kabul was a city-state, surrounded by guerilla-infested mountains, and linked only tenuously to the regime's other urban outposts, like Mazar-i-Sharif in the north and Khost in the south-east. Yet to control Kabul meant a great deal. Before the Soviet invasion, Kabul was home to about half a million people, less than five percent of a total population of fifteen million. By 1987, possibly as few as nine million people were still living in Afghanistan. The rest had fled abroad, or were dead. Of those still living, many had migrated to the relative safety of the capital, and by early 1987, its population had swollen to between two and three million people – nearly a third of the country's entire population.

Life was not particularly comfortable for internal refugees. Even Babrak Karmal admitted in October 1982 that there were food shortages and malnutrition. But the regime did what it could, in ever-worsening economic circumstances, to make conditions in the capital tolerable. Refugees might hope to find work, and even to get access to subsidised food. To make up for the disruption of normal trade by the war, the Soviet Union provided essential items like food, soap, shoes, clothing and kerosene, which were distributed free, or at subsidised prices, through a system of coupons. Only state employees were eligible, but by 1983, 250,000 people throughout Afghanistan were receiving coupons, and many families living in the 'liberated areas' tried to arrange for at least one relative to get work in a government organisation.

Most importantly, the city offered security. In the surrounding rural areas life became increasingly hazardous in 1982. For the first time, aerial bombardments and major military offensives were carried out in heavily populated areas close to Kabul, like the Shomali plain, the Panjshir valley and the province of Logar. Refugees streamed into the capital. Depopulation of the countryside was adopted as a deliberate policy. Moscow, it seemed, had concluded that the mujahedin were like Mao's fish in the sea, and rather than trying to hook them out one by one, it decided to drain the sea itself.

It's uncertain how long Brezhnev expected Soviet troops to stay in Afghanistan when the invasion took place. Soviet generals had unsuccessfully argued that their troops should be deployed in the main cities and military bases, leaving active operations against the rebels to be carried out by Afghan government troops. Presumably they reasoned that those operations could succeed. The Kremlin may also have hoped that its troops would be regarded more as liberators than conquerors. The brutal dictator Hafizullah Amin had been overthrown, and his successor Babrak Karmal was thought to represent the acceptable face of socialism. A former minister from the Daoud era, Siddiq Farhang, who was co-opted into the first post-invasion administration, was given a firm undertaking by Karmal that Soviet troops would return home within months.[1]

Sent in to solve one problem, though, the Red Army created an even worse one merely by its presence. The Afghan army, already in bad shape, haemorrhaged in a steady series of mutinies. To keep up the numbers, pay rises, re-enlistment bonuses and other incentives were offered; later, with numbers still dropping, boys of sixteen and even younger were pressganged in the streets, given at most a few days' training, and sent off to remote garrisons surrounded by barbed wire and minefields to stop them defecting to the mujahedin.

With the rebellion spreading fast, it quickly became clear that Soviet troops would have to be used extensively in military operations, even though their combat role was long hidden from the Soviet public. An early withdrawal was clearly impossible, and from mid-1980 onwards, a strategic infrastructure began to be built for Soviet military operations, including new airbases, all-weather runways, new roads, permanent barracks, ammunition- and fuel-storage facilities and heavy bridges across the Amu Darya.

Full-scale occupation, though, does not appear to have been seriously envisaged. By the summer of 1980, 85,000 Soviet troops had been deployed in and around Kabul and other provincial towns. In 1983 Soviet generals decided that at least 300,000 troops would be needed to rout the resistance; yet throughout the war, Western military intelligence never put the Soviet troop presence higher than 125,000, with another 30,000 stationed just across the northern border for use in specific operations. When the troops were finally withdrawn in 1988/89, the first official Soviet figures released since the invasion put the departing contingent at 105,000 men.

Operating against disorganised guerillas in mountainous territory presented the Soviet army with a challenge it had not been trained to meet. Its early tactics were more suited to the European theatre of war: conventional offensives with heavy armour, supported by helicopter-gunships and jet-fighters. A typical example of an early Soviet operation was described by Dr Claude Malhuret, a doctor working with the French medical organisation Medecins Sans Frontières who first visited Afghanistan in 1980. 'In the province of Hazarajat,' he wrote later, 'several hundred armoured vehicles would leave either Kabul or Jaghori and occupy a valley that could easily be entered. The population, which had warning either by rumour or because they had seen the helicopter movement, fled into the mountains. The Soviet troops, therefore, entered empty villages where they remained for a few days, harassed by the Muslim resistance groups – the mujahedin – who also barred access to the upper valleys. During those few days, the soldiers pillaged and burned homes, set fire to crops and dragged off with them the few inhabitants left behind – mostly old people, whom they interrogated or summarily executed.'[2]

The first frustrations of dealing with irregular guerillas operating in mountainous terrain eventually led to the adoption of new tactics. By 1983 the emphasis was shifting from large-scale sweep operations by armour and infantry (20,000 troops were reportedly used in an offensive up the Panjshir valley in 1982) to smaller, more surgical counter-insurgency operations. Heliborne troops were dropped on the high ground behind guerilla positions to seal off strategic passes, while Afghan government forces advanced from the front. Special airborne troops were also used to carry out raids on targets deep in guerilla-held territory, either bases or large villages known to be co-operating with the mujahedin. Massive Soviet firepower – artillery, tanks and aircraft – penned the mujahedin into 'hunting zones', while small groups of Spetsnaz commandos conducted night-time raids and ambushes against mujahedin caravans.

Although tactics were continually modified, overall Soviet military strategy remained the same. Soviet forces never attempted to pacify areas where they encountered resistance, or to expand the area under their control. Their policy was to terrorise the local population into refusing to help the mujahedin, or to drive civilians out entirely by bombing villages and destroying crops, orchards and irrigation systems. Another terror tactic involved the scattering over the countryside of hundreds of thousands of anti-personnel mines. They were designed to maim, which caused greater inconvenience to the guerillas than the outright death of a comrade. One thing Kabul and Peshawar have in common is the sight of men and young boys hobbling along on one leg; livestock also suffered. Claude Malhuret, on his first trip into Afghanistan, was struck by 'the number of goats and cows that had legs in splints made of bamboo sticks and tied with wire.'[3]

Many of the atrocities carried out against the civilian population have never been documented. Only very rarely have Western journalists been at hand to witness the bombing of an Afghan village. One incident which received widespread attention was attested to by three eyewitnesses before an international human rights tribunal in Paris in December 1982. To avoid a conscription drive in Logar province, they said, 105 villagers, including old men and a dozen boys under the age of thirteen, took cover in an underground irrigation system. Soviet troops damned one end and forced the water up to chest level. Then they poured in an inflammable liquid, set it on fire, and burned everyone to death.[4]

Many refugees in Pakistan have similarly horrific tales to tell. One old man living in a makeshift camp just outside Peshawar said he was one of the few survivors of a massacre by Soviet and Afghan troops in the village of Chardara, in Kunduz province, in 1984. 'Tanks came,' he told me, 'and then the soldiers entered the village and started stabbing, killing and shooting. We don't know why.' He claimed that 680 people had been killed in the space of an hour and a half. In the same year, a *New York Times* correspondent reported conversations with two Soviet soldiers who had been captured and were now fighting alongside the mujahedin. One, who had been stationed near Qandahar said that, 'we were ordered by our officers that when we attack a village, not one person must be left alive to tell the tale. If we refuse to carry out these orders, we get it in the neck ourselves.'[5]

In the towns, and in areas where the resistance was less active, particularly in the less mountainous regions north of the Hindukush, Soviet strategists hoped that economic and cultural incentives, combined with a more tolerant attitude towards Islam and intensive propaganda against the mujahedin, would eventually isolate the mullahs and feudal reactionaries who were thought to be the main instigators of the rebellion. 'You can't turn mullahs into communists', a Soviet diplomat told a visiting British journalist at the end of 1981. 'The government must win people's hearts and minds by showing the right direction for reform, provided it is gradual.'[6]

Islam's powerful role as both a source and a focus of opposition was hammered home to Babrak Karmal's new government immediately after the Soviet invasion. As soon as the initial shock wore off, a nationwide agitation swept through the main cities, starting in Qandahar and reaching Kabul by the second half of February. Traders in the bazaars went on strike, soon to be joined by civil servants and students. Daily demonstrations were organised. In some places they remained peaceful, but in Kabul they culminated in a mini-uprising, in which 300 people were reportedly killed. Mosques were used to call the faithful to rise instead of to prayer, and at night, the entire population climbed onto their rooftops, crying 'Allah-o-Akbar' ('God is Great') and chanting the *azan*, the Muslim call to prayer.

Babrak was well aware of the need to neutralise the opposition of the mullahs. At the end of 1980, his brother, Mohammad Baryalai, openly admitted that 'the thinking of the predominantly illiterate population is still being formed mainly by the mullahs.'[7] If that was so, and if mullahs couldn't be turned into communists, the regime would have to conceal its communist colours. The task Babrak set himself, as he put it later, was to 'incorporate Islam into the revolution'.[8]

In a bid to make a clean break with the past, Babrak bitterly denounced Hafizullah Amin for carrying out wholesale massacres of religious leaders, which he described as a 'tragedy'.[9] The new regime's provisional constitution – entitled 'Basic Principles' – promised official respect for 'the sacred religion of Islam', and the old tricolour of red, black and Islamic green was restored as the national emblem. The support of mullahs and religious scholars was sought in frequent meetings, and to bring the clergy more closely under government supervision, Babrak established Afghanistan's first Department of Islamic Affairs, which was given control over the private finances and endowments of mosques throughout the country. In effect, the clergy were converted into state employees, whose stipends depended on their denunciations of the 'counter-revolution' in their Friday sermons. By 1987, Dr Najibullah was able to claim that there were 16,000 mullahs on the government's payroll. The money acquired from the nationalisation of religious institutions also enabled the department to undertake a major programme of mosque building and renovation, which became an important ingredient of the regime's propaganda drive.

Religious leaders were not the only key group to be wooed by the new regime. To convince businessmen and landlords that doctrinaire socialist policies would not be followed, Babrak put non-Marxists in charge of the ministries of commerce, agriculture and land reforms. Private sector trade was tolerated, and later even encouraged. Babrak's professed aim, as outlined in his initial policy statement, was the creation of 'a broad front of all the national and democratic forces' under PDPA leadership.

Babrak's real strategy, though, was to give the illusion of heading a popular government without conceding political power. In January 1980, several thousand political prisoners were released from Pul-i-Charkhi jail, and non-Marxists were initially appointed to many senior government positions. In June 1981, even the Revolutionary Council was opened to non-PDPA members. But as in any communist system, all matters of real significance were decided by the PDPA Politburo rather than the Council of Ministers. Even the 'National Fatherland Front' (NFF) which was founded in June 1981, turned out to be a sham. Its constitution obliged it to attract the 'vast masses of the people' to 'participate actively and consciously in constructing a democratic and progressive Afghanistan'. Yet the fact that it took nearly eighteen months to establish illustrates the problems Babrak faced in trying to build popular support from the top downwards. The NFF consisted mainly of PDPA front organisations set up to 'represent' groups such as youth, teachers, women, poets, journalists, religious scholars, peasants and industrial labourers. Most were headed by active communists, and the majority of members – even of workers and peasants associations – were drawn from the middle-class professions. Despite claiming a total membership of 100,000 by early 1983, few of the groups making up the NFF had any significant representation outside Kabul, and the Front's activities were largely confined to holding pro-government demonstrations and sending telegrams to the UN.

In the provinces, or at least in areas where the civilian population was not being bombed into submission, the regime tried to win support through bribery and promises. Border tribes like the Shinwari Pashtuns were the prime beneficiaries of the regime's largesse, receiving cash and weapons in return for keeping their territory free from mujahedin activity. Tribal leaders who pledged support to the government and landlords willing to sell their surplus produce to the regime were exempted from land reforms.

None of these measures had much effect. Babrak Karmal was in a classic Catch 22 situation. While Moscow bullied and cajoled him into broadening the base of his support, his dependence on Soviet backing made the task impossible. Clandestine pamphlets, known as *shabnama*, distributed at night by underground resistance cells, denounced him as a puppet and a traitor. 'You reached power by rubbing your nose like a dog in front of the Kremlin's doors,' one said.[10]

Russian civilians in the capital lived in special housing complexes, surrounded by barbed wire and armour. Babrak's own movements were equally restricted. His bodyguards, cook and chauffeur were Russians or East Germans, and only once did he feel safe enough to take a hurried walkabout in the streets of his own capital. One joke popular among Kabulis probably sums up the general attitude to the people's leader. A young Pioneer, a kind of PDPA cadet, was asked by Babrak to choose a prize for himself, and the boy asked for a television set with windscreen wipers. Babrak was extremely puzzled, and when the boy came to collect his prize asked him what he wanted a television set with windscreen wipers for. 'Well,' said the boy, 'when you deliver your speeches, all the members of my family keep spitting at our TV screen and then ask me to wipe it clean. Now this new TV will save me the bother!'

Babrak was not even able to fulfil Moscow's bottom-line political objective: uniting the two wings of the ruling party. Inevitably the PDPA grew in size, swelled by soldiers, government employees and others acting out of self-interest rather than ideological conviction. In mid-1982, Babrak claimed that the PDPA had 70,000 members (a claim considered wildly exaggerated by Western diplomats, who put the figure closer to 20,000). But the rift between Parcham and Khalq was if anything sharpened by the invasion. Khalqis, the majority faction, deeply resented Amin's assassination by Soviet troops and Babrak's subsequent denunciation of him as a CIA agent. As early as March 1980, Asadullah Sarwari, the most senior surviving Khalqi, was openly saying that the Soviet army should hand over power to 'us' and go home.[11] Meanwhile, Parchamites who had been imprisoned, tortured or exiled under Taraki and

Amin – some of them by Sarwari personally – were thirsting for revenge.

Babrak was unable to move against the Khalqis too quickly or too openly. Moscow demanded at least a show of unity, and – more crucially – the officer corps of the armed forces were solidly Khalqi. Officially, the two wings of the PDPA were subsumed in a single organisation, and many senior Khalqis initially retained their positions in the Politburo and the Revolutionary Council. As soon as he felt reasonably secure, however, Babrak began easing out his main rivals. In June 1980, thirteen Khalqis, including three former ministers, were arrested and executed, and, in the same month, Sarwari was posted off to Mongolia as ambassador. At a lower level, hundreds of Khalqi activists were either jailed or had their weapons confiscated, leaving them defenceless against urban guerillas – or against their Parchamite opponents.

The summer of 1980 marked one of the high points of Khalq-Parcham rivalry. Western diplomats attributed most of the daily assassinations and bomb-blasts taking place in the capital at that time to factional rivalry within the ruling party rather than mujahedin activity. Between June 1980 and February 1981, diplomats also reported rumours of four separate coups being plotted by Khalqi army officers.

The weakness of Babrak's grip on the army was demonstrated by his attempt to replace seven provincial army commanders with loyal Parchamites in May 1980. The seven men, all Khalqis, simply tore up their transfer orders and packed their replacements back to Kabul. Subsequent efforts to purge the armed forces only exacerbated the ill-feeling between the two factions. Dozens of Khalqi officers who were detained on suspicion of plotting against the regime in 1980–81 were later released for lack of evidence and sent back to their units to serve under newly appointed Parchamite commanders and political commissars. What with a resentful and divided officer corps and a conscripted rank and file, it's hardly surprising that the armed forces dwindled to less than 30,000 men, a third of their former size, within the first year of the Soviet invasion.

To supplement the crumbling armed forces, a bewildering array of militias were established. The earliest, known as Soldiers of the Revolution, drew on committed party activists. Later, ordinary government employees were coerced into performing nighttime guard duties, and additional civil defence units were set up to defend farms, factories and government departments. There were women's militias, youth militias, ethnic militias and frontier militias. Some, particularly in the tribal areas, were entirely mercenary; others had a hard core of party members. In 1987 Najibullah claimed that the regime had half a million people under arms.

Khalq-Parcham rivalries were quickly institutionalised in the regime's two most important paramilitary organisations, KHAD and Tsarandoy. When Babrak took power, the Interior Ministry was headed by a staunch Khalqi, Mohammad Gulabzoi, the young air force officer with Napoleonic pretensions who played a crucial role in the 1978 coup. It was a powerful portfolio. The Interior Ministry not only controlled a large armed police force, but also the intelligence department with its own political police. It was an intolerable situation. In a deft administrative manoeuvre, Babrak hived the intelligence department off from its parent ministry and gave it independent status under his young protégé Dr Najibullah. The political police – renamed KHAD – were taken under the wing of the KGB and East German intelligence experts and became the main bulwark of the regime's security.

KHAD gradually assumed an enormous range of responsibilities, from internal intelligence, arrests, and interrogations to the subversion of border tribes, assassinations, counter-insurgency operations, the infiltration of refugee organisations and sabotage in Pakistan. KHAD was also given its own army division, complete with tanks and helicopters, and its troops, many of them hardened party activists, provided most of the Afghanistan's élite units. Not to be outmanoeuvred, Gulabzoi set about building up his armed police force, attracting recruits from those sympathetic to Khalq. By 1984 the police force was estimated to be nearly twice the size of the army and many of its units were converted into a light infantry force called Tsarandoy, which participated in regular military duties.

The two organisations took their rivalries with them to the battlefield. Rumours of armed clashes between KHAD and Tsarandoy were frequent, and in 1984 Babrak Karmal felt compelled to ask a Tsarandoy audience in Kabul not to use their weapons to settle intra-party disputes. It made no difference. In 1988 mujahedin officials in Peshawar were still happily telling tales of Khalqi militiamen tipping off guerillas to the movements of their Parchamite rivals so that ambushes could be laid, and vice versa. The troublesome Gulabzoi remained firmly in control of Tsarandoy until he was finally posted off as ambassador to Moscow in the last months of the Soviet troop withdrawal.

Despite the protection which Moscow extended to Gulabzoi, it was the Parcham-dominated KHAD which became the Kremlin's most favoured instrument. Special training courses offered in the Soviet Union turned it into a far more deadly and efficient organisation than any of its predecessors. For ordinary citizens, KHAD was synonymous with terror and mind-control. A family-planning official who defected to Pakistan in 1984 was one of many to describe the continual fear of midnight raids. 'They searched everything,' he said, 'looking for members of the resistance, arms, youths to conscript, subversive literature. If you objected you were in danger of being taken away.'[12] 'Everywhere you go,' said another Kabul resident, 'you are under the scrutiny of KHAD.' Communist party cells headed by a KHAD agent were set up in each city neighbourhood and citizens were required to register all members of their families and make weekly reports on their activities.[13]

Increasingly aware of the unpopularity and unreliability of the Babrak regime, Soviet advisers turned their attention towards building a youthful new élite, which would run the administration loyally and stay committed to a pro-Soviet future for Afghanistan. Indoctrination began early. At the age of ten, schoolchildren were encouraged and sometimes forced to enrol in the 'Young Pioneers', where they were trained to spy on classmates and even on their families. By 1982 a nationwide membership of 40,000 was claimed; mass education was imparted twice weekly in the Palace of Pioneers, two double-storied buildings in the eastern outskirts of Kabul with a cinema, library and workshops attached.

At the age of fifteen, Young Pioneers were expected to join the Democratic Youth Organisation of Afghanistan (DYOA), where they were split up into small groups and assigned responsibilities such as surveillance and propaganda work, or guarding schools and government buildings. Membership of the DYOA led straight on to enrolment in the party, and, in 1987, Dr Najibullah claimed that thirty percent of all students belonged either to the DYOA or the PDPA. Orphans, and children kidnapped from bombed villages, had the least chance of escaping indoctrination. They were educated in 'Fatherland Training Centres', or 'Watan Nurseries', where there was no check on communist propaganda. Mrs Karmal was official patron of the nurseries, but they were under the supervision of KHAD, and were designed to turn out highly committed agents. Children as young as ten years old were occasionally discovered infiltrating mujahedin groups.

Even those who avoided enrolment in these organisations did not escape the process of 'sovietisation'. The school curriculum was changed; learning Russian was made compulsory, and political-science courses were introduced which included topics such as 'Revolutionary movements of the proletariat class'. New textbooks were prepared under the supervision of Soviet advisers, and in 1985 all

187

teachers were directed to lecture their students regularly on Afghan-Soviet friendship.

At the University, student numbers plummeted from 15,000 at the time of the invasion to less than 5000 in 1983, mainly because of defections and military conscription. All remaining students, many of them girls, were required to attend courses in Marxist-Leninist political theory, including scientific sociology and dialectical materialism. Independent-minded professors were purged or imprisoned and replaced by young party activists recruited for their loyalty rather than their qualifications. Soviet influences gradually percolated through the entire system. One textbook I glanced at during a visit to the university in 1987, a B.A. course in spoken English, contained the following exchange:

Dina: Did you see the gymnastics? The Russian girls were very good, I thought.
Mary: Yes, it's nice to see a sport in which women are actually superior to men.

It's hard to imagine two sentences more alien to traditional ways of Afghan thinking!

To isolate young Afghans even further from their roots, tens of thousands were sent to study in the Soviet Union. By 1984, the US State Department estimated that 4,000 students a year were being sent to the USSR for 'advanced political indoctrination'. In the same year, the regime announced what it described as a 'magnificent friendly gesture by the Soviet Union towards the Afghan people'. Two thousand young Afghan children aged between seven and ten were to be sent annually to the Soviet Union for at least ten years' schooling.[14] The programme began in November. The first batch of children sent off to Soviet central Asia included many taken from the Watan Nurseries; but weeping relatives were also seen gathering at the airport to wave goodbye. They had not been consulted. The return of the 'lost Afghans' was one of the demands of mujahedin leaders at the time of the Soviet troop withdrawal.

Children may have been the primary target for the programme of long-term 'sovietisation', but adults were not left in peace either. Radio, television, the cinema and the press all provided an unrelieved diet of Marxist propaganda, designed to promote the image of the Soviet Union and contrast Afghanistan's ugly past with the PDPA's utopia. Soviet advisers controlled all news programming, and at least four Russian films were shown each week, many showing how the Soviet Union singlehandedly defeated the Nazis in World War II. The evening news regularly featured interviews with mothers of Afghan soldiers talking about their pride in having a son fighting 'foreign imperialists'.[15]

Far more subtle was the regime's Soviet-inspired policy of stressing and encouraging ethnic and linguistic differences. Traditionally, the Afghan variant of Persian, Dari, has been the lingua franca in Afghanistan and the main medium of instruction in schools. But Babrak Karmal's government assiduously promoted the language and culture of Tajiks, Uzbeks, Turkomen, Baluchis and other minority nationalities. Kabul Radio began broadcasting in different languages – even, as I discovered during my visit there, in obscure Nuristani dialects. Newspapers, magazines, pamphlets and books were imported from Soviet central Asia, and for the first time, provincial schools began teaching children in their own mother-tongues. Soviet propaganda specialised in fuelling the resentments felt by minority ethnic groups against the pro-Pashtun policies of Daoud and Zahir Shah. At the same time, great stress was placed on the historical and cultural affinities between the ethnic groups of northern Afghanistan and their cousins living across the Soviet border.

Afghan intellectuals saw this policy as a replica of Lenin's successful experiments in Soviet central Asia, in which ethnic groups were labelled as separate 'nationalities', and isolated from each other and the wider Muslim world, making it far easier for Moscow to impose Russian as the lingua franca and, eventually, centralised Soviet control. The USSR's intensive economic exploitation of northern Afghanistan, particularly its enormous gas deposits, only heightened anxieties that Moscow's long-term plan was to integrate the resource-rich north into the rest of Soviet central Asia.

In the Pashtun south, the game of divide and rule was played in a slightly different way – with offers of money and local autonomy. The usual procedure was for KHAD to make contact through a go-between with an influential tribal malik who was known to have a rivalry with a neighbouring malik supporting the resistance. The subsequent bargaining might lead to a mutual non-aggression treaty, in which the malik received weapons and subsidies in return for turning his kin group into a pro-government militia. It could be a risky business, though. In September 1980 Babrak's minister for tribal affairs, Faiz Mohammad, set off from Kabul with three hundred Afghanis and several fattened sheep to celebrate the conclusion of lengthy peace negotiations with his own Zadran tribe. The tribal elders feasted themselves on mutton, and then shot him dead.

Opposition from doctrinaire Marxists committed to centralised communist control hampered Babrak's efforts to incorporate individual pact-making into a coherent strategy. Babrak originally promised to devolve power to autonomous local bodies as early as 1981, but it wasn't until March 1984, after a bitter dispute within the PDPA, that legislation was introduced which effectively gave tribal chiefs control over local government development funds. At around the same time, in a bid to cut mujahedin supply lines from Pakistan, the regime adopted a conciliatory new policy towards the Pashtun tribes straddling the southern border. Some tribes, like the Mohmands, were won over by offers of food, fuel, weapons and cash subsidies, and Babrak announced in a major policy speech that 'no-one will be allowed to interfere or encroach on the national matters, the customs and the traditions of the tribes'. Radio broadcasts in different Pashto dialects began stressing tribal virtues and the deeds of Pashtun folk-heroes, rather than the glorious achievements of the PDPA. The regime also tried to enhance its legitimacy by reviving the practice of holding jirgas, an integral part of the Pashtun tribal code. Nearly four thousand delegates attended a 'High Jirga of the Tribes' in September 1985, a third of them from Pakistan. In an amazing about-turn, the PDPA was not only offering to exempt the Pashtun tribes from the Revolution, but was even trying to pose as the champion of tribal traditions.

Until 1985, the regime's attempts to attract popular support were at best halfhearted. In the spring of that year, though, something crucial happened: Mikhail Gorbachev took up residence in the Kremlin. Almost at once a spate of political initiatives started to flow from Kabul, all designed to show that the PDPA was now prepared to share power.

In April Babrak finally redeemed his 1981 pledge to hold a Loya Jirga in Kabul. It received great attention at home and abroad, even though it was packed with party officials and 'independent' members were handsomely paid for their attendance. In August local elections began. They too were badly flawed: in Kabul, candidates were introduced only moments before the vote, which took place by a show of hands under the watchful eyes of KHAD agents. In most rural areas, the war made voting impossible; the elections were such a farce that some winning candidates didn't even know they were standing.[16] Nevertheless, by the end of 1986, the regime claimed that elections had been completed in all twenty-nine provinces. Of more significance, according to official figures only forty percent of successful candidates were members of the PDPA.

A similar process was underway throughout the administrative structure. In March 1985 the National Fatherland Front was given a non-party chairman, a tea-merchant from

Qandahar called Abdul Raheem Hatef, who had served in Parliament under the monarchy. At the end of the year, on the eve of the annual UN General Assembly vote on Afghanistan, Babrak Karmal announced a new initiative (known as the 'Ten Theses') which was designed to 'broaden the social pillars' of the revolution. In addition to non-socialist incentives such as tax breaks for the private sector, the Revolutionary Council was to be doubled in size to include members of the clergy, the intelligentsia and the private business community. Over the next few months, the Kabul media carried the names of dozens of non-Marxists appointed to posts in the government and the Revolutionary Council, and by March 1986, when the *Guardian*'s Johnathan Steele paid a return visit to Kabul, a Soviet official told him that 'the only argument the counter-revolution has against this government now is the presence of Soviet troops.'[17]

Back in the Kremlin, though, Mikhail Gorbachev could see that more concessions still had to be made. Babrak Karmal himself would have to go. His domestic and international credibility had never recovered from the humiliation of being installed in power by Soviet tanks. General Zia of Pakistan had specifically ruled out any direct negotiations with him. Among the mujahedin he was an object of loathing and ridicule, and in Kabul, rumours constantly circulated about his mistresses and his hard drinking habits. Even within the PDPA, he had exacerbated rather than healed party divisions. No government led by Babrak Karmal could be expected to survive the withdrawal of Soviet troops for which Gorbachev was now preparing.

Perceptive observers already had their eye on a potential successor: the KHAD chief, Dr Najibullah. A Babrak protégé and full member of the Politburo since 1981, he had 'all the makings of a future Soviet strongman', an anonymous Western diplomat prophesied in January 1985.[18] At the end of that year, 'Comrade Najib' (as he then liked to be called) began his climb to power. In November, he quit his security post to take up full-time party work, and was appointed Secretary to the PDPA Central Committee. In April 1986, amidst mounting rumours, Babrak was unexpectedly summoned to the Soviet capital on the eve of the annual celebrations of the Saur Revolution. Najibullah took the salute at the military parade. The silent coup had begun, but Moscow was taking no chances. As Babrak returned home, Soviet troops disarmed their Afghan colleagues and took up key positions around the city. The next day, Babrak 'resigned' and the Politburo unanimously elected Najibullah as the new General Secretary of the PDPA.

On the face of it, Najibullah was an odd choice to preside over the dramatic new programme of 'national reconciliation' planned by Moscow. Even leaving aside the manner of his installation, he too risked being labelled a Soviet puppet. As head of KHAD since 1981, he was a much-feared figure who was reputed to have ordered the torture of thousands of people. But his attractions far outweighed his disadvantages. His long association with KHAD had given him an unparalleled understanding of the Pashtun tribes on both sides of the border. Although a leading member of the Parcham wing of the PDPA, his Ghilzai Pashtun origins improved his chances of working closely with the Ghilzai-dominated Khalqis. As an added bonus, he was related to the royal family through his wife Fattan. He even had good connections in Peshawar, where his father had been Afghanistan's Trade Commissioner under the monarchy.

Najibullah's personal qualities were as impressive as his family and clan connections. His youthful enthusiasm for wrestling, weightlifting and volleyball had built him into a massive and imposing man, whose physique fully justified his nickname, 'The Ox'. His early involvement in politics, beginning when he was still at high school, meant that he never finished his medical degree; yet he was intelligent, as well as shrewd and stubborn. Unlike Babrak, Najibullah was not a demagogue. But he was fluent in both Pashto and

193

Dari, and as time went on his simple yet forceful speeches calling for peace began to have a growing impact on his countrymen. Again unlike Babrak, his private life was beyond reproach. He lived in a modest bungalow with his wife and three daughters, one of whom was disabled. Most important of all, he was loyal to Moscow. As the KGB's leading protégé, Gorbachev believed, Najibullah could be trusted to do as he was told.

To smooth over the first few difficult months, stress was laid initially on the notion of a collective leadership, with Najib as party chief, Babrak as head of state (in his capacity as Chairman of the Revolutionary Council) and Prime Minister Keshtmand running the government. But Babrak's supporters were not fooled. On the day he was replaced, his former mistress Anahita Ratebzad organized a procession of college girls who marched through the streets shouting anti-Najib slogans. Western diplomats reported a go-slow in the work of government ministries, and attributed a series of bomb blasts in the capital to Babrak loyalists. In November 1986, Babrak was finally stripped of all his remaining posts and packed off to Moscow for 'medical treatment'. Yet even a year later, Najib was embarrassed by attempts to elect his predecessor as a delegate to the PDPA's second party conference. Instead of uniting the party, as Moscow had hoped, Najib's elevation split Parcham into two rival factions.

Najibullah was not brought to power simply to provide a change of face. Three months earlier, Gorbachev had stunned the world by publicly referring to Afghanistan as the Soviet Union's 'bleeding wound', announcing at the same time that Soviet troops were ready to pull out as soon as a political settlement could be reached. International negotiations (whose progress is chronicled in chapter 13) needed to be matched by major changes at home, and Najibullah was Gorbachev's chosen instrument. At first, he seems to have been unaware of quite how far his master in the Kremlin was preparing to go in his search for a face-saving settlement. Najib's first speeches as party chief were as hardline as any that Babrak had made. 'To ensure peace in the country', he declared in May 1986, we must 'decisively crush the last bands of counter-revolution (sic) . . . the ringleaders of these treacherous bands are traitors to the national interest and are committing crimes against our people and homeland every day.'[19] Within nine months, though, Najib was offering to meet representatives of the mujahedin on neutral ground, and to recognise their status as equals. In July 1987 he offered specific Cabinet posts to leaders of the 'moderate' mujahedin parties; soon after, during a further trip to Moscow, he announced that he would be willing to retire gracefully if he became an obstacle to peace.

The centrepiece of Najibullah's overtures to the opposition was the programme of 'national reconciliation', which he announced on 1st January 1987. It involved three main elements: a six-month unilateral ceasefire, the formation of a government of 'national unity' including representatives of the opposition, and the return of the estimated five million refugees from Pakistan and Iran. A huge propaganda offensive began in the Afghan media, which carried daily reports of streams of refugees returning home and former guerillas laying down their weapons. Instead of calling the mujahedin 'bandits', Kabul radio started referring to them as 'angry brothers'.

An 'Extraordinary Supreme Commission for National Reconciliation' was set up, ostensibly at the request of religious leaders, which opened hundreds of branches all over the country. Their job was to make contact with friends and relatives in exile or fighting in the hills and pass on the government's message of peace. Some, like the committee I visited in Paghman in March 1987, had already been supplied with wheat, sugar, blankets, household utensils and other essential items for the use of returning refugees. No-one had yet arrived. Other inducements offered to refugees included tax concessions, promises to restore confiscated property and the deferment of military service. A halt was also called to pressgang operations, and about 4000 political prisoners were released from jail.

By June 1987, just before the expiry of the six-month ceasefire (during which fighting had been heavier than usual), Dr Najib claimed that 59,000 refugees had returned to Afghanistan, and that 'tens of thousands of armed men' were negotiating with the government. Four thousand 'representatives of the opposition,' he claimed, had been included in reconciliation commissions, and coalition governments had already been formed in 'several villages, sub-districts, districts and provinces'.[20] Inevitably, the figures were questioned by Western diplomats, who covered their bets by pointing out that even if they were correct, 59,000 refugees were only about one percent of the total refugee population.

The national reconciliation programme was undoubtedly less successful than Moscow and Kabul had hoped. By the end of 1987, more new refugees had arrived in Pakistan than had left. Only a few weeks after the programme was announced, I stumbled across a small encampment of refugees near Peshawar. They had just arrived from northern Afghanistan after a harrowing journey in which they had been bombarded time and again by Soviet MIGs. They showed me their horrible injuries, and an old man broke down in tears. His wife had been blown to pieces.

The guerilla alliance in Peshawar turned down each new proposal with angry contempt. Yet national reconciliation struck a raw nerve in the refugee camps in Pakistan. In the days following the announcement, refugees rushed to exchange their hoarded Pakistani rupees for Afghan currency, and vehicles were sold off in an effort to beat an anticipated rush to dispose of property in Pakistan. 'You get the impression in the camps these days that if anything happens, ninety percent of the refugees are ready to move' said an experienced Afghan refugee official working in Peshawar. Privately, even mujahedin officials were dismayed by the alliance's flat rejection of Najib's offer, and recognised that Kabul had seized the political initiative.

Heartened by the confusion amongst his opponents, and driven on by Gorbachev's determination to withdraw Soviet troops as soon as possible, Najibullah pressed on relentlessly. In June 1987 the 'ceasefire' was extended for a further six months. In July the regime published a draft constitution and invited suggestions for changes. In October Najib specifically named the seven-party Peshawar alliance in his appeals for a coalition government, and said they would be allowed to open offices in Kabul and publish newspapers if they ended their resistance.

The new constitution was formally adopted by a Loya Jirga in November 1987. It established Islam as the state religion and converted Afghanistan, in theory at least, into a multi-party parliamentary democracy. In practice, though, strong powers were concentrated in the hands of the President, a post to which Najibullah himself was elected, and the PDPA retained an 'organising and leading role'. PDPA-sponsored parties representing 'the peasantry' and the 'patriotic clergy' materialised out of nowhere, and obscure left-wing splinter groups were allowed to establish themselves as independent political entities. Five months later, in a move deliberately timed to coincide with the political settlement signed at Geneva in April 1988, elections were held under the new constitution. A quarter of the seats in the lower house of Parliament were left vacant for 'the opposition', while others were contested by candidates sponsored by the NFF, or by the newly-formed parties. The result of what amounted to 'rigging in reverse' was that the PDPA ended up with only twenty-two percent of the seats. As Soviet troops prepared to leave, the totalitarian Marxist state they had come to protect was in the process of dissolving itself.

Each new stage of the fast-moving Afghan *perestroika*

undertaken by Najibullah during his first two years in power was publicly ridiculed by the mujahedin and their Western backers. The Loya Jirga held in November 1987 was denounced from Peshawar as 'a meaningless puppet show staged by the Soviet Union for the benefit of foreign audiences.' When the regime claimed that a million and a half people voted in the national elections the following April, the US State Department insisted that the turnout was minimal and that the results were based on coercion and fraud.[21] The non-party Prime Minister appointed after the elections, Mohammad Hassan Sharq, was instantly labelled by guerilla officials as a KGB agent of long-standing.

Most, or even all, of these allegations may have been true. Undoubtedly, Najib's offers and concessions were intended to divide the resistance and secure a dominant role for the PDPA in any future government. The PDPA never publicly offered to relinquish control over crucial instruments of state control, such as the Interior and Foreign Ministries, or of KHAD. Yet by focusing attention on what they saw as the regime's grand policy of deception, and by rejecting the idea of negotiations of any description with the regime, the mujahedin leadership and its US backers were ignoring some important realities.

The first reality was that Najibullah's government was not quite so universally loathed as Western propaganda had always made out. In Kabul, with its hugely expanded population, the regime had developed over the years a sizable constituency of passive, if not active, support. The attitude of the assistant manager of the Kabul hotel where I stayed in early 1987 was fairly typical of the urban middle-class. He wasn't a supporter of the government. He had migrated to Kabul to escape persecution by KHAD after refusing to act as a government informer in his own village. But he was fed up with the war, and wanted to be left in peace to get on with his life. 'What's the difference?' he countered when I asked him whether he preferred the regime or the mujahedin. 'Najib brings the Soviets, Rabbani brings the Americans.'

Even some Western diplomats recognised that their propaganda was misleading. While publicly maintaining that Najibullah's regime would fall within weeks of a Soviet withdrawal, a senior Western envoy to Kabul privately admitted in February 1988 that a large minority of urban people had developed the outlook of 'better the devil you know'. Reflecting on the bitter divisions within the resistance, he admitted that if completely free and fair elections were to be held in Afghanistan, 'it wouldn't surprise me if the PDPA ended up as the largest single party.'

The second reality was that Najib's *perestroika* was laying the groundwork for his regime's survival in the post-Soviet era. National reconciliation had a chance of succeeding even without the capitulation of the mujahedin leaders in Peshawar. While offering them the role of junior partners in a national unity government in Kabul, Najib was simultaneously trying to build a coalition from the bottom upwards, offering more and more autonomy to local leaders in exchange for peaceful co-existence. The offer would look increasingly attractive to war-weary Afghans once Soviet troops had left.

The PDPA had gone a long way towards transforming its image. The Islamic republic which Najibullah claimed to have built by the beginning of 1988 was a far cry from the fanatically socialist Khalqi regime of ten years before. No-one really believed that Najib, or other die-hards in the PDPA, had altered their inner beliefs. 'How could a Marxist come to Islam, for goodness sakes, sir?' was Pir Gailani's response when I met him on my return from Kabul in March 1987, and pointed out that the regime had made a good job of changing its spots. But even the hardliners in Peshawar estimated the number of hardcore communists in Kabul at no more than 5000, and as national reconciliation gathered momentum, the more thoughtful guerilla leaders recognised the dramatic change in the regime's posture, and were afraid. 'The PDPA is softening its position every day,' Pir Gailani confided to me in January 1988. 'On Kabul television, Najibullah's government is showing itself to be even more Islamic than the government of Pakistan. People may be deceived. If the war goes on for another two years and the Soviets leave, the PDPA regime might survive because of the programmes they have now. And then it would revert to full Marxism.'

Two years have not yet elapsed since the last Soviet soldier left Afghanistan, but Pir Gailani's words are already beginning to look prophetic.

THIRTEEN

The Man from the UN:
Diego Cordovez and the Peace Talks
1982–1988

On 14th April 1988, the foreign ministers of Afghanistan, Pakistan, the Soviet Union and the United States congregated in the Palais des Nations in Geneva. There was a scrawl of signatures on four separate documents. Together, the documents comprised what United Nations officials had been trying to piece together during six years of tireless diplomacy: a negotiated settlement to what had become known as the 'Afghanistan problem'. All Soviet troops would withdraw within nine months. Pakistan and Afghanistan would refrain from interfering in each other's affairs. Refugees would be encouraged to return home on a voluntary basis. In a separate document, the USSR and the US pledged to 'guarantee' the settlement.

The world applauded. From the point of view of the international community, the accords were a diplomatic triumph. By mid-February of 1989, a poor, Third World country would have regained its independence. The Geneva accords appeared to herald the start of a new era of superpower *détente*, providing a model for the resolution of other regional conflicts. Moscow described them as of 'exceptional importance and tremendous international significance'.[1] Britain's Foreign Secretary, Sir Geoffrey Howe, expressed the hope that they would 'pave the way for the Afghan people as a whole to reach a comprehensive internal political settlement'.[2] Pakistan took a more exultant line. The withdrawal of Soviet troops, trumpeted the Pakistani Prime Minister Mohammad Khan Junejo in a nationwide broadcast, 'would mean that imperialism had come to an end for ever'.

Strangely, though, the 'determined and patriotic' mujahedin to whose anti-imperialist struggle Mr Junejo paid lavish tribute, were less than enthusiastic. Only a few weeks earlier, Gulbuddin Hekmatyar had warned Pakistan that signing the accords would be 'a very great and historical treason committed against the *jehad* in Afghanistan.'[3] Moderate guerilla leaders like Sibghatullah Mojadedi were more ambivalent. Mojadedi welcomed the Soviet troop withdrawal, and privately accused some of his colleagues of 'trembling with fear', because 'their life and survival depends upon the *jehad*'. But as usual the moderates were outflanked. Two days after the Geneva signing ceremony, tens of thousands of refugees were bussed to a field just outside Peshawar to hear all seven leaders, including Mojadedi, denounce the accords. Those who spoke in the harshest terms got the greatest applause. Gulbuddin was heard in pin-drop silence. In a corner of the field, I asked a shaven-headed Afghan teacher what *he* thought of the Geneva accords. Without replying, he turned to his young pupils and led them in a shrill chant of 'We reject! We reject! We reject!'

The mujahedin had good reason to be wary of the Geneva accords. The agreement addressed only the external aspects of the 'Afghanistan problem', leaving the PDPA regime, albeit under conciliatory new management, sitting tight in Kabul. The United States was well aware of this drawback. In an extraordinary move, the US Secretary of State George Shultz announced immediately after the signing ceremony that Washington had no intention whatsoever of halting its military support to the resistance. Arms supplies would continue to the mujahedin as long as Kabul continued receiving weapons from the USSR. Pakistan, on the other hand, had signed detailed and specific undertakings, among other things, to 'prevent within its territory the presence, harbouring, in camps and bases or otherwise, organizing, training, financing, equipping and arming of individuals and political, ethnic and any other groups'.[4] If the Geneva accords were rigorously implemented, the mujahedin would be disarmed and herded back into Afghanistan to fend for themselves. Even if Pakistan simply ignored its commitments, they would still have to fight their way to Kabul. The Geneva accords guaranteed the continuation of the war.

This unfortunate outcome to a 'peace process' which had taken six years to bring to fruition was the result of many factors: Washington's suspicions about Soviet intentions, Pakistan's manipulation of the mujahedin leadership and the obduracy of the mujahedin themselves. The major share of the blame, though, lies with the Kremlin. The *de facto* recognition of the PDPA government it installed at the time of the invasion was the price demanded by Moscow, and tacitly accepted by the United Nations, for allowing negotiations to begin in 1982. In January 1980 an emergency session of the UN General Assembly voted for an immediate withdrawal of unnamed 'foreign troops' from Afghanistan. Moscow was startled by the size of the vote against it, but the damage had already been done. Brezhnev soon laid down what he called the Soviet Union's 'fundamental position'. Since the USSR's 'limited contingent' of troops had been invited in by a legitimate Afghan government, they would be withdrawn, he insisted, 'only with the agreement of the Afghan government'. It was strictly a bilateral affair between Moscow and Kabul, not a subject for international negotiation. Moreover, troops would only be pulled out after all 'counter-revolutionary' activities against the PDPA were 'completely stopped' and on the basis of 'accords between Afghanistan and its neighbours', which would be required to give 'dependable guarantees' that they would no longer support the 'counter-revolutionary gangs'.[5]

Brezhnev's unbending position doomed to failure the various international peace conferences proposed by statesmen such as the French President Giscard d'Estaing and the British Foreign Secretary Lord Carrington. Even less acceptable to Moscow was Iran's proposal, put forward in November 1981, for Soviet troops to be replaced by an Islamic peacekeeping force, and for the PDPA to relinquish power to a caretaker council of Islamic clergymen.

The only hope for negotiations lay in mediation by the United Nations. In November 1980, reacting to hints of Soviet flexibility, Pakistan proposed that the UN Secretary-General should appoint a representative to initiate talks between Pakistan, Iran and Afghanistan. Accordingly, in February 1981, Kurt Waldheim appointed the Peruvian diplomat Javier Perez de Cuellar as his special representative.

The prognosis was not good. Tehran flatly refused to have anything to do with the negotiations unless the mujahedin were directly involved. Islamabad refused to talk to Kabul except through a UN intermediary; it wanted a Soviet troop withdrawal and Afghan self-determination to be at the top of the agenda. Kabul demanded direct, bilateral talks with Pakistan with minimal UN involvement, focusing on the halting of aid to the mujahedin and avoiding all reference to a troop withdrawal.

In early 1982 a new actor took the stage. Perez de Cuellar, who had replaced Waldheim as UN Secretary-General, appointed as *his* special representative for Afghanistan a fellow Latin American, Diego Cordovez. Cordovez was a brilliant diplomatic illusionist: a small, rather vain, cigar-smoking Ecuadorian who was highly persuasive, often charming, always volatile and, above all, tenacious.

To break the deadlock, Cordovez proposed that the divergent priorities of Kabul and Islamabad be included in a single package. He persuaded Pakistan to drop its insistence on discussing Afghan self-determination, and Kabul to accept the UN as honest broker. In June 1982 delegations from the two capitals arrived at the UN headquarters in Geneva for the first round of 'indirect' talks – so-called because the participants only met face-to-face six years later

204

when the accords were finally signed. Instead, Cordovez held alternate sessions with the two delegations, one in the morning, the other in the afternoon. The only refinement in the format of the talks came in 1984, when Pakistan agreed that the two delegations could sit simultaneously, but in separate rooms, at the Palais des Nations. This enabled the peripatetic Cordovez to shuttle more quickly between them, and provided journalists with a little light relief as they watched the delegates trying to avoid bumping into each other in the canteen and corridors.

It was an incredibly cumbersome negotiating mechanism for resolving the Afghan war. The central issue – the withdrawal of Soviet troops – could not be directly addressed, since Moscow considered it a strictly bilateral affair. Apart from the senior Soviet diplomats lurking behind the scenes to 'advise' the Kabul delegates, the Soviet Union did not participate in the talks at all. Pakistan claimed to represent the interests of the mujahedin and the Afghan refugees, but its negotiating partner was the Kabul regime, which, even at Moscow's behest, could hardly be expected to agree to its own dissolution. There was suspicion all round that each side was participating in the talks mainly with an eye to the gallery, either to placate domestic public opinion – in the case of Pakistan – or to win international legitimacy, in the case of Kabul.

Despite the topsy-turvy negotiating process, 1983 began with a surge of optimism that a solution could be found. In November 1982 Leonid Brezhnev had died. His successor, the former KGB chief Yuri Andropov, was a far more subtle man who was rumoured to have advised against the invasion. Andropov immediately began sending out signals of moderation, using the occasion of Brezhnev's funeral for unusually intense diplomatic activity. Even General Zia of Pakistan got the red carpet treatment, and he came away from his meeting with Andropov believing that there was 'a new freshness and flexibility on the Soviet side'.

Perez de Cuellar and Diego Cordovez were equally heartened by the discussions they held with Yuri Andropov in Moscow in March 1983. Andropov privately conceded that a definite timetable for a Soviet withdrawal could be included in a comprehensive settlement package. Cordovez later recalled that Andropov ended the hour-long meeting 'by holding up his hand and pulling down his fingers, one by one, as he listed the reasons why the Soviet Union felt a solution had to be found soon to the Afghan problem. The situation was harmful to relations, not only with the West, but also with socialist states, the Muslim world, and other Third World states. Finally, he said, pointing his thumb down, it was harmful for the Soviet Union internally, for its economy and its society.'[6] Meanwhile, Pakistan seemed to be signalling its readiness to curb the activities of the guerillas. On the eve of the next round of Geneva talks, convened on 11th April, the Pakistani authorities quietly told the guerilla leaders in Peshawar to close down their newspapers, and to move their political offices out of the city.

The second round of Geneva talks resulted in what Cordovez described as 'substantial progress' in setting out 'the principles and objectives of a comprehensive settlement'. By the time the session ended, he had drafted a twenty-page agreement, which he rashly claimed was 'ninety-five percent complete'. Pakistan tentatively accepted draft clauses on 'non-interference', which obliged it to prevent its territory being used by the mujahedin. In return, it wanted the Soviets to come up with a firm withdrawal timetable of not more than six months, and to replace Babrak Karmal. The Afghan side hinted that Soviet troops could be out within eighteen months, and promised to come to the next round of talks armed with a formal proposal.[7] But it still insisted on face-to-face talks to discuss the withdrawal, and also wanted guarantees that Washington would refrain, like Pakistan, from aiding and arming the mujahedin.

Buoyed by the sense that both Moscow and Islamabad

wanted a settlement, Cordovez hoped that the remaining differences could be ironed out within a few months. Taking the draft document with them, the two delegations returned to their respective capitals for consultations and journalists covering the talks reported that the two sides would reconvene in mid-June for what was expected to be a brief session to finalise the agreement. When the talks did reopen, however they ground to a halt. Both sides went back on their provisional undertakings. Pakistan's Foreign Minister Yaqub Khan reopened the issue of 'non interference', and laid new stress on the need to 'consult' the Afghan refugees. The Kabul delegation failed to deliver a timetable for the withdrawal of Soviet troops.

What went wrong? In the interlude between the two rounds of talks, Yaqub Khan visited Washington, where he was informed by senior US officials of their 'serious doubts' about any settlement which would leave the Kabul regime in place.[8] Pakistan later denied that it had buckled under American pressure, but a senior Pakistani foreign ministry official conceded that 'it is recognising a reality that if the Afghans call for international guarantees and the US is one of the guarantor powers, then an agreement has necessarily to be acceptable to Washington.'[9]

The Kremlin was also divided. Visiting Moscow just before the talks reconvened, Yaqub Khan was received by the hardline Foreign Minister Andrei Gromyko, who appeared to back-track on Andropov's promise to give a formal timetable. The doves on each side were outflanked by the hawks. The opposition of Washington and Riyadh to the deal persuaded General Zia to rein in his own Foreign Office, while in Moscow, Andropov's declining health paralysed the decision-making process. With the main elements of the settlement still based on verbal commitments rather than written undertakings, the general atmosphere of mistrust was sufficient to kill off the fragile hopes of an agreement.

It was becoming increasingly clear that agreement

between Islamabad and Kabul would be impossible without the full backing of the superpowers. Unfortunately for the people of Afghanistan, the international climate was growing worse. A South Korean airliner was shot down over Soviet airspace in September 1983, precipitating near hysteria in the United States. The US deployed Cruise and Pershing missiles in Europe, provoking the Soviets to walk out of the arms reduction talks in Geneva. Then, in February 1984, after a long illness, Yuri Andropov died. His successor, the inflexible Konstantin Chernenko, refused to receive Zia at Andropov's funeral, and gave a long audience to Babrak Karmal instead. The mujahedin recall Chernenko's time in office as the most brutal period of the Afghan war.

Afghanistan was caught in the freezing grip of a new cold war. Soviet forces conducted massive military offensives against mujahedin strongholds in the spring of 1984, and in the autumn the US Congress started voting huge increases in funds for covert CIA operations. Moscow accused Pakistan of direct military involvement in Afghanistan, and retaliatory shelling and bombing raids across the Pakistan border became commonplace.

Diego Cordovez, indefatigable as always, continued to shuttle between the regional capitals and convened a third round of Geneva talks. But even he recognised that the UN negotiations were in danger of collapsing. A fourth round of talks scheduled for February 1985 was postponed twice, once at the request of Pakistan, which was about to hold elections, and the second time at the insistence of the UN, which demanded better assurances of progress from all parties involved.

It was not until mid-1985 that there was any detectable movement on the part of the superpowers. At the fifth round of Geneva talks, Moscow signalled its willingness to give an internationally binding guarantee that its troops would withdraw within a given period. Retracting one of Brezhnev's 'fundamental' conditions, it also conceded that the withdrawal could begin on the same day that foreign aid was halted to the mujahedin. After much hesitation, the US followed suit, formally pledging itself to guarantee a settlement so long as all the other elements of the package were acceptable (which Washington considered highly unlikely). In March 1986 Cordovez announced that he now had 'all the elements of a comprehensive settlement of the Afghan problem.' Two months later, at the eighth round of Geneva talks, Kabul finally dropped its insistence on direct talks with Pakistan.[10] Now nearly two years of bartering over the length of the withdrawal timetable was about to begin.

What broke the superpower stalemate was the death of another Soviet leader. In March 1985 Chernenko died, and Mikhail Gorbachev – a protégé of Andropov – succeeded to the Kremlin leadership. The impact of Gorbachev's 'new thinking' took some time to be felt in Afghanistan. After a secret CPSU Politburo review in April, Gorbachev is believed to have authorised his generals to break the back of the resistance, but within a specified timeframe. The US administration raised the military stakes at around the same time: in April 1985 President Reagan signed a National Security Directive which called for efforts to drive out Soviet forces 'by all means available'.

Nevertheless, Gorbachev was not relying solely on a military solution to staunch what, in February 1986, he described as the 'bleeding wound' of Afghanistan. In that same speech, made to the 27th CPSU Congress, he announced publicly that a withdrawal schedule had already been worked out with Kabul, and would be implemented as soon as a political settlement was achieved. On 28th July, in a major foreign policy speech at Vladivostock, he underlined his commitment to a solution by announcing that six Soviet regiments would withdraw from Afghanistan by the end of the year. Washington was adamant that the fulfilment of Gorbachev's promise in October 1986 was just a cynical public relations exercise which left Soviet military capabilities in Afghanistan unimpaired. But, in retrospect, it seems probable that Gorbachev *had* made a firm political decision to extricate all Soviet troops from Afghanistan by the time he made his Vladivostock speech.

Gorbachev's problem was how to ensure that a friendly, pro-Soviet government remained in power in Kabul after Soviet troops had left. The speed with which he could afford to pull Soviet troops out of Afghanistan depended on the stability of the Kabul regime, which in turn depended on broadening the regime's base so as to make it more acceptable. At the end of 1985, an article in *Pravda* made the unprecedented admission that Babrak Karmal's government was not universally popular, and called it to undertake a 'positive' dialogue with its opponents. Three days later Karmal started inducting non-Marxists into his administration; a few months later he was replaced. At the end of the year, his successor Dr Najibullah unveiled his grand strategy of 'national reconciliation' (see chapter 12).

What is still unclear is how far Gorbachev was prepared to go in diluting communist control in Kabul. Was he committed to the PDPA retaining a dominant role in a coalition? Or would he have agreed to the installation of a caretaker government excluding both the communists and the Islamic fundamentalists? Early in 1987 Soviet officials started expressing growing concern that a 'bloodbath' would follow a withdrawal, and insisted that prior agreement would have to be reached on a government of national unity. Moscow made indirect approaches to Zahir Shah, and there was talk of the former king returning from Rome to head such a government. Moscow also indicated that it might be satisfied with a non-PDPA government formally committed to neutrality. Pakistani officials hurriedly boned up on the Finnish and Austrian models of neutrality, but were then told that they had taken the idea too literally. In the autumn of 1987 Western diplomats in Islamabad were saying that Moscow had still not come up with any specific proposals on how power might be equitably shared in Kabul.

The limited success of Najibullah's programme of national reconciliation strained Moscow's patience with its increasingly wayward clients in Kabul. Not unnaturally, even the loyal Najibullah was reluctant to sign his own regime's death warrant. At the Geneva talks, Kabul tried desperately to apply the brakes to a settlement. In May 1986, its delegates put forward an absurd proposal for a withdrawal spread over four years, compared to Pakistan's demand for a pull-out within three to four months. The following summer, Moscow reportedly warned Najibullah that he only had a year left to come up with a genuine power-sharing arrangement before Soviet troops started pulling out.[11] Yet in September 1987, when even *Pravda* was advocating a twelve-month timetable, Kabul refused to go below sixteen months.

Diego Cordovez, meanwhile, had also begun working on what became known as the 'second track' – parallel negotiations to secure a coalition or caretaker government in Kabul acceptable to all sides. In September 1987 he circulated a memorandum to Moscow, Kabul, Islamabad and Washington which suggested that a dialogue be started under UN auspices between the PDPA, the mujahedin alliance and Afghan nationalists in exile. The proposal was not adopted formally, but Moscow encouraged Cordovez to meet Zahir Shah, and even General Zia conceded in November 1987 that any caretaker government would have to have the confidence of 'the three main elements in the Afghanistan conflict: the freedom fighters, the refugees and the present Kabul government.'[12]

Zia's apparent readiness to contemplate a continued role for the communists in Kabul in late 1987 suggests that, with sufficient political determination, some sort of power-sharing arrangement could have been worked out which might have averted full-scale civil war. At heart, Zia was still committed to the establishment of a government in

Kabul dominated by his fundamentalist mujahedin clients. But growing impatience within Pakistan for a settlement, and Moscow's insistence that a government of national unity be formed prior to its troop withdrawal, persuaded him to adopt a more flexible public posture. Even Cordovez, who harboured few illusions about Zia's ultimate goal, believed that once Moscow, Washington and Islamabad were convinced of each other's sincerity, a deal could be worked out within a matter of weeks.

Zahir Shah was the obvious person to head a neutral caretaker government. He seemed to be acceptable both to Moscow and to the majority of refugees. Even Zia's former military governor of the Frontier Province, General Fazle Haq, privately expressed his belief that 'all you have to do is get Zahir Shah into Kabul and there will be general euphoria'.[13] The bitter hostility of the fundamentalist guerilla leaders towards the former king, though, made the Zahir Shah option problematical. According to Pakistani diplomats, Zia finally ruled it out after India, anxious to strengthen its hand in the end game, sent its own envoy to Rome. The mutual paranoia which has always existed between Delhi and Islamabad put the final nail into the old king's political coffin.

Instead, Cordovez began working on the idea of a 'government of personalities', compiling, in consultation with Kabul and prominent Afghan exiles in Pakistan and the West, a list of well-known figures who might be acceptable to both sides. Moderate guerilla leaders in Peshawar discreetly let it be known that they would agree to individual members of the Kabul regime joining such a government, so long as the PDPA was not officially represented. In the opinion of Fazle Haq, the alliance's public refusal to accommodate the regime was 'all humbug'.

Cordovez's attempt to arrange a UN-sponsored dialogue between the resistance and the regime, however, was hamstrung by Pakistan's ambivalent attitude. Despite General Zia's stated willingness for the PDPA to occupy a third of the seats in a coalition government, Islamabad did nothing to facilitate an intra-Afghan dialogue. The prevailing opinion among hardliners in Islamabad and Washington was that the Kabul government would only survive for a few months after the withdrawal of Soviet troops and Cordovez was actively discouraged from holding a formal meeting with the Peshawar resistance leaders until February 1988. Disingenuously disclaiming any influence over the alliance, Islamabad told Moscow that it would have to discuss arrangements for a transitional government directly with the mujahedin themselves, a humiliation which Moscow was not prepared to accept at that stage.

Moderate guerilla officials privately accused General Zia and the ISI of deliberately sabotaging progress on the 'second track'. Frustrated and impotent, their allegations are understandable enough. But in fact, all Zia had to do was to remain inactive. Having ensured at the start of the war that a united guerilla leadership could not emerge, the composition of the Peshawar alliance did the rest. In a set-up where, in the words of one insider, 'they can't even agree where to put the ashtrays', the alliance's decision-making process (which required unanimous agreement) led to complete political paralysis. Outnumbered and outvoted, the three moderate alliance leaders appealed to Pakistan to allow them to hold either a jirga or a referendum among the refugees, which would throw up a united leadership confident enough to undertake negotiations without fear of being accused of betraying the cause. Pakistan refused. The Peshawar alliance's own proposals about when and how to convene a *shura*, or elected assembly, were repeatedly shelved because of internal disagreements. Throughout the time when a deal on power-sharing seemed possible, chronic disunity prevented the Peshawar alliance from advancing beyond the lowest common denominator of its demands: the unconditional withdrawal of Soviet troops and the unconditional surrender of the Kabul regime.

In late October 1987, Gorbachev concluded that he could

not afford to delay a withdrawal until the fractious Afghans reached agreement on a coalition government. On 8th February 1988, he publicly announced that Soviet troops could start leaving on 15th May and complete their withdrawal within ten months. Moscow was ready to sign an agreement at Geneva irrespective of the progress of inter-Afghan talks on power-sharing, and any further delay, Soviet officials made clear, would be entirely the responsibility of Pakistan.[14]

Pakistan was bemused by Moscow's change of tack, and suddenly fearful that the Najibullah regime might after all be able to consolidate itself, leaving Islamabad to cope with three million discontented and well-armed refugees. Zia's response was to try to engineer a U-turn in Pakistani policy. To the consternation of his own foreign ministry officials, he stated categorically in a newspaper interview that Islamabad would never sign an agreement at Geneva with the Najibullah regime. He gave the same message to Yuli Vorontsov, one of Moscow's top Afghan negotiators, who visited Islamabad just after Gorbachev's announcement. Vorontsov countered by saying that the formation of a coalition government in Kabul was 'nobody's business but the business of the Afghans themselves.'[15]

Only then did the ISI begin bullying the Peshawar alliance to come up with a slightly more constructive counter-proposal to Najibullah's offer of a government of national reconciliation. After weeks of bitter argument and just ten days before the final round of Geneva talks began, the alliance announced the formation of an interim government, intended to replace the Najibullah regime, oversee the Soviet troop withdrawal, and hold elections within six months for a constituent assembly. Although a quarter of the Cabinet seats were left for 'Muslims presently living in Afghanistan' (a euphemism for non-communist members of the Najibullah regime), the proposed government was to be dominated by the seven Peshawar parties, whose leaders

214

would constitute a 'grand council' to oversee the government.

The moderate guerilla leaders were bitterly disappointed by a scheme they alleged had been forced on them by the ISI. Pir Gailani described the proposal as 'so rigid that it requires the complete capitulation of the Kabul regime.'[16] 'It is Pakistan's brainchild,' one of his chief lieutenants added. 'Zia wants to close all other doors, torpedo all other efforts, by erecting this government.' Pakistani foreign ministry officials were equally disappointed with the mujahedin proposal. 'Urgent action is needed on our part,' one official told me later, 'to convince these buggers to come up with something credible.' But the Foreign Ministry had virtually no contacts with the Peshawar leaders. Only Zia and the ISI could influence the outcome of the alliance's deliberations.

Nevertheless, Zia was under growing pressure at home not to block a settlement altogether. The installation of a civilian administration in early 1985 had gradually undermined the absolute power he formerly enjoyed as an outright military dictator. Although the main opposition parties were excluded from the 1985 elections, even the tame politicians of the ruling Muslim League had their own interests to pursue. With fresh elections promised for 1990, they could not afford to ignore the hostility felt by a growing number of Pakistanis to 'Zia's' Afghan war. On top of heroin and sophisticated weapons saturating the country, a KHAD-sponsored bombing campaign hit Pakistan's cities in 1987, designed to increase public pressure on the government to accept a settlement on Moscow's terms. After a bomb blast in Karachi which killed over seventy people, even Zia's handpicked Prime Minister Mohammad Khan Junejo said pointedly that the terrorist campaign was 'only because of the Afghanistan problem and the influx of three million Afghan refugees to our soil'.[17]

The divide between the civilian and military members of Pakistan's ruling establishment over Afghan policy became increasingly acute as Moscow's determination to conclude a settlement became more evident. At the end of 1987, Prime Minister Junejo finally asserted his own authority in the hitherto sacrosanct area of foreign affairs, by engineering the replacement of Zia's long-serving Foreign Minister Yaqub Khan and taking over the portfolio himself. Around the same time, on Junejo's instructions, the Foreign Ministry stopped automatically clearing decisions with Zia. According to Cordovez, Zia telephoned him almost every night during the final round of Geneva talks to find out what Pakistan's delegates were doing and to express his own views.[18]

Junejo strengthened his hand further by convening an unprecedented all-party conference on the eve of the talks, to hammer out what he called a 'national consensus' on Afghanistan. Even Benazir Bhutto was invited – her arrival at the Prime Minister's house was the first time she had been seen on Pakistani television since returning from exile nearly two years before. No clear-cut statement was issued, but the mood of the conference and of the nation was summed up by a centrist opposition leader, who said, 'we must take this opportunity of a lifetime'.

Pressure from the civilian politicians was only one of several factors which finally persuaded General Zia to back down from his earlier refusal to sign a treaty with the Najibullah regime. Strong advice to go ahead with the settlement was coming from his closest allies, the United States, Saudi Arabia and China. But probably the most crucial factor in Zia's thinking was Washington's last-minute decision not to honour its commitment to halt military supplies to the mujahedin on the day that Soviet troops started to withdraw.

The commitment was made public by the US State Department in December 1986, but as soon as Gorbachev announced a definitive date for the withdrawal in February 1988, right-wing US senators began to denounce the 'Day One deal' as an 'indecent' sell-out of the guerillas, secretly negotiated by the State Department without the knowledge of Congress or even the White House.[19] Buckling under the pressure, the State Department announced that aid to the mujahedin would not be stopped without 'a symmetrical cessation of military supplies to the regime in Kabul'.

Washington's new demand nearly scuppered the final round of Geneva talks. In two weeks of intensive bilateral exchanges between Soviet and American officials, Moscow refused to halt its own military supplies to Kabul, arguing that its treaty obligations to the Kabul government dated back to the 1920's. Gorbachev was incensed by what he saw as American backsliding, but he was left with no choice. In early April, according to US accounts which have never been acknowledged by Moscow, the USSR finally agreed to a formula of 'positive symmetry', whereby both superpowers could continue to supply their respective allies with weapons.

On 14th April 1988, just before the Geneva signing ceremony, the UN Secretary General received a formal US notification that Washington reserved the right to continue supplying the mujahedin, although it would 'meet [Russian] restraint with restraint'. When US Secretary of State George Schultz signed the accords a few hours later, he knew that Washington's formal guarantee of the settlement was totally meaningless.

Islamabad's position was rather different. As one of the two 'high contracting parties' to the accords, it formally bound itself to close down all mujahedin training camps, offices and even newspapers in Pakistan, and prevent all movement of guerillas and weapons across the border into Afghanistan. Yet Washington could only continue to supply the mujahedin through Pakistan. US officials fudged the issue, hinting that legal experts would be able to find a way around Pakistan's new treaty obligations. Zia also felt the need to tread carefully at first. At a luncheon on the day of the signing, he announced with masterly ambiguity that 'we will try our best to fulfil the Geneva accords, without any effect on the Afghan mujahedin efforts inside

Afghanistan'. But if there was ever any real doubt about his meaning, it disappeared as soon as the accords came into effect on 15th May. Although great care was taken to keep the fifty-man UN monitoring team and journalists in ignorance of what was going on, the flow of US weaponry to the mujahedin through Pakistan continued exactly as before. For General Zia and the Pakistani army, the Geneva accords were – in the pithy words of Foreign Minister Yaqub Khan – 'just an inconvenient episode which interrupted play'.[20]

The 'second track' was not abandoned entirely, but with the signing of the accords, both Moscow and Islamabad lost some of their former leverage over their respective Afghan allies. The chance of negotiating a coalition government into power in Kabul may have existed in late 1987, but now it was too late. The Peshawar alliance hardened its terms for a settlement, and packed its provisional government with fundamentalist guerilla officials. Diego Cordovez was empowered by the four signatories of the accords to promote an intra-Afghan dialogue, but only in his private capacity, rather than as the UN Secretary-General's special representative.

His last attempt to avert a civil war was brave but futile. Hardline mujahedin leaders like Yunis Khalis had long been convinced that Cordovez was a Soviet agent, and when he returned to Pakistan in July 1988 to unveil a new proposal for a neutral caretaker government of 'peace and reconstruction', the idea was summarily rejected both by Kabul and the Peshawar hardliners, who once again refused to meet him. Before returning to Ecuador to take up the post of Foreign Minister, one of his last actions as would-be peace-maker was to visit Nasir Bagh, a show-piece Afghan refugee camp on the outskirts of Peshawar. It was the first time that he had made direct contact with the refugees in over six years of mediation, and sitting in serried ranks under multi-coloured awnings, the camp elders listened politely as Cordovez made a passionate appeal to them to 'solve the remaining problem in a traditional way, in an Afghan way, by using your own traditions'. It was all over within twenty minutes, and then the man from the UN was whisked off in a cavalcade of jeeps to visit the Afghan border. After the dust had settled, the elders yawned and stretched. 'He didn't say directly that we should hold a jirga with Najib, but that's what he meant', one of them commented. 'But how is it possible when the communists hold power? We have to continue our struggle.'

FOURTEEN:

The Struggle for Kabul:
Soviet Withdrawal and its Aftermath

Eleven days before General Boris Gromov took his famous last walk out of Afghanistan, Western diplomats in Kabul staged their own strategic withdrawal. After shredding a handful of documents and immobilising their vehicles, Britain's gallant few ate a final dinner of champagne and army rations, lowered the Union Jack and took a plane for Delhi. Exactly sixty years earlier, Western diplomats attending the court of the reformist king, Amanullah, had fled in much the same way before the advancing forces of the fundamentalist Tajik bandit Bacha Saqao. This time their sympathies were with the advancing mujahedin, but they expected the same result. 'We hope to be back soon', the British chargé d'affaires Ian Mackley said as the party headed for the airport.[1] The greater the distance, the more certain the predictions of the regime's imminent collapse. Arriving in Delhi, the US chargé, John Glassman, gave it six months at the outside; back in Washington, Congressman Charlie Wilson – an ardent pro-mujahedin lobbyist and supplier of Tennessee mules to the resistance – predicted that Kabul would fall within three weeks.

Kabul's predicament certainly seemed grim as the last Soviet troops pulled out. The steady stream of Soviet armoured traffic heading up the Salang highway to the Soviet border over the preceding months, together with the massive airlift of Soviet ammunition into Kabul airport, severely restricted the import of the essential civilian commodities on which the capital had come to depend in wintertime. Taxis queued all day for a few litres of petrol. Diminishing stocks of food and cooking fuel disappeared into the backrooms of hoarders and profiteers. As black market prices soared, women and young boys from the shanty towns waited hours for a pitiful ration of bread or wheat flour. In the bitter cold of one of the worst winters in living memory, the weakest froze to death.

The situation eased slightly in late-February, when Moscow mounted a huge airlift of food which helped stabilise prices. But despite the harrowing television pictures beamed back into sitting rooms in the West, our governments declined to support the UN's relief efforts in Kabul. It was necessary to be cruel to be kind, they argued. A well-fed citizenry would only prolong the longevity of the Najibullah regime. By early May, UN emergency food stocks had run out and officials were saying that 400,000 people were in need. When its last thirteen sacks of flour and sugar were distributed, journalists reported that women in *chadors* fought like wild dogs. In the backstreets sparrows were being grilled for kebabs.

Except for Charlie Wilson and a few others like him, no informed observer expected the mujahedin to launch an immediate frontal assault on the capital; but there was much talk of a tightening siege, of popular uprisings, or of the possibility of a military coup by Khalqis or nationalist army officers. Mass defections from the army were widely expected, and guerilla reports claimed that 11,000 Afghan troops and militiamen defected in different parts of the country the very first day after the Soviet withdrawal ended.[2] House-to-house searches undertaken by KHAD led to the arrest of hundreds of suspected guerilla sympathisers, and secret stashes of weapons were seized in and around the city. Najibullah himself had no doubt about the gravity of the crisis he was facing. On 18th February, he declared a state of emergency, sacked the non-party Prime Minister, and transferred the powers of the newly-elected government to a twenty-member Supreme Military Council, vested with draconian powers.

Outside Kabul, the outlook for the regime was even bleaker. For most of the previous nine months, as Soviet troops had geared up for withdrawal, the regime's forces had been retreating before the mujahedin. The rout began completely unexpectedly just ten days after the Geneva accords were signed. On 25th May 1988, under cover of an intensive aerial bombardment, dozens of helicopters clattered up the Kunar valley in eastern Afghanistan and landed at the small border garrison of Barikot. The defenders – several hundred strong – were herded on board, possibly at gunpoint; even the KHAD officers had not been forewarned: freshly-baked bread was later found lying half-eaten in their houses. Tanks, trucks, ammunition and other equipment too heavy to take away were blown up by the departing troops. Then, as quickly as they had come, the helicopters took off again for Jalalabad, leaving the garrison protected against the mujahedin only by its minefields.

Over the next few months, dozens more government posts and garrisons were either captured or abandoned in similar fashion. In mid-August 1988, by which time 50,000 Soviet troops had left, US intelligence calculated that over one hundred former government strongholds had fallen into guerilla hands, many of which had been fought over for years. By the end of the year, the mujahedin were controlling the whole of the Panjshir and Kunar valleys as well as five provincial capitals. Najibullah's announcement that the evacuation was part of a deliberate policy of creating 'demilitarised zones' to which refugees could return safely was met with jeers of scepticism. In its annual report for 1988, the US State Department predicted that 'the shift of military momentum towards the resistance, or mujahedin, probably is irreversible.'[3]

That tiny note of official caution was more than justified. More than one year later, the mujahedin have yet to capture a single important town, and the regime is growing in confidence daily. Even vulnerable regime strongholds like Khost, which needed the active intervention of Soviet troops to withstand a concerted mujahedin siege in the winter of 1987–88, are still holding out today. What went wrong?

The full answer is complex, but some of its ingredients are clear enough. In purely military terms, the relative balance of strength was badly misrepresented. The regime's evacuation of the border areas may have seemed like a rout, but in reality it was a carefully-planned re-deployment of its diminished military resources. Soldiers posted in vulnerable border positions were pulled back to towns, major bases and vital lines of communication, formerly defended by Soviet troops. Concentrated in larger, better-fortified positions, their morale was less likely to crack and the opportunities to defect were smaller. More thoughtful mujahedin were taken aback by the deep bunkers, underground passages and other fortifications they found at abandoned border garrisons like Jaji; the positions to which the troops had been withdrawn were undoubtedly even stronger. The regime was digging itself in for a protracted defensive war.

The mujahedin were ill-prepared for the switch they were now compelled to make from guerilla insurgency to conventional warfare. They had no airforce, and were still vulnerable to the regime's bombers and helicopter-gunships (the US administration, deeply nervous about evidence that dozens of Stingers had been sold off to Iran by renegade guerilla commanders, decided to discontinue the supply in February 1988).[4] The mujahedin had only a handful of captured tanks, and a little mine-clearing equipment. Equally important, they had no unified military command. In 1988, in spite of improving cooperation between local commanders in the field, each guerilla party still jealously maintained its own separate military committee and supply lines. Even the joint offensives which were occasionally planned in Peshawar foundered, through lack of co-ordination and a general reluctance to follow up rocket and artillery bombardments with ground assaults.

In the north-east, Massoud's forces had captured half a

dozen minor garrisons since 1986, but only after months of planning by a commander with an unusually acute grasp of military strategy and well-disciplined fighters. In the Pashtun south, no government stronghold of any significance had been captured during the entire war. The mujahedin, in the words of one of their number, had inflicted 'ten years of pinpricks' on the regime, and even NIFA's military supremo Rahim Wardak, not normally renowned for his modesty, admitted in a rare moment of introspection in May 1988 that 'in all these years we've tried we haven't achieved a damned thing'.[5]

The regime's military strength, by contrast, had been badly underestimated. Perhaps Western and Pakistani intelligence organisations fell victim to their own propaganda. For years, diplomats based in Kabul had assiduously fostered the impression that the Afghan army was in tatters. They embroidered their cables with second-hand tales of defections, of teenagers pressganged in the streets, of drunken Khalqi officers misbehaving with local women and of mutinous Afghan conscripts forced into battle by Soviet infantrymen. What they failed to mention was that intensive Soviet training had implanted a stiff backbone of hard core professionals within the Afghan army by the mid-1980's. Increasingly, Soviet troops were used only for special operations, and the forces which spearheaded the relatively successful government offensives of 1986 were composed predominantly of Afghan troops. In addition, according to Yossef Bodansky, a consultant with the US Defense Department, a force of 20,000 recruits from northern Afghanistan was trained and held in permanent reserve in the USSR for most of the 1980's.[6] The exact number is disputed, but there's no doubt that several thousand Afghan military personnel stationed in the USSR were summoned home when the Soviet withdrawal began, which may account for the sudden appearance in the Qandahar area of a brutal and highly-motivated militia force known to the mujahedin as 'Jowzjanis', after the northern province of Jowzjan.

The most important instrument at the regime's disposal was the Afghan airforce, estimated in May 1989 to consist of nearly three hundred aircraft, including ninety Sukhoi bombers, twenty MIG-27s, fifty MIG-21s and ninety heli-copters, mostly MI-17s and the dreaded MI-24 'Hinds'.[7] Airforce personnel were recruited with great care, and all pilots were required to join the party. The commander of an Afghan air brigade who defected in early 1989 estimated that forty percent of pilots were loyal to the regime – a significant figure, particularly in view of the tendency of defectors to tell their new comrades what they wanted to hear.[8] The vital role the Afghan airforce would continue to play was underlined in the summer of 1988, when the mujahedin briefly overran the defences of two provincial capitals, Kunduz and Maidan Shahr. In both cases, heavy artillery bombardments and air strikes drove them out again with heavy losses. Even if the guerillas were able to capture a major city, they still had to find a way of holding on to it.

The militias were another source of the regime's military strength, although their reliability varied enormously from place to place. Many 'pro-government' militias were simply the opportunistic tribal rivals of a nearby resistance group; when it suited their interests they traded information and ammunition with the guerillas while keeping a wary eye out for the government helicopters which periodically brought them supplies of hashish and alcohol. Mohammad Es Haq, who acts as a spokesman for Massoud in Peshawar, once told me 'it's all a big game, and the enemy knows it'. Some militia forces, though, were highly effective; Es Haq himself admitted that women militias armed with grenades and machine-guns held up Massoud's forces for several hours during their attack on the garrison of Keranamunjan in 1987.[9]

As Soviet troops prepared to pull out, the regime raised

extra militias and military units, including a new force called the Guard Corps, designed to take over the defence of the capital from Soviet troops. Later that year it was absorbed into the élite Special Guard, a 10,000 man strike-force which also included the army's crack commando brigades, the Presidential Guard (which had fought so valiantly to defend Hafizullah Amin during the Soviet invasion) and some Tsarandoy units.[10] By early 1989 Western military analysts reckoned that Najibullah could call on somewhere between 80,000 and 150,000 security force personnel, while the Soviet deputy Defence Minister, General Varenninkov, formerly in charge of military operations in Afghanistan, claimed that the Afghan armed forces consisted of about 300,000 men – almost as many as the number of active mujahedin as estimated by Pakistani military intelligence.[11]

Even so, the Peshawar politicians were not overly concerned. Most held it as an article of faith that Najibullah presided over a hated, repressive regime, whose support would melt away once Soviet troops had left. Hajji Deen Mohammad, deputy to Yunis Khalis and 'Defence Minister' in the alliance's provisional government, told me he expected entire Afghan army units to change sides and take part in the the final mujahedin assault on Kabul. Civilians would also have a role to play. 'Cities only fall when there's some resistance from within', he said, his boyish face shining ruddily beneath a sky-blue turban. 'We're banking on that. All these years the citizens of Kabul have been assuring us that they're with us. Now's the time for them to translate that into action, to rise in revolt and make our task easier.'[12]

Others, though, harboured private doubts. NIFA's Rahim Wardak argued that the mujahedin should hold off from major military operations and concentrate on 'psychological operations' to encourage defections. 'Otherwise', he warned in his Sandhurst drawl, 'it'll be backs-to-the-wall. The regime will be fighting for its life, and that's the toughest fight of all.' Once again, the most realistic assessment came from Mohammad Es Haq of Jamiat-i-Islami, drawing conclusions from the battle experience of Massoud over the previous two years. 'The Americans are over-optimistic about the situation', he told me. 'They think everything is hollow. But the regime will not fall by itself. It has learned to fight. Even to attack a small garrison takes two months of preparation, and to get one garrison to submit, you have to take two by force.'[13] Massoud's own response to the Soviet withdrawal, announced after a meeting of his 'Supervisory Council of the North' in mid-1988, was to build a regular 13,000 man army capable of progressing from the occasional capture of minor garrisons to the seizure of major bases and the blockade of cities. One year on, in late 1989, he was still expecting it to take four more years before he would be ready to move on Kabul.

Mujahedin politicians, of all shades of opinion, agreed on the need to keep the regime under military pressure in one form or another. Despite their interminable rhetoric, they were more-or-less aware that, in Es Haq's words, 'a lot of people are sitting on the fence, waiting for a catalyst in the form of a big military attack to force them to decide which way to jump'. At that point, though, agreement abruptly ended. Some favoured full-scale assaults on regime-held cities; others wanted to gradually tighten the noose by blocking roads and attacking military bases outside the towns; yet others hoped to topple the regime from within. Broadly speaking, the divisions over strategy followed two natural fault lines in the resistance: the first was between the Peshawar politicians and the foot-soldiers of the jehad; the second was between the 'moderates' and the 'fundamentalists'.

Once it began to dawn on ordinary Afghans that the Soviet withdrawal was for real, the *'jehad* spirit' slowly started to seep away. The Najibullah regime was not any the less loathed, but – so many rank-and-file mujahedin must have reasoned – its universal unpopularity made its

227

collapse inevitable without them risking their lives unnecessarily. In areas vacated by regime troops, the first priority of petty commanders was to consolidate the authority of their clan, lay claim to land and settle local disputes, rather than press on to the nearest government stronghold. And even when commanders recognised the need to go on fighting, rocketing towns and cities posed a serious dilemma for local fighting fronts. Relatives and friends living there would be in as much danger as military targets. Like many of his peers, Commander Anwar, a Jamiat commander in charge of 500 mujahedin around Jalalabad, was unhappy with plans drawn up by the ISI and the Peshawar alliance in May 1988 for a major assault on his home city. 'This is our national treasure', he complained. 'The regime will counter-attack and the city could be destroyed. We don't want to inflict a lot of casualties.'[14] In the end, the opposition of the local commanders to the plan won the day, and 'Operation Jalalabad' was postponed.

With the enviable detachment of men who knew that they and their relatives were not in the firing line, the politicians in Peshawar had fewer scruples about inflicting civilian casualties. During the planning of 'Operation Jalalabad', Hajji Deen Mohammad – one of the few politicians who also took part in military operations – recognised that firing rockets into civilian areas could be counter-productive. 'They are all Afghans', he said, 'why should we offend them?' Yet he was insistent that the KHAD headquarters in the centre of the city would be the first target, and his only suggestion was that local residents should 'ask' KHAD to move outside the city, where, presumably, it could be safely bombarded to extinction. Later, in token recognition of the risk of driving city-dwellers into a closer embrace with the regime, the Peshawar alliance issued several amnesties for 'collaborators' who contacted their local resistance front within a specified period.

The division between the 'moderates' and 'fundamentalists' over military strategy was even more significant than between ordinary mujahedin and the politicians. The split was a reflection both of their relative military strengths and their contrasting political constituencies. Hardliners – Gulbuddin Hekmatyar in particular – were insistent on the need for swift and decisive military action. Journalists – and the Kabul regime – got to know that 'Operation Jalalabad' was being planned because Gulbuddin boasted openly in his party journal that by 1st June 1988, he would be saying his prayers in the city's main mosque. Mujahedin bands affiliated to Hezb and Jamiat were also largely responsible for a premature attack on the northern city of Kunduz, in August 1988, which provoked a savage counter-attack by Afghan and Soviet forces. As the guerillas withdrew from the city, they burned down cinemas, looted shops and raped women, fuelling the growing anxieties of city residents everywhere about the implications of a mujahedin victory.

Gulbuddin's impatience stemmed from the realisation that time was against him. Now that its weapons were no longer killing Russians, Washington's promise of continued military support could not be relied on indefinitely; equally serious, the unexpected death of General Zia in August 1988 suddenly made Pakistan a less-than-certain partner in the *jehad* enterprise. Inspired by his vision of a fascist-style Islamic state, and with little popular support among the traditional sectors of Afghan society, Gulbuddin's best chance of dominating the future set-up in Kabul lay in a fast victory; in the chaos which would inevitably follow the toppling of the Najibullah regime, his party's formidable military muscle would almost certainly guarantee him the pre-eminent position in the mujahedin regime. For much the same reason, he made little attempt to conceal his abhorrence of Massoud's plans to create a 'regular' army. The rivalry between the two men, which had existed since the mid-1970's, had long since grown into mutual loathing, and Gulbuddin knew that Massoud, rather than the old men in the alliance, would be his greatest challenger in a 'revolutionary' Islamic Afghanistan.

The 'moderate' leaders in Peshawar, particularly Pir Gailani, had quite different hopes and ambitions. Their strength lay not in military muscle, but in their ties with traditional Pashtun tribal forces, educated nationalists and the old royal establishment. Although equally committed to overthrowing the communist-dominated regime, they viewed the prospect of rule by 'extremists' like Hekmatyar as no better than rule by Amin, Babrak or Najibullah. Without any definite vision of the kind of Afghanistan they were fighting for, they were less efficient, but also less ruthless. Hezb's attitude was summed up by one mujahed who told a BBC *Panorama* crew that 'we have given more than a million martyrs during this ten years of war. So what if we give 50,000 more . . . because we are fighting to bring an Islamic state in Afghanistan.'[15] The moderates, by contrast, hoped to settle the civil war in the 'traditional' Pashtun way: by sitting down and talking, reactivating the clan and family networks fragmented by the war. As Pir Gailani's son Mohammad told me in August 1988, 'Now even government ministers and committed communists are seeking contacts with us. They send someone to ask "What will happen if we join you?" We have to keep up the military pressure, but we also have to provide a breathing space. If they see there is a possibility for negotiations, eighty percent will surrender. Otherwise they will continue to fight, and another million people could die.'[16]

As a recipe for seizing power in Kabul, NIFA's attitude was arguably as naive as Hezb's was ruthless. In the Durrani-dominated area of Qandahar, though, it might have succeeded. The mujahedin commanders around Qandahar, though theoretically affiliated to the Peshawar parties, held them in deep contempt (a sentiment returned with interest by many eastern Pashtuns, especially Ghilzais, who tend to view Qandahar as an Afghan version of Sodom and Gomorrah, rife with homosexuality, pederasty, drug addiction and

every other known vice). On visits to the area, I had discovered that even some Hezb commanders were royalists at
heart (Amanullah, you may recall, fled to Qandahar when
he was overthrown in 1929). In addition, links between the
city residents and the surrounding mujahedin were particularly close. One respected local commander, Haji Abdul
Latif – the Lion of Qandahar – was particularly outspoken.
'This rocketing on the city is killing small children, women
and other innocent people, all for the sake of killing a
few communists', he told *Panorama*. 'It's not achieving
anything. My mujahedin won't stand for it. They have
fathers and mothers and sisters living inside the city.'
Shortly afterwards, Haji Latif was poisoned by less reason-
able men.[17]

By the summer of 1988, local negotiations between the
resistance and figures in the regime were already underway
in the Qandahar area. A senior NIFA official told me in
confidence in September that the party had made contact
both with the Governor of the city and with senior army
officers in the local garrison. Earlier that year, a separate
deal had been reached with a key militia commander, Esmatullah Muslim Achakzai, an outrageous drunkard and wom-
aniser who had swapped sides once before in 1985 and now
controlled the road between Qandahar and the Pakistani
border on behalf of the regime. Esmatullah had agreed, my
NIFA source told me, 'to put all his forces under our
control in order to find some direct or indirect way for
Zahir Shah to come back'.[18] The purpose of the subsequent
negotiations with the Governor, the source continued, was
to effect a 'transfer of power without bloodshed'. If successful, the next step would almost certainly have been the
convocation of a Loya Jirga in Qandahar, at which Zahir
Shah would have been summoned home.[19]

Whether or not these contacts would have come to anything, NIFA officials were convinced that Gulbuddin and
his patrons in the ISI sabotaged their attempts to negotiate
a bloodless transfer of power in Qandahar. Gulbuddin

certainly knew of the plan, and in August 1988, without specifically mentioning NIFA, denounced it publicly as a Soviet-inspired plot.[20] General Zia, according to Pir Gailani, was right behind Gulbuddin. 'Pakistan wants a frontal attack, it doesn't want negotiations' he grumbled angrily. His lieutenants supplied the details. The deal NIFA had reached with Esmatullah Muslim, they said, was deliberately wrecked by the local ISI chief Colonel Faizan, who had supplied huge quantities of weapons to Esmatullah's tribal rivals, the Nurzai clan, and even sent Pakistani artillery units across the border to bombard his positions. A few months later, as Pir Gailani was preparing to begin negotiations with the Governor of Qandahar, Hekmatyar was hastily flown to the region (by the ISI, according to the rumours) and spent two weeks trying to bribe local commanders to launch an attack on the city. Today, Qandahar is still controlled by the regime.

In view of the bitter power-struggle already going on beneath the superficial 'unity' of the Peshawar alliance as Soviet troops began to withdraw, it's hardly surprising that the Peshawar politicians found it impossible to construct a coherent mujahedin government when they had all gone. There was a pressing need for such a government. The struggle was now between Afghans, and the resistance needed to prevent the Najibullah regime securing the recognition of the international community by default. With an 'alternative' government, preferably based inside Afghanistan, the mujahedin could lobby for the Afghan seat in international organisations such as the UN and the Islamic Conference Organisation; and if it could establish its claim to be the legitimate representative of the majority of Afghans, the mujahedin government could then demand control over the $1.6 billion of international aid being sought by the UN's 'Operation Salam' for post-war relief and reconstruction in Afghanistan.

Inside Afghanistan, the need for a credible mujahedin government was equally urgent. The provisional government, announced from Peshawar the previous year, had failed to win any credibility, even amongst the alliance's own commanders. It was becoming increasingly clear that Peshawar could no longer convincingly claim to represent the entire resistance. Since ending its war with Iraq, Iran had started to play a much more active role in Afghanistan, and was pressing the claim of its own tame 'eight-party alliance' to a quarter share in any future Afghan government. A few individual commanders, particularly Massoud, were demonstrably more powerful than some of the smaller parties either in Peshawar or Tehran, yet they had no political voice; and among field commanders generally, there was a growing disillusionment with the political machinations and interminable power-struggles of their nominal leaders in Peshawar. If the Kabul regime fell quickly, an authoritative mujahedin government would be needed to forestall a bloody struggle between different resistance factions for the spoils of war. If Najibullah managed to hang on, co-ordinated military and political action would be needed to bring the regime down. Already Pakistani officials were privately arguing that the main reason the regime's troops were not defecting was because they didn't have anything to defect *to*.

Accordingly, just five days before the end of the Soviet withdrawal, around 500 carefully selected Afghans gathered inside the Hajj complex at Islamabad airport to elect a mujahedin government. As originally envisaged, the shura, or consultative council, was to be representative of the entire resistance, bringing together mujahedin politicians from Peshawar and Tehran, field commanders, religious leaders, nationalist exiles from the West and refugee elders. In the event, though, it turned into a farce. The Peshawar parties packed the shura with their own delegates, many field commanders refused to attend and the Tehran politicians flew home early, complaining that they were not being offered due representation in the new government. After thirteen days of acrimonious public debate and behind-the-scenes deals, a vote was taken and a new interim government was elected. To the disgust of all, but the surprise of none, it was nothing but the old Peshawar alliance in a different guise. The seven Peshawar leaders took over all thirty-five ministries in the new government. As the BBC correspondent in Islamabad reported at the time, 'it's taken thirteen days for the shura merely to select the seven leaders they've already got.'[21]

The most damaging blow to the credibility of the Afghan Interim Government (AIG) was the fact that it was created in the Pakistani capital Islamabad, under the watchful eye and guiding hand of the ISI. In the circumstances, its campaign for international recognition was doomed from the start. To date, only a handful of Muslim governments, led by Saudi Arabia, have recognised the AIG as the legitimate government of Afghanistan. Even the Islamic Conference Organisation has not given it full recognition. Pakistan is taking its lead from Washington, which has played a damaging double hand by withholding formal recognition while channelling millions of dollars worth of military and 'humanitarian' aid through the appropriate AIG ministries. As a result, a handsome new mujahedin 'Defence Ministry' building is now under construction in Peshawar, but the minister in charge lacks any real authority to plan a proper 'defence' policy. Amongst Afghans themselves, even amongst officials of the seven Peshawar parties, the AIG's credibility is almost zero.

The only way the new government could hope to prove its legitimacy, wipe out the taint of foreign sponsorship, and secure the recognition and funds it craved, was to establish itself inside Afghanistan. At his inaugural press conference, the provisional mujahedin 'President' of Afghanistan, Professor Sibghatullah Mojadedi, declared it would do just that within a month.[22] The question was, where? Of the major cities, Qandahar was by far the most vulnerable. But it was too far away from Kabul for its loss to be a decisive strategic blow to the regime as well as a damaging psychological one; moreover, from the ISI's point of view, the local guerillas were too independent-minded and pro-royalist. Instead, the choice for a mujahedin capital fell on Afghanistan's third-largest city, a communist redoubt strategically located half-way between Kabul and Peshawar, where the majority of local guerillas were loyal to Yunis Khalis and other 'fundamentalists'. 'Operation Jalalabad', shelved the previous year after vociferous opposition from local commanders, was about to be resurrected.

According to one account, when the ISI outlined its plans for an attack on Jalalabad to the mujahedin on 2nd March 1989, it encountered considerable resistance. 'Why should we who have never lost a war take advice from people who have never won one?', one commander is reported to have demanded.[23] A month later, even the newly-appointed mujahedin 'chief of staff' General Yayha Nauroz, a former Afghan army officer, publicly pointed out the folly of attacking a city when the defenders outnumbered the attackers by an estimated ratio of three to one, the reverse of what conventional military wisdom demanded.[24]

It's hard to believe that the mujahedin were *quite* so reluctant to attack as they later made out; thousands of mujahedin poured to the war-front in whatever transport was available. Initially, morale was high. One journalist reported a ride he hitched with a guerilla officer who 'stuck a tape-recording of battle into his tape deck and bounced happily along to the bloodcurdling cacophony of automatic weapons fire, explosions and screams'.[25] Less well-heeled guerillas struggled for seats in battered civilian buses, their rocket-launchers competing for floor-space with the live chickens and vegetables being transported to market by their fellow passengers. There is no doubt, however, that the ISI approved the operation, drew up the original battle-plans and arranged the logistics, the intelligence and the communications. In an effort to spread the blame, the ISI Director-General, Hameed Gul, later claimed that the decision to attack was pushed through against his advice by Benazir Bhutto and her civilian colleagues; Ms Bhutto herself told confidants that Gul had pressed strongly for the assault, insisting that it would fall 'within days'.[26]

At first, all went well. On 7th March NIFA guerillas swarmed up the road from Pakistan to the outskirts of Jalalabad and captured the base of Samarkhel, twelve miles to the south-east. Formerly a major Soviet army camp, it had been expected to put up a fierce fight, but instead it collapsed within two hours. Several hundred Afghan troops surrendered, possibly according to an agreement reached beforehand with the local NIFA commander; the rest fled to the relative safety of the city. From Samarkhel, the mujahedin advanced a few miles up the road to the airport, where they ran into stiff resistance and dug themselves in. Over the next four months, despite chaotic human assaults and the expenditure of a vast amount of rocketry (Soviet military intelligence later estimated that the bombardment was heavier than at the seige of Stalingrad), they advanced little further. Then, in early July, when many mujahedin had returned to Peshawar to observe the holy fasting month of Ramadan, the regime's armoured columns swept out of the city and re-captured Samarkhel with minimal resistance. In the most prolonged, if not the bloodiest battle of the entire war, more than two thousand lives were lost on the side of the regime, the majority of them civilians. Estimates of mujahedin losses ranged anywhere between a few hundred and a few thousand.

The battle pitilessly exposed the weaknesses of the mujahedin as a conventional fighting force. The original ISI plan for a co-ordinated attack from three different directions never materialised, and the fighting was 'directed' by two separate shuras (councils) of commanders acting independently of each other. Even the easiest part – the blockade of the city – was made ineffective by poor coordination and party rivalries, particularly between the Hezb of Yunis Khalis and NIFA, both strong in the area. Each party took turns to guard the only road leading to Jalalabad from Kabul, and several large re-supply convoys managed to slip through the mountains into the city when the guard was being changed.

Mujahedin tactics were appalling. Timothy Weaver, a British journalist, described in graphic detail how a group of 500 guerillas posted near the airport started advancing in all directions, through a hail of fire, after hearing false rumours that a nearby government post had surrendered. Finally under cover, prayers were held; then Weaver 'watched incredulously as the mujahedin, having gained so much ground in their spontaneous assault, began to withdraw. Their ammunition spent, and with no conception of holding on to ground dearly won, they moved back to the rear. The next day they would have to do it all over again.'[27]

Armed with raw courage, mortars and multi-barrelled rocket-launchers, the mujahedin inflicted heavy damage on the city and the string of security posts around it, but they were still vulnerable to the superior hardware of the regime, particularly its airpower. For the first time, the regime found itself confronted with a concentrated enemy force on ground ideally suited for its superior conventional strength. Jalalabad lies towards one end of a broad plain, surrounded by minefields more than a mile wide, and protected on one side by a wide canal. The lack of cover made the regime's airpower particularly effective. Antonov-12 bombers flew high overhead, dropping cluster-bombs which fragmented on impact and seemed, in the words of one eyewitness, 'to leapfrog towards you'. The Afghan airforce flew with extreme bravery, making low-level bombing raids so daring that the mujahedin automatically assumed the pilots were Russians. Another fearsome weapon used with devastating psychological effect were the regime's newly-acquired long-range Scud-B missiles; fired from Kabul, the only warning of a Scud's arrival was the double-bang it made as it passed through the supersonic barrier just seconds before its 1,700-pound warhead exploded.

Although the Peshawar politicians and their ISI patrons must have taken into account the formidable firepower the regime had at its disposal, they seem to have under-estimated the resolve of regime troops to stand their ground. Up to 20,000 troops and militiamen assembled in and around Jalalabad, brought in from as far afield as Herat. The reinforcements, particularly when they were not Pashtuns, were unlikely to risk surrendering to unknown local guerillas. Even the troops stationed permanently in the city had relatively few contacts with nearby resistance groups, partly because the fiercely competitive nature of tribal politics in Nangrahar province had always made it an effective recruiting ground for pro-government militias. The heavy KHAD presence in Jalalabad lessened the likelihood of a popular uprising by citizens who, in any case, were too busy trying to save their lives. According to aid officials, fifty thousand people fled to Pakistan from Nangrahar during the first three months of the seige, and after less than two weeks of fighting, one hardline guerilla told a Western journalist that 'anyone who is still left must be communist supporters who deserve to die'.[28] Perhaps most significant of all, any government troops tempted to defect were deterred by the news that prisoners were being massacred by fundamentalist guerilla groups. At least seventy Afghan troops, mostly officers, were reportedly murdered by a fanatical Khalis commander after the fall of Samarkhel, an atrocity which the Minister for Reconstruction in the Kabul government later pointed to as the 'turning point' of the campaign.

The battle for Jalalabad was a watershed in the Kabul regime's struggle for survival. Until that point, even its supporters had been pessimistic about its fate. I still recall quizzing my government 'minder', just before setting off to interview Najibullah in March 1987, about what *he* would ask the party chief if given the chance. After much hesitation, he whispered his unmentionable fear: 'can we survive without Soviet troops?' The Afghan army's successful defence of the country's third-largest city, without Soviet help, against the most massive assault ever mounted by the mujahedin, must have done wonders for his morale.

Militarily, the regime had won itself a breathing space. In the summer of 1989, after months of static defence, its forces resumed active operations and gradually regained control of most of the road between Jalalabad and the Pakistani border. Another offensive against Khost was beaten off with heavy mujahedin casualties. In the autumn, Kabul pushed huge supply convoys through by land to Qandahar and Khost, for the first time since the Soviet withdrawal.

Politically, too, the regime has grown in confidence since Jalalabad. Faced with the threat of extinction, the factional rivalries within the PDPA have grown less intense. In April 1989, Babrak Karmal's brother, Mohammad Baryalai, was released from house-arrest and two months later he was appointed first deputy Prime Minister. Several Khalqi ministers who served under Hafizullah Amin have also been rehabilitated and re-instated in the government.

Regime spokesmen who pointed to these appointments as evidence of 'national reconciliation' in action convinced no-one. All they showed was that the PDPA was closing ranks. Nevertheless, Najibullah's appeals to his real opponents – the guerillas – to lay down their arms and share power continued unabated. The real split within the regime now, according to journalists who have spent time in Kabul recently, is not between Khalq and Parcham *per se*, but between those committed to the policy of national reconciliation and those favouring a less conciliatory line. Najibullah is generally counted among the 'doves', but his future stance will probably depend on whether the mujahedin can mount a more credible military or political challenge than they have so far. Five months after the Soviet withdrawal, a non-aligned diplomat based in Kabul told the visiting Western journalist Hamish Macdonald that 'when Diego Cordovez was here, representation of twenty to thirty percent was being talked about for the PDPA . . . Today they would laugh at twenty percent – though they would [still] concede that they cannot have lasting peace unless they share power.'[29] Since then, with the mujahedin gripped by military and political paralysis, the initiative has slipped further from their hands.

The battle for Jalalabad also strengthened the PDPA's outrageous claim to be the new champion of Afghan nationalism. After more than ten years of overt Soviet sponsorship and support, it's an uphill struggle; but many factors – including the widespread reporting of the ISI's influence in Peshawar, the regime's own propaganda that the battle was directed by Pakistani and US advisers, and the influx and growing influence of fanatical Wahhabi volunteers from the Gulf – have started to convince more and more Afghans that the Peshawar-based leaders are at least as much puppets of foreign masters as their PDPA rivals.

By contrast, the regime has gone to great lengths to eradicate signs of Russian influence. As soon as the withdrawal was complete, shops changed their names: overnight, 'Misha's Boutique' became 'Ittifaq Store', Afghans fluent in Russian suddenly found they had forgotten how to speak it, and the Soviet-made Volgas driven by KHAD agents were hastily 'converted' into Toyotas or other acceptable models.[30] Hamish Macdonald even found government officials starting to claim that Najibullah had single-handedly persuaded Moscow to withdraw its troops – a claim Moscow was willing to back up with documentary proof.[31] Meanwhile, the regime has relentlessly polished up its Islamic credentials. Ceasefires have been declared to coincide with holy days and Kabul's large Shia population has been permitted to hold traditional Moharram processions, despite the night-time curfew imposed on other citizens. Najibullah himself laces his perorations liberally with quotations and proverbs from the Quran, which he appears to have learnt off by heart.

In the past twenty years, there have been three coups in

240

Afghanistan; the fourth, invisible coup which Najibullah is trying to pull off is less dramatic, but far more surprising. In effect, he is trying to stand the Saur Revolution on its head. Instead of imposing the dictatorship of disgruntled lower-middle class activists on an entire nation, he is trying to forge an extraordinary coalition of forces: the Marxist left, secular nationalists and the educated middle classes, religious and ethnic minorities and – most amazingly of all – the traditional, tribal strata of society from which the *jehad* has always drawn its main strength and its legitimacy. Unlike his PDPA predecessors, Najibullah has a profound understanding of his countrymen. Through both words and action, he is now trying to draw them into collaboration with the regime by appealing to everything that matters most to them: their pockets, their pride and their traditions, their love of anarchy and above all their yearning for peace.

However tainted his background and intentions, Najibullah has learned to speak straight to the heart of ordinary Afghans. His simple yet powerful speeches, now shorn of revolutionary gobbledegook, appeal directly to their desire for an end to the senseless conflict. Mujahedin commanders are no longer 'counter-revolutionaries', they are 'patriots', whose rightful influence is being ignored by the corrupt and luxurious politicians in Peshawar. Najib's continual offers of negotiations, of free elections, of guaranteed neutrality, contrast sharply with the promise of bloody and indefinite warfare still being held out by the guerilla leadership in Peshawar.

If it was no more than rhetoric, the mujahedin would have no need to worry. But in order to consolidate his power at the centre, Najibullah is now delivering to Afghan warlords in the provinces exactly what they have always sought from Kabul: full local autonomy, with huge subsidies of money and weapons to go with it. Quite how far this process has gone is still unclear; in July 1989, the Soviet ambassador in Kabul, Yuli Vorontsov, claimed that local guerilla commanders in three-quarters of the country were engaged in truces and negotiations with the regime at different levels. It was, he said, a 'very Afghan process' which would take time but was likely to succeed.[32] Vorontsov's claim is impossible to verify. No sensible guerilla chieftain would openly announce he was negotiating with the regime for fear of being denounced as a traitor and attacked by his rivals. In at least one place, though, there has been no attempt to conceal the truth: in Qandahar, talks between local resistance leaders, tribal elders and the Governor have even been filmed by Western cameramen, and *Panorama*'s peripatetic crew shot some extraordinary footage of mujahedin, on a day's excursion to Qandahar, depositing their weapons, like coats at a cloakroom, at a militia checkpoint on the city outskirts.

No well-known commander has yet 'defected' to the regime, but it's noticeable that the powerful non-Pashtun commanders of the north, including Ahmed Shah Massoud and Ismael Khan of Herat, took little part in the fighting during 1989. Persistent rumours that Massoud has sold out to the regime are just Hezb propaganda. He is a nationalist rather than a local warlord, too committed to the establishment of an Islamic republic, and too powerful in his own area, to risk his position by recognising the authority of Kabul. Like other commanders, though, he's probably in indirect contact with the regime; as Massoud demonstrated in the Panjshir Valley in the mid-1980's, such talks can be used to tactical advantage, to gain time, military or material support, in order to continue the war. Massoud himself says that his failure to block food supplies coming down the Salang Highway to Kabul after the Soviet withdrawal was deliberate policy. 'We don't want ordinary people in Kabul to suffer from food shortages', he told *Panorama*. 'We won't cut food supplies until a properly planned, co-ordinated offensive is launched against Kabul.' According to his own account, the first time Massoud heard that a major offensive had been launched against Jalalabad was on the BBC Persian Service.[33]

More susceptible to the regime's offer of power-sharing are the smaller ethnic and religious minorities which have traditionally suffered at the hands of the Pashtun majority. In Baghlan province, where most of Afghanistan's small Ismaili minority live, the son of the community's religious leader has been appointed Governor. Now, claiming to control 13,000 militiamen, he runs the province as his personal fiefdom, in the old-style feudal tradition, and says he is entirely neutral between the regime and the mujahedin.[34]

The regime has also made repeated overtures to the Shia mujahedin groups controlling the Hazarajat. In talks with Tehran and its eight-party Afghan Shia alliance at the end of 1988, Yuli Vorontsov reportedly offered the Shias an autonomous state within Afghanistan in return for reconciliation with Kabul. They turned him down, but in April 1989, according to hostile mujahedin intelligence reports, the discussions were continued at secret talks in Kabul. So far these contacts have not borne fruit; my own occasional meetings with Shia leaders gave me the impression that most of them still supported a unitary Afghanistan, with constitutional guarantees for their religion and community. In any case, since the war began the Hazarajat has been enjoying *de facto* autonomy, and its inhabitants have prospered greatly. Should the war end, though, Afghanistan's Shias could hardly be blamed for being tempted by offers of complete autonomy; the alternative is a potentially totalitarian Sunni regime led by Peshawar leaders like Yunis Khalis, who by his own admission despises Shias as much as he does the communists.

Most unlikely of all, Najibullah is trying to co-opt the support, or at least the toleration, of traditional tribal elders. Exploiting the rivalries of the Pashtun tribes has always been a policy of PDPA regimes. The boozing, hash-smoking, pro-government militia forces found in some parts of the country are none other than tribal rivals of their local counterparts in the resistance. On the whole, though, previous regimes in Kabul have only managed to recruit weaker clans to its standard, or those engaged in especially bitter ethnic, religious or territorial disputes with their more powerful cousins. But now, the regime's policies are starting to make a deeper impact.

To some extent, it's a question of material incentives: huge quantities of cash and weapons – including tanks – are being supplied to tribal militias in exchange for only token allegiance to Kabul, or just a promise to keep mujahedin out of their territory. In some cases, however, individual clans and tribal elders have come to view the regime as actually preferable to the mujahedin. Among the new provincial governors appointed by Najibullah in May 1988 was Wakil Azam, a Shinwari tribal chieftain with considerable influence in half a dozen districts in Nangrahar province. For years, Wakil Azam had been an active member of Hezb-i-Islami, but eventually he became disillusioned with the growing influence of the mullahs. Falling out with Gulbuddin Hekmatyar, he held a jirga of Shinwari tribesmen at which he declared that 'if you don't accept tribal traditions, I will have to go to the other side and start my attempts from there'. Not long afterwards, possibly in fear of his life, he left Pakistan with sixty Shinwari families in tow, and was appointed Governor of Nangrahar. Those who stayed behind understood his action. 'People don't have the impression he went to surrender to the regime', my informant said. 'They feel that he will hand all power and authority back to the Shinwari tribes.'[35]

Najibullah still has a long way to go before he can be sure of cementing together the red, black and green coalition he is trying to build. Afghans are not fools, nor are they quick to forgive. Najibullah's communist beliefs and his long stewardship of KHAD make it highly unlikely that any regime which he himself heads will win widespread acceptance, however dilute the PDPA's dominant role becomes. In their increasingly confused state, though, many Afghans sympathetic to the resistance have begun to identify Najibullah as almost the last symbol of continuing communist domination in Kabul. If he and a few other prominent PDPA colleagues were eventually to step down, it's not impossible that a PDPA-led regime could consolidate its authority on a permanent basis.

How desirable that would be is a different question. In some ways, the policies which the regime has gradually adopted under Najibullah are well-suited to Afghanistan's long-term needs. If it is to become a coherent and stable nation, an accommodation based on equality and toleration needs to be reached between its constituent ethnic and religious communities. In particular, the Tajiks of the north-east and the Shias of the Hazarajat have won, through their armed struggle, the right to be treated, for the first time in the country's history, as first-class citizens. The two-hundred-year-old dominance of the Pashtuns is over. Moreover, the secular ideals favoured by the PDPA – particularly the emancipation of women – will continue to spread and undermine ancient Afghan prejudices. Afghanistan can no longer isolate itself from the twentieth century.

In practice, though, the survival of the regime in its present form could be a recipe for further disaster. In spite of the programme of national reconciliation, communists, or former communists, are still in control of all the main levers of central power. In the provinces, the bookshelves of local regime officials and KHAD officers still contain translations of the works of Stalin and Engels rather than the Quran. Whatever disguise their leaders have adopted, the Afghans who so readily embraced Marxism Khalqi-style are still committed ideologists, who harbour a deep-rooted disrespect for the tribal traditions and Islamic beliefs of their fellow-countrymen. After visiting the unabashedly feudal mini-state of Kayan, where the Ismailis have been given full autonomy, Hamish Macdonald reported that his accompanying Soviet and PDPA guides expressed 'unease when asked about the apparent return to the past, and make it clear they see it as a temporary measure'.[36] It is quite possible, as Pir Gailani predicted, that once the resistance has been neutralised by the deceptive policies of national reconciliation, Khalqi totalitarianism could gradually re-assert itself, sparking off a new cycle of repression and resistance.

The opposite scenario is perhaps even more dangerous. If central authority cannot be restored, and if the Kabul regime is forced to devolve power piecemeal to those warlords and petty chieftains willing to collaborate with it, Afghanistan could disintegrate as hopelessly as Lebanon has done. Weak, locally autonomous units would be even more susceptible to the influence and interference of interested foreign powers like Iran, Pakistan, Saudi Arabia and India. The people of Afghanistan deserve better than to have their country turned from a theatre of superpower confrontation into a playground for regional ambitions. Nor can the rest of us afford to shrug off their troubles as a little local difficulty. If Gorbachev's gamble should fail and the Soviet empire begins to come apart at the seams, anarchy in Afghanistan would add considerably to the dangers the world would face.

Despite the West's fast-changing attitude towards the Afghan resistance since the Soviet withdrawal, the mujahedin represent the majority of the Afghan people. For the past ten years, the majority of Afghans have *been*, in the broadest sense, mujahedin. What has let them down is their bankrupt political leadership. The 'moderate' leaders of the resistance have been too short-sighted, too weak, sometimes even too cowardly, to make a real stand for what they believe in. Leaders like Sibghatullah Mojadedi and even Burhanuddin Rabbani, who profess to believe in a tolerant, pluralistic Islamic state, have protested in public or worried in private but have always stayed on the bandwagon. For more than a decade, sponsored and supported by outside powers, a small minority of extremists on both sides have written and directed the tragedy of Afghanistan.

There can be no easy solution. A whole generation of young Afghans has been radicalised by the war. Over a million young refugees have been born outside their homeland. Brought up in claustrophobic camps on the heat-baked plains of Pakistan and Iran, they've been uprooted from their culture and traditions and deprived of the liberty and sense of pride which has always marked out the Afghan people, however poor, as somehow special. In many Afghans, the *jehad* has instilled a new spirituality, a new faith in Islam. But where it has been turned into narrow channels, it has also bred hatred and xenophobia, not only against foreigners, but against other Afghans. The chants of 'death to Russia', 'death to America', which youngsters are taught to chant in Gulbuddin Hekmatyar's training camps inside Afghanistan, could easily turn in to chants of 'death to Massoud' or 'death to Zahir Shah'. As Gulbuddin told me during one of our increasingly tense meetings, 'in the liberated areas, children are being trained in a system totally against the Soviets and their agents. They will be much harsher mujahedin in the next generation.'[37]

It's too simple, though, to view Gulbuddin Hekmatyar as a bogeyman whose disappearance would bring instant peace and harmony. His ambitions and his ruthlessness are all his own, but he represents a significant new trend in Afghan society. The tensions between Islam and Western secular materialism which produced both the communist and Islamic radical movements in the 1960's have not been resolved. In their search for a modern Islamic identity, a sizeable number of educated young Afghans have gravitated to Hezb over the past ten years, and as the modern world continues inexorably to undermine Afghanistan's old ideas and beliefs, the search will intensify. An end to the war and an end to outside interference is the best hope for ensuring that the answers found are less fanatical and intolerant than the philosophy promoted and practised by Hezb.

Gulbuddin is significant in another way too. Like Ahmed Shah Massoud, like Sibghatullah Mojadedi, like Dr Najibullah, he is also, in his way, an Afghan nationalist – one who thinks in terms of the entire country rather than his own particular community. The war against the Soviet Union has created many more such nationalists, most of whom are becoming increasingly depressed by the grave danger their country is facing after its heroic victory against Soviet aggression and occupation. Such men and women are the best hope for Afghanistan's future, and to them I dedicate an old Dari couplet sent to me by an Afghan exile who has been forced to flee from both Kabul and Peshawar during the course of the war. Its (probably quite inadequate) translation reads:

> In hopelessness, hope abounds
> As a dark night ends with a bright dawn.

EPILOGUE:

The Headless Goat

The United States embassy in Islamabad, the nerve centre of American influence in Pakistan and Afghanistan, is a sprawling, self-contained complex, surrounded by huge walls and complete with shops, restaurants, a swimming pool, a full-sized cinema, a communications centre and much else hidden to the eye of the casual visitor. At one end is the ambassador's spacious open-plan residence, and in April 1988, selected Western journalists gathered there for an informal briefing by the incumbent, Arnie Raphel, who was to die four months later alongside Zia ul Haq and his top generals in an unexplained air-crash.

The final round of Geneva talks had already begun, and we were anxious to know how the ambassador envisaged a post-Soviet Afghanistan. Mr Raphel, a cultivated and intelligent State Department official with years of experience in Afghan affairs, did not need to ponder the question. It would, he speculated, either be run by tribal maliks, mullahs and traditional religious leaders – a variation on the old ruling establishment – or it would become an orthodox Islamic state controlled by Wahhabi-style fundamentalists. In either case, he said, 'the chances of a progressive, secular state in Afghanistan are negligible'. As for the dangers of fragmentation, Mr Raphel admitted it was likely, but, he said, 'eventually an Abdur Rahman Khan will be found who can weld the country together again'.[1]

Any would-be twentieth-century version of the 'Iron Amir', though, faces quite different conditions. Abdur Rahman ruled ruthlessly, stifling dissent, conquering,

249

converting and enslaving religious and ethnic minorities and creating a nation-state based on Pashtun dominance. Today, that would guarantee a state of permanent civil war. Equally important, having extricated itself from Afghanistan after the second Anglo-Afghan war, Britain left Abdur Rahman largely to his own devices to re-establish order in his own way. Today's great powers, by contrast, are still deeply involved in Afghanistan's internal affairs.

In spite of the Geneva accords, both sides in the Afghan civil war are still receiving vast quantities of lethal weaponry from their respective patrons. According to US intelligence, Moscow's military aid to the Najibullah regime since its withdrawal has totalled between $200 and $300 million each month.[2] In May 1989 alone, six hundred Soviet cargo planes flew into Kabul with hundreds of tons of weapons and ammunition; Moscow has also provided the regime with 500 Scud-B missiles, 120 new tanks, and advanced ground-attack fighters. The US is less prompt to disclose details of its own aid to the mujahedin, but some estimates put it at around $500 million during 1989, with Saudi Arabia probably pumping in roughly the same amount.[3] All in all, during 1989, probably more than $200 dollars-worth of lethal 'aid' was donated by outsiders for every Afghan man, woman and child.

In strategic terms, the result is a military stalemate, but in human terms the toll has been appalling. According to figures published by the regime, five thousand civilians were killed or wounded and nearly two thousand government troops died in the first five months after the Soviet withdrawal.[4] Mujahedin casualties were also heavy. Letters sent to the BBC Pashto Service from listeners in both Kabul and Peshawar, indicate that they would prefer the money to be spent on something else. The feeling of the silent majority is best summed up by a listener in one of the refugee camps in Pakistan's North West Frontier Province, who requested the BBC to:

Please convey my message to George Bush, tell him from my side that the Afghan people don't need weapons anymore. What they now desperately need is peace and tranquillity.[5]

The continuing supply of weapons to both sides in the conflict is the result of the 'positive symmetry' agreement secretly struck between Moscow and Washington just before the Geneva accords were signed. Last-minute attempts to negotiate a 'negative symmetry' deal, whereby both superpowers would discontinue military aid, were rejected out of hand by Moscow at that time. Since the end of 1988, though, the positions have been reversed. The USSR has publicly announced its willingness to implement 'negative symmetry', while the US has declined to discuss the issue, arguing that Moscow's massive re-supply operation has unfairly tilted the military balance in Kabul's favour.

Since the Soviet withdrawal, the Bush administration has followed a short-sighted policy which has ensured that the fighting continues without significantly improving the mujahedin's prospects of military or political victory. The number of Congressional critics urging a halt in military supplies to the resistance has grown, and in July 1989, after bitter complaints from Peshawar leaders (including the AIG Defence Minister) that they were being starved of weapons and ammunition, the US special envoy to the mujahedin admitted that there had been what he called a 'downswing' in supplies.[6] A few days later, though, the *Washington Post* reported that the Administration had decided to increase the flow and quality of arms to the mujahedin, and another report from Washington quoted a senior US official as saying 'we are determined to stay the course with the mujahedin and hang tough with the Soviets. The mujahedin deserve one more fighting season which will decide the outcome of the war in their favour.'[7]

As Afghans continue to die, international efforts to

promote a political settlement have made little progress. Various ideas have been put forward (including Kabul's own proposals for an international conference) and a host of would-be peace-makers from Yassir Arafat to Lord Bethell have offered their services as mediators. The UN Secretary-General's annual report for 1989, though, contained barely-concealed signs of frustration with the failure of the 'international community' to co-operate in promoting a political settlement. Perez de Cuellar didn't specifically mention the United States, but US officials have made it abundantly clear that they do not consider it either 'appropriate or possible for the UN to try and force a settlement at this time'.[8] So far, all Washington's hopes for peace have been pinned on 'broadening the base' of the Afghan Interim Government in Peshawar.

Under its new Prime Minister, Benazir Bhutto, Pakistan's position has shifted, but not radically. In May 1989, she sacked her hardline ISI chief Hameed Gul, a Zia appointee and the man who advised her that Jalalabad would fall 'within days'. During a visit to Britain in July, she said she believed that there were 'good Muslims' within the PDPA (not including Najibullah) with whom a settlement could be negotiated.[9] On the whole, though, Pakistan's popularly-elected government has followed much the same Afghan policy as did General Zia. Ms Bhutto's political position is too precarious for her to risk alienating Washington or jeopardise her already suspect domestic credentials as an 'Islamic' leader. Her private inclinations are certainly not in favour of a fundamentalist-led regime in Kabul, but she has little innate sympathy with the Afghan moderates either. I was present during a tense but amusing exchange between Ms Bhutto and Pir Gailani's eldest son at a party in Islamabad, about a year before she became Prime Minister; she was bickering with her fellow opposition allies in the Movement for the Restoration of Democracy. 'When are you going to sink your differences and get united?' she asked him abruptly, to which his instant reply, accompanied by a charming smile, was 'we'll unite as soon as you do'.

Other players in the 'Great Game', meanwhile, are fishing with growing zest in the muddy Afghan waters. Iran's historic interests in Afghanistan, neglected during its exhausting war with Iraq, have been re-activated with a vengeance; Tehran's relations with Kabul improved noticeably during 1989 as it sought to increase its influence through its tame eight-party Afghan Shia alliance. The extent of Iran's military support to fighting groups inside Afghanistan is unknown, but it is unlikely to be diminishing. The intense rivalry between Iran and Saudi Arabia for leadership of the Islamic world is now being played out in the mountains of Afghanistan. Riyadh has put its full weight behind the AIG in Peshawar; the wealthy Wahhabi movement, also Saudi-based, has consolidated its position in the Kunar valley (where two Wahhabi-influenced 'Islamic republics' have been set up) and is now sending growing numbers of wealthy volunteers to buy Afghan converts to its puritanical and intolerant version of Islam.

The longer outside powers continue to fuel the multi-faceted civil war in Afghanistan, the greater the danger of permanent 'lebanonisation'. Political authority there is now so fragmented that no foreign power, perhaps not even the international community acting in concert, can hope to impose a political settlement that would endure. Even the UN's cautious attempts to stimulate a process of consultation between different Afghan factions are, I believe, unlikely to succeed. In a country as polarised and radicalised as today's Afghanistan, any process which bears the hallmarks of foreign involvement is automatically doomed to failure.

Whole-hearted international co-operation, however, can make a difference. The most urgent need is for Washington and Moscow to negotiate a new agreement on 'negative symmetry' under which military aid to both sides would be halted. That is the only way in which the two countries which have done most to fuel and stoke the civil war, can help create conditions in which the people of Afghanistan would have a better chance of working out their own destiny.

For most of the past ten years, US policy towards Afghanistan has been based on the presumption that the mujahedin *could not* force the Soviet army out. Bankrolling the Peshawar leaders was the easiest, if not the most effective way of killing Soviet troops. But it is not the best way for the US to guarantee friendship with, and future influence in, a free, independent Afghanistan. Over the past year, Washington has gradually started to wake up to the fact that its long-term interests are not served by favouring the 'fundamentalist' factions in the resistance; it now needs to recognise that its patronage of the bankrupt mujahedin leadership in Peshawar as a whole is untenable, and probably in the end counter-productive.

Washington's main argument against a 'negative symmetry' agreement (and possibly Moscow's main hope) is that it would ensure the PDPA's 'victory'. That reasoning, I believe, is spurious. The United States was not responsible for the popular revolt against the Khalqi revolution in 1978, or for the spontaneous opposition to the Soviet occupation: it was the Afghan people, armed with rusty swords and Lee Enfield rifles, who rose up against overwhelming odds. Commanders like Massoud have got on very well without much help from the US or Pakistan. Why, then, does Washington now believe that only its military support stands between Afghanistan and communist domination? In a world where the Soviet Union has renounced its self-appointed right to intervene in the affairs of even its crucial East European allies, the United States should allow the Afghan people to work out their own destiny without fear that Afghanistan is the exception to Mr Gorbachev's 'Sinatra doctrine'.

In 1972, just seven years before the Soviet invasion, the US Department concluded in its annual policy review

254

report that 'Afghanistan has a natural political, economic, commercial and cultural relationship with Russia. Any effort on the part of other nations to reduce Soviet-Afghan relations below this natural level would be contrary to the interests of both and *the resulting situation could not persist* [my italics].'[10] If it was true in 1972, it remains true today. Washington cannot hope to impose and sustain its favourite Afghans in power in Kabul. It is too far away, and its congressmen are too fickle. But the US can protect its interests by doing the Afghan people a final favour and negotiating an end to the flow of superpower weaponry which is now killing only Afghans.

With no outside support to sustain them, it is possible that both the present Kabul regime and the Peshawar alliance would eventually wither away. Few Afghans would grieve. Neither represents the majority of the Afghan people, and it may be that neither will be able to form the nucleus of the loose broad-based government which is the only solution to the country's savage conflict. Afghanistan's revolution is still unfinished, and as it completes the transition to some uniquely Afghan version of an Islamic republic, more blood is certain to be spilled. It does not need, though, to be spilled with the 1700-pound Scud-B warheads, the multi-barrelled rocket-launchers, the cluster bombs and the 120mm mortars now being supplied by the superpowers.

Afghanistan's national game, buzkashi, is a wild kind of rugby played on horseback, with the headless carcase of a goat or calf used as the ball. It is an exhilarating sport which was borrowed enthusiastically from the Mongols, and is now played all over Afghanistan as well as by the refugees in Pakistan. To the untutored eye, buzkashi seems to be a frantic, anarchic mêlée in which every man is out for himself and his own glory. As such, it has lately become a favourite metaphor both for the Afghan character and for the present power-struggle inside Afghanistan.

In reality, though, buzkashi does have rules, not least of

which is that there are two teams of roughly equal size, whose players are all invited to participate. After ten years in which Afghanistan itself has become the headless goat, torn and ripped apart by contending foreign powers, it is time for the Afghans to be left to play out their own power-struggle and their own national destiny according to their own rules.

London, 14th November 1989.

Notes

ONE: Birth of a Nation

1. Juvaini, quoted in Nancy Hatch Dupree, *An Historical Guide to Afghanistan*, Afghan Tourist Organisation, Kabul, 1971. p. 35.
2. Quoted in P. Macrory, *Signal Catastrophe*, London, 1966.
3. Soviet Prime Minister Nikolai Rhzykov told the Congress of People's Deputies in June 1989 that the USSR spent $7.8 billion a year on the war, approximately double the amount estimated by US intelligence.
4. Quoted by David Hirst, the *Guardian*, 7th March 1989.
5. Bruce Wannell, unpublished manuscript made available to the author.
6. Quoted in W. K. Fraser-Tytler, *Afghanistan*, Oxford University Press, London and New York, 1950, p. 51.
7. Quoted in Andre Singer, *Lords of the Khyber*, Faber and Faber, London, 1984, p. 27.
8. Quoted in Singer, op. cit., p. 38.
9. Quoted in Anthony Hyman, *Afghanistan under Soviet Domination*, Macmillan Press, London, 2nd edition 1984, p. 5.
10. *Oxford History of India*, edited by Percival Spear, Oxford University Press, Delhi, 1958, pp. 601–2.
11. Quoted in Louis Dupree, *Afghanistan*, Princeton University Press, 3rd edition 1980, pp. 400–1.
12. Quoted in W. K. Fraser-Tytler, op. cit., p. 153.
13. Quoted in John Griffiths, *Afghanistan, Key to a Continent*, Andre Deutsch, London, 1981, p. 36.
14. Quoted in Nancy Hatch Dupree, op. cit. p. 56.
15. Quoted in *Afghanistan, The Great Game Revisited*, edited by

Rosanne Klass, Freedom House, New York, 1987, pp. 2–3.
16. See for instance Yossef Bodansky in Klass, op. cit., pp. 230–31.

TWO: A Clutch of Kings:
from Amanullah to Daoud

1. W. K. Fraser-Tytler, *Afghanistan*, Oxford University Press, London and New York, 1950, p. 200.
2. Quoted by Andro Linklater, in the *Spectator*, 25 February 1989.
3. W. K. Fraser-Tytler, op. cit., p. 210.
4. Quoted by Andro Linklater, the *Spectator*, 25 February 1989.
5. The *Independent*, 15 February 1989.
6. Conversation with S. K. Singh, former Indian ambassador to Pakistan.

THREE: Embracing the Bear:
Foreign Policy 1919–1973

1. Raja Anwar, *The Tragedy of Afghanistan*, Verso, London and New York, 1988, p. 27.
2. The phrase was borrowed by the resistance from Babrak Karmal, the man installed in power by Soviet tanks in December 1979. Referring to Daoud, Karmal once said that 'the power socialism has gained forces many princes to join this movement. They are the red princes.'
3. D. Gibbs, 'Does the USSR have a Grand Strategy?' *Journal of Peace Studies*, 1987, p. 368.
4. Quoted in Henry S. Bradsher, *Afghanistan and the Soviet Union*, Duke University Press, 1984, p. 23.
5. Henry S. Bradsher, op. cit., p. 30.
6. Nikita Krushchev, *Krushchev Remembers*, Boston, 1971, p. 560.
7. Quoted in Steven R. Galster, 'Rivalry and Reconciliation in Afghanistan', *Third World Quarterly*, October 1988.
8. Quoted in Galster, op. cit.

9. Louis Dupree, *Afghanistan*, Princeton University Press, 3rd edition 1980, pp. 523–4.

FOUR: The Dangerous Decade:
Islam, Marxism and the Democratic Experiment
1963–1973

1. Louis Dupree, *Afghanistan*, Princeton University Press, 3rd edition 1980. pp. 590–91.
2. Bruce Wannell, unpublished manuscript.
3. S. B. Majrooh, *The Sovietisation of Afghanistan*, Afghan Jehad Works, Peshawar, 1986, pp. 129–30.
4. S. B. Majrooh, op. cit., p. 133–34.
5. James Rupert, *Washington Post*, 25 June 1986.
6. Quoted in Henry S. Bradsher, *Afghanistan and the Soviet Union*, Duke University Press, 1984, p. 41.
7. Quoted in Henry S. Bradsher, op. cit., p. 44.
8. As told by Mrs Taraki to Raja Anwar, see Raja Anwar, *The Tragedy of Afghanistan*, Verso, London and New York, 1988, p. 41.
9. Conversation in March 1987 with Shafika Razminda, vice-chairwoman of the All-Afghanistan Womens' Council.

FIVE: Revolution in Two Acts:
Daoud's Republic and the Communist Coup
1973–1978

1. Five months after defecting to Britain, in June 1982, from his post in the USSR's Tehran embassy, Kuzichkin gave a wide-ranging interview to *Time* magazine in which he alleged among other things that Babrak Karmal was a KGB agent of long standing.
2. Quoted in R. Gartfhoff, *Détente and Confrontation: American-Soviet Relations from Nixon to Reagan*, Brookings, Washington DC, 1985, p. 938.
3. Conversation with General Nasirullah Babar, former Governor of the North West Frontier Province, October 1986.
4. Taraki's biography, published by the armed force's Political

Department, was reproduced in *The Democratic Republic of Afghanistan Annual*, Kabul, 1979.

5. Anthony Arnold, *Afghanistan's Two-Party Communism*, Hoover Press, 1983, pp. 48–55.
6. Most of the details of this account of Daoud's death are drawn from Raja Anwar, *The Tragedy of Afghanistan*, Verso, London and New York, 1988, p. 102.
7. Quoted in Henry S. Bradsher, *Afghanistan and the Soviet Union*, Duke University Press, 1984, p. 87.
8. Raja Anwar, op. cit., p. 123.
9. Quoted in Raja Anwar, op. cit., p. 110.
10. John Fullerton, *The Soviet Occupation of Afghanistan*, Far Eastern Economic Review Ltd, Hong Kong, 1983, p. 32.
11. Quoted by Victoria Schofield, *Every Rock, Every Tree*, Century, London, 1987, p. 281.
12. Amnesty International report, September 1979.
13. The French scholar Olivier Roy makes a strong case for this argument in chapter 5 of his *Islam and Resistance in Afghanistan*, Cambridge University Press, 1986.
14. Story recounted to the author by M. Ishaq Negargar, former associate professor at Kabul University, now in exile in England.

SIX: Prelude to Invasion:
Hafizullah Amin and his Downfall

1. US diplomats in Kabul were well aware of Moscow's attitude, as demonstrated by secret US cables to the State Department which became available in 1985. See Claudia Wright, 'What They Were Really Up To', *New Statesman*, 12th September 1985.
2. *The Economist*, 23rd June 1979.
3. Raja Anwar, *The Tragedy of Afghanistan*, Verso, London and New York, 1988, p. 165.
4. As reported by Vladimir Kuzichkin, *Time* magazine, November 1982.
5. See Claudia Wright, op. cit., and Steven R. Galster in *Third World Quarterly* Vol. 10 No. 4, October 1988.
6. *New York Times*, 'Did Moscow fear an Afghan Tito?', 13th January 1980.

7. Claudia Wright, op. cit.
8. *Indian Express*, Delhi, 13th February 1980.
9. *International Herald Tribune*, October 1989.
10. State Department memorandum, quoted in Steven R. Galster, op. cit.
11. State Department cable, quoted in Galster, op. cit.
12. See, for instance, Geoffrey Stern, 'The Soviet Union, Afghanistan and East-West Relations', in *Millenium: Journal of International Studies*, Autumn 1980, pp. 135–46.
13. Quoted in Henry S. Bradsher, *Afghanistan and the Soviet Union*, Duke University Press, 1984, p. 155.
14. *International Herald Tribune*, 20th March 1989.
15. Yuri Gankovsky, chief researcher of the Institute of Oriental Studies, in an interview with *Izvestia*, 4th May 1989.
16. As told by Mrs Taraki to Raja Anwar in *The Tragedy of Afghanistan*, Verso, London and New York, 1988, pp. 187–89. A different version of the poisoning story is told by John Barron in *KGB Today*, Hodder & Stoughton, London, 1986. Barron claims that the KGB assassin attached to Amin's kitchen staff tried to poison Amin's fruit-juice on several occasions, but failed because Amin was in the habit of filling his glass from different containers. He also claims that Amin was discovered with a 'lovely female companion' when the KGB assassination squad stormed the palace. An Afghan source, Ishaq Negargar, was told while in jail by Amin's Cabinet ministers that Mrs Amin and her children were not in the presidential palace on the day of Amin's death at all, and speculates that she may have concocted the poisoning story she told to Raja Anwar in order to conceal her husband's infidelity.
17. Tass, 27 December 1979, quoted in Henry S. Bradsher, op. cit. p. 180.

SEVEN: The Bearded Warriors:
Resistance Inside Afghanistan 1978–1988

1. Sir Olaf Caroe, *The Pathans*, Oxford University Press, Karachi, 4th impression, 1985, p. 526.
2. Foreword to Sandy Gall, *Afghanistan: Travels with the Mujahedin*, Hodder and Stoughton, 1985, p. xiii.

3. For a case study of the reactions of a particular Uzbek community to the Saur Revolution and the Soviet invasion, see Audrey Shalinsky, 'Ethnic Reactions to the Current Regime in Afghanistan', *Central Asian Survey*, Vol. 3 No. 4, 1984.
4. Bruce Wannell, unpublished manuscript.
5. Frederik Barth, 'Cultural Wellsprings of Resistance in Afghanistan' in *Afghanistan: The Great Game Revisited* edited by Rosanne Klass, Freedom House, New York, 1987, p. 198.
6. Ibid.
7. Story told first hand to Ishaq Negargar.
8. Shalinksy, op. cit., p. 53.
9. Bruce Wannell, unpublished manuscript.
10. *The Times*, 12th December 1984.
11. Bruce Wannell, unpublished manuscript.
12. Overheard in Pul-e-Charkhi jail by Ishaq Negargar.

EIGHT: The Bearded Politicians:
the Resistance in Exile 1975–1989

1. Press conference in Islamabad, August 1988.
2. Author's conversation in January 1988 with General Fazle Haq (Retd.), military governor of the North West Frontier Province in the early 1980's.
3. Conversation with the author in Peshawar, January 1988.
4. Conversation with the author in Peshawar, March 1988.

NINE: Uncle Sam and the Grinning General:
US and Pakistani Involvement in the Resistance

1. Quoted in Mohammad Asghar Khan, *Generals in Politics*, Vikas Publishing House, New Delhi, 1983, p. 180.
2. Quoted in Galster, 'Rivalry and Reconciliation in Afghanistan', *Third World Quarterly*, October 1988.
3. Quoted in Henry S. Bradsher, *Afghanistan and the Soviet Union*, Duke University Press, 1984.
4. Z. Brzezinski, *Power and Principles: Memoirs of the National Security Adviser, 1977–1981*, Farrar-Straus-Giroux, New York, 1983, p. 427.

5. Steven R. Galster, 'Destabilising Afghanistan', *Covert Action* No. 30, Summer 1988, p. 53.
6. Ibid.
7. *Washington Post*, 23rd and 24th September 1981.
8. Selig Harrison, 'The Afghan Arms Alliance' in *South*, March 1985.
9. *Wall Street Journal*, 16th February 1988.
10. *Philadelphia Enquirer*, 28th February 1988.
11. Ibid.
12. Ibid.
13. Olivier Roy, *Islam and Resistance in Afghanistan*, Cambridge University Press, 1986, p. 122.
14. *New York Times*, 28th November 1984.
15. *Philadelphia Enquirer*, 28th February 1988.
16. Quoted by Bob Woodward and Charles Babcock, *Washington Post*, 13th January 1985.
17. 'The Missing Millions', *Far Eastern Economic Review*, 5th March 1987.
18. *Washington Post*, 13th January 1985.
19. Steven R. Galster, 'Destabilising Afghanistan', op. cit., p. 58.
20. *Philadelphia Enquirer*, 1 March 1988. See also *Washington Post*, 13th January 1985.
21. Press briefing in Islamabad, 12th April 1988.
22. Conversation with the author in Peshawar, March 1988.
23. Conversation with the author in Islamabad, May 1988.
24. Sandy Gall, *Afghanistan: Travels with the Mujahedin*, Hodder and Stoughton, 1985, p. 155.
26. Because of the atmosphere of fear and intimidation in Peshawar, this source, like many others, asked to remain anonymous.
27. Conversation with the author in Peshawar, October 1987.
28. Conversation with the author in Peshawar, May 1988.

TWELVE: The Puppet Regime:
War and National Reconciliation 1979–1988

1. Anthony Hyman, *Afghanistan Under Soviet Domination 1964–83*, Macmillan, London, 1984, p. 194.

2. 'Afghanistan, The Struggle in its 5th Year', US Information Agency, June 1984, p. 16.
3. Ibid.
4. Afghanistan Report, Foreign and Commonwealth Office, March 1983.
5. Arthur Bonner, *New York Times*, 1st November 1985.
6. Johnathan Steele in the *Guardian*, 11th November 1981.
7. Budapest radio, 11th December 1980, quoted in Henry S. Bradsher, *Afghanistan and the Soviet Union*, Duke University Press, 1984, p. 232.
8. Interview with Patricia Sethi in *Newsweek*, 11th June 1984.
9. DRA White Book, cited in Bradsher, op. cit., p. 232.
10. Anthony Hyman, op. cit., appendix C.
11. Quoted in Raja Anwar, *The Tragedy of Afghanistan*, Verso, London and New York, 1988, p. 210.
12. *Guardian*, 16th February 1984.
13. Faiz Khairzada, 'An Afghan looks at his homeland', US Information Agency pamphlet, June 1984.
14. Rasul Amin, 'The Sovietisation of Afghanistan', in *Afghanistan, The Great Game Revisited*. p. 324.
15. Edward Girardet in the *Christian Science Monitor*, 2nd July 1983.
16. 'Afghanistan, Six Years of Occupation', US Department of State Bureau of Public Affairs, December 1985, p. 10.
17. *Guardian*, 'Why the War must go on', 19th March 1986.
18. *Financial Times*, 5th January 1985.
19. Foreign Affairs Bulletin, No. 7, Afghan Government Publications, Kabul, 1986; quoted by Raja Anwar, op. cit., p. 247.
20. 'Afghanistan: Taking the Path of Reconciliation', Government Committee of Press and Publication, Kabul, 1988, p. 49.
21. 'Afghanistan: Soviet Occupation and Withdrawal', US Department of State Bureau of Public Affairs, December 1988.

THIRTEEN: The Man from the UN:
Diego Cordovez and the Peace Talks 1982–1988

1. Foreign and Commonwealth Office, Background Briefing, May 1988.
2. Ibid.
3. Press conference in Islamabad, 17th February 1988.
4. 'Agreement between Afghanistan and Pakistan on the Principles of Mutual Relations, in particular on Non-Interference and Non-Intervention', Article 2, subclause 12. (Annexure to FCO Background Briefing, May 1988.)
5. L. I. Brezhnev, Report of the Central Committee of the CPSU to the XXVI Congress, Novosti Press Agency Publishing House, Moscow, 1981, p. 18.
6. Quoted in Selig S. Harrison, 'Inside the Afghan Talks', Foreign Policy #72, Fall 1988, p. 42. Harrison held forty-one discussions with Diego Cordovez from 1982 to 1988, and has provided the most detailed published account of the Geneva talks.
7. *International Herald Tribune*, 10 January 1984.
8. Selig S. Harrison, 'US Fighting to the last Afghan', *Washington Post*, 15th January 1984.
9. Quoted by Malheea Lodhi, 'What Happened at Geneva III', South Syndication Service, September 1984.
10. 'Afghanistan: 7 Years of Occupation', US State Department Bureau of Public Affairs, December 1986.
11. *Washington Post*, 17th April 1988.
12. *Guardian*, 28th November 1987.
13. Conversation with the author in Peshawar, 9th January 1988.
14. US State Department Annual Report on Afghanistan, December 1987.
15. *Guardian*, 2nd February 1988.
16. Conversation with the author in Islamabad, February 1988.
17. *Guardian*, 16th July 1987.
18. Selig Harrison, Foreign Policy #72, p. 57.
19. See William Safire, 'Afghanistan: how a sellout was foiled', *New York Times*, 26th March 1988.
20. Conversation with the author during his brief spell out of office. Yaqub Khan was re-instated as Foreign Minister after General Zia sacked the civilian government at the end of

May 1988, and has retained the post in Benazir Bhutto's administration.

FOURTEEN: The Struggle for Kabul: Soviet Withdrawal and its Aftermath

1. *Sunday Times*, 5th February 1989.
2. The *Daily Telegraph*, 27th February 1989.
3. 'Afghanistan: Soviet Occupation and Withdrawal', US Department of State Bureau of Public Affairs, December 1988, p. 1.
4. David Ottaway in the *International Herald Tribune*, 28th March 1988. The supply of Stingers was later resumed by the US administration.
5. Conversation with the author in Islamabad, 26th May 1988.
6. Yossef Bodansky, 'Soviet Military Operations in Afghanistan', in *Afghanistan: The Great Game Revisited*, edited by Rosanne Klass, Freedom House, New York, 1987, pp. 271–72.
7. Mark Urban, 'Afghanistan Reassessed' in *Janes Defence Weekly*, 27th May 1989.
8. *AFGHANews* Vol. 5 No. 5, 1st March 1989 (a publication of Jamiat-i-Islami from Peshawar).
9. Conversation with Mohammad Es Haq of Jamiat in Peshawar, 28th May 1988.
10. *Janes Defence Weekly*, 27th May 1989.
11. BBC World Service news story, 19th March 1989.
12. Conversation in Peshawar, 27th May 1988.
13. Conversations in Islamabad and Peshawar, April–May 1988.
14. Conversation with the author, 27th May 1988.
15. *Panorama*, 'Afghanistan: The Squandered Victory', broadcast on BBC1 on 2nd October 1989. Two film crews spent seven months in Afghanistan to make this programme.
16. Conversation with the author in Peshawar, August 1988.
17. *Panorama*, 2nd October 1989.
18. These remarks, like a number of others I have quoted, were made to me 'off the record' during my stay in Pakistan. I have chosen to breach the journalistic code of confidentiality in an attempt to chart as accurate a course as possible through the thick tangle of lies and deliberate deceptions

woven by all parties to the Afghan conflict. (Pakistani leaders and officials, for instance, denied unequivocally, throughout the course of the war, that they were involved in helping the mujahedin.) However, where I feel the source could be in danger, I have protected his identity.

19. In mid-September 1988, Pir Gailani told me outright (again off the record) that 'if any city falls into my hands, especially Qandahar, I'd call for a real elected jirga'. Although he denied that Zahir Shah would automatically be summoned home, he clearly believed that would be the outcome.

20. Press conference in Islamabad, 15th August 1988.

21. Despatch from Islamabad by Phil Jones, 23rd February 1989.

22. *The Times*, 1st March 1989.

23. Christina Lamb in the *Financial Times*, 20th March 1989.

24. Ian MacWilliam, 'The Jihad's Last Gasp', *Afghanistan* Issue No. 11, Summer 1989, p. 8.

25. John Kifner in the *New York Times*, 5th May 1989.

26. Confidential source, London.

27. Timothy Weaver in the *Independent*, 14th March 1989.

28. *Financial Times*, 16th March 1989.

29. Hamish Macdonald, 'Stay of Execution', *Far Eastern Economic Review*, 13th July 1989.

30. Christopher Walker in *The Times*, 22nd February 1989.

31. *Far Eastern Economic Review*, 13th July 1989.

32. Interview with Yuli Vorontsov by Lyse Doucet for the BBC in Kabul, 9 July 1989.

33. *Panorama*, 2nd October 1989.

34. Hamish Macdonald, 'Back To Feudalism', *Far Eastern Economic Review*, 13th July 1989. See also the wacky film about the Ismailis of Kayan by Jeff Harmon, 'Afghanistan: Year of the Warlord', broadcast in the Channel 4 *Despatches* series, 15th February 1989.

35. Conversation with a reliable Afghan source in Peshawar.

36. *Far Eastern Economic Review*, 13th July 1989.

37. Conversation with the author in Peshawar, 28th February 1987.

EPILOGUE: The Headless Goat

1. Briefing at the US Embassy in Islamabad, 12th April 1988.
2. *Washington Post*, 16th July 1989.
3. See, for instance, Ahmed Rashid, 'The Big Push', *Far Eastern Economic Review*, 13th July 1989.
4. BBC despatch from Lyse Doucet in Kabul, 26th June 1989.
5. Extracts from BBC Pashto Service 'Listeners Letters', June 1989.
6. BBC despatch from Islamabad, 10th July 1989.
7. *Washington Post*, 16th July 1989, and *Far Eastern Economic Review*, 13th July 1989.
8. Deputy Assistant Secretary of State Howard Schaffer, speaking to the Congressional subcommittee on Asia in mid-June 1989, quoted in *Far Eastern Economic Review*, 13th July 1989.
9. Interview with the BBC Urdu Service, 12th July 1989.
10. Quoted in Steven Galster, 'Rivalry and Reconciliation in Afghanistan', *Third World Quarterly*, October 1988.

Index

269

271